All proceeds from the sale of this book go to sexual assault survivor causes.

———

Praise for Torah Bontrager's

An Amish Girl in Manhattan

Reader Reviews

Melanie Jones: **Absolutely a must read. It is an easy yet well written read that deals with incredibly complex themes. . . .**
As someone who has read quite a few books and memoirs dealing with themes of trauma and overcoming obstacles, I have to say this memoir has it all. It is an easy yet well written read that deals with incredibly complex themes. I found this book and the author's personal journey to be so inspiring and empowering, as she describes and reflects on her escape from a terrible situation at a young age as well as her entrance into a culture (and even a language) quite different from her own. Her journey from Amish upbringing to graduating from one of the most elite universities in the USA is amazing. Highly, highly recommended, and my congratulations to the author for her success and hard work in processing so many traumas allowing her to be able to share her story in written form with us!

Brian: **She guides us through various moments in her life with such honesty and artistry that I**

felt like I was there by her side

Torah's tale is one of immense trials followed by towering triumphs. She guides us through various moments in her life with such honesty and artistry that I felt like I was there by her side. It's less a book and more a confession from a close friend. She brings to light a serious subject in Amish communities that is overlooked in favor of stereotypical depictions of Amish people and culture. It's done with her strong sense of storytelling such that you devour her sentences and are anxious to see/read her next project. I don't reread often but this is a book with chapters and sections that I will reread just to remind myself that if Torah can get through what she has, then I can, too.

Elam Zook: **Torah's work is a tribute to the resilience of the human spirit.**

Her fierce determination to claim her story while simultaneously not giving up on her people is what saints are made of! We Amish are lucky to have her.

Lindsay Gibson: **A Must Read!**

This book had me reading it to the end in almost one sitting! A very well written memoir, capturing the author, Torah Bontrager's life growing up in her Amish community, how she escaped and the obstacles she faced. As a rape survivor myself, my eyes were in tears reading the horror of sexual abuse and rape she suffered through - yet I smiled after reading how she conquered. She is a hero and a strong inspiration to those who are suffering from trauma.

Keerthi Vemulapalli: **managed to escape from a terrible and situation**
Congratulations to Torah for being able to process her traumatic childhood experiences enough to be able to write a memoir. This is a very inspiring and engaging story about how the author, a 15-year-old female, managed to escape from a terrible and situation. Despite being uneducated at the time of her escape and not speaking English as her first language, she then goes on to graduate from one of the most elite universities in the USA. I highly recommend this to anyone looking for inspiring true life stories about overcoming trauma, self-empowerment (especially female empowerment), and succeeding in life despite all odds.

Tina: **This book awakens one to the awful potentials of the closed Amish community**
This book kept me riveted until the end. The emotional lows that she went through were so painful and traumatizing that I could empathize with her pain and hope now she can live a better life.

MW: **I am struck with how my perception of the Amish and your childhood are such sad conflicts. I am also dumbstruck with all that ...**
I finished your book last night. Wow! Jaw dropping story! Each time I sat down to read a few pages, I found myself wondering what I would find next. And each page that I turned was more sensational than the one before. At the moment, I am struck

with how my perception of the Amish and your childhood are such sad conflicts. I am also dumb-struck with all that you have achieved Torah, and your path along the way as you juggle burdens from your childhood. You amaze me.

Kindle Customer: **The devastating effects of us-ing others....**
Torah gets very real with the reader about what she felt growing up Amish, and the abuses she endured at the hands of selfish people. She has a very en-gaging personality, and is a natural leader.
The end of the book, however, leaves the reader wondering if maybe the story isn't finished yet. Hopefully she can find peace and forgiveness in her heart for those who committed these hideous acts and rise to her true potential...
Looking forward to book two.

AN AMISH GIRL IN MANHATTAN

AN AMISH GIRL IN MANHATTAN

ESCAPING AT AGE 15,
BREAKING ALL THE RULES,
AND FEELING SAFE AGAIN

a memoir

TORAH BONTRAGER

Know-T Publishing
New York | USA

Portions of this work were published by the author in 2014, 2015, 2016, 2017, 2018, and 2019.

Know-T Publishing, an imprint of Know-T, LLC
New York | Texas | USA
646-653-0654
AmishGirl@TorahBontrager.com

Ordering Information: Discounts are available on quantity purchases. Special editions, which include personalized or branded covers, excerpts, and corporate or nonprofit imprints, can be created when purchased in large quantities. For details, please email or call us at the info above or via www.TorahBontrager.com

Book Design by Torah Bontrager
Author photos © Torah Bontrager

An Amish Girl in Manhattan: Escaping at Age 15, Breaking All the Rules, and Feeling Safe Again (A Memoir) / Torah Bontrager. —revised 2nd ed.

Library of Congress Control Number: pending
ISBN: 978-0-9894200-7-5 (paperback)
ISBN: 978-0-9894200-5-1 (ebook)

Printed in the United States of America
Revised Second Edition

For my children,
so you know more about
the mysteries of your origins

Love yourself.

Listen to your heart.

Trust yourself.

You are not alone.

Founder + Executive Director
TORAH BONTRAGER
speak@AmishHeritage.org
AmishHeritage.org
212.634.4255 (mobile/text/WhatsApp)

#AmishHelp #WIvYoder

Invite Torah to speak on Amish issues. We provide training in cultural awareness, female-driven entrepreneurship, and sexual assault survivor advocacy.

SPEAKING + TRAINING TOPICS:

Overturning *Wisconsin v. Yoder*
We are attempting to overturn *Wisconsin v. Yoder*, the 1972 Supreme Court case that denies Amish children—and consequently *all* children in the US and Native/indigenous lands—an education beyond the eighth grade. Learn why *Yoder* violates a child's Constitutional right to a quality education.

Amish Entrepreneurship
The Amish cannot compete with Big Ag and Silicon Valley. Learn about our programs to help Amish women, and men, transition to sustainable farming practices and produce food that can compete in today's marketplace. Programs include industrial hemp growing and financial literacy training.

Sexual Assault Survivor Advocacy + Cultural Awareness
We wrote an 8-Step Guide to help survivor advocates better support Amish victims. We are LGBTQ+ welcoming and provide cultural awareness training for sexual assault survivor advocates, law enforcement, and attorneys. We also created the SNAP Amish chapter and hold monthly, free online sexual assault survivor support meetings.

Ketamine for PTS(D)
Ketamine for post-traumatic stress is legal in all 50 states, if administered by a licensed doctor. Learn what exactly ketamine is and how it helps with PTSD, depression, and pain. Torah relies on this medicine for relief from repeat rape and extreme childhood traumas.

Feel free to request a topic not on this list. Torah is available in-person and online.

Author of the memoir
An Amish Girl in Manhattan

What Audiences Say:
"We were stunned into silence." - 30th Annual SNAP (Survivors Network of those Abused by Priests) Conference

"We need more conferences like AHF's. . . ." - Sarah Haider, *Executive Director*, Ex-Muslims of North America

"I didn't know my culture had so much in common with the Amish. . . ." - Attendees

Torah's story has been featured:

**DONATE
BECOME A PARTNER
BECOME A SPONSOR**
www.AmishHeritage.org/donate

Contents

Preface

When I was a kid, I told myself that if I made it, I'd write a book about my experiences so those left behind inside the Amish Church would know that it's possible to have a happy life in the devil's playground. This is that book.

Teenage Torah

This book is for teenage Torah.
    For the girl who believed in herself.
For the girl who didn't give up.
For the girl who dared to dream,
    dared to defy,
    dared to do the unthinkable.

This is for the girl who was born into the wrong family.
For the girl without a mother and father.
For the girl who knew (and knows)
She was (and is)
More
Than the restrictions imposed upon her.

This is for the

heartbreak
abuse
rape
loneliness
desolation
isolation
suicides
dark nights—
All that she went through.

This book is for that girl.

. . . Who still believes that love
    is the most powerful force in the universe.
And that she deserves to be seen and heard.

(written on February 25, 2017 while listening
to David Bowie's "Heroes", the song that
carried me through my darkest teenage hours)

Music for the Soul

_____

*Here are several selections that helped me get through the
events or period of this chapter, or reflect musically what I
felt during this time. I understood very little of most
lyrics—even today my ears don't process most words—but
the melodies and instruments fed my soul. Had it not been
for music, I wouldn't have survived until I finally got to
therapy at age twenty-nine.*

- Armin van Buuren. "Alone (feat. Lauren Evans)." *Intense*, 2013.

- Bob Dylan. "Forever Young." *Planet Waves*, 1974.

- Bob Marley & The Wailers. "No Woman, No Cry." *Legend, the best of*, 2002.

Introduction

This memoir reflects a very brief sketch in time over the course of my life thus far. It hardly scratches the surface of all that I've experienced and all that's shaped my worldview as of today. This version of my story is not the end result I envisioned—there are so many missing pieces—but I'd never have gotten it finished if I hadn't finally just picked a date and said, "It's done." I've lived a very unusual and colorful (and heartbreaking and soul-ripping) life that is impossible to convey in only one book. I see myself writing a second book, so look for more to come.

Please opt in to my email list if you'd like to stay informed about national and international book tour dates, appearances I make, and projects in the works:

- A short film based on the memoir
- A TV series based on the memoir and my life
- New episodes on the podcast
- Writing workshops to help you leverage your personal story

If you're Amish with no internet access, ask one of your English friends to sign up for my newsletter on your behalf. Or go to the public library and ask the librarian/staff for help with creating a free Gmail account and finding my website. Or call me at 212-634-4255 and leave a message with your contact information. That's also the number to call if you need help escaping or assistance post-escape, no matter how many years it's been. In the future I'll come up with a way via my nonprofit, The Amish Heritage Foundation (www.AmishHeritage.org), to distribute this book and much-needed resources offline among us Amish.

You can order the print version of this book through Barnes & Noble or other bookstores by giving them the ISBN 978-0-9894200-7-5 and asking them to order the book for you. The digital, printable version is free for all sexual assault survivors. You can request a copy by emailing AmishGirl@TorahBontrager.com or leaving a message by phone.

Each Chapter Can Be Read on Its Own

This book is formatted into twenty-six chapters, symbolically representing each of the letters of the English alphabet as an acknowledgment to the role that language played, and still plays, in my life. I didn't learn how to speak, read, and write English until I was six years old. English opened up other worlds for me, lifting me out of intellectual and spiritual poverty as an Amish child. Amish was an oral-only language until I was around fifteen years old, at which point someone translated the Bible into the Pennsylvania dialect of Amish—which is very different from the Midwestern dialect that I speak. In practical terms, Amish is still only a spoken language.

Each chapter is designed to be read as a standalone piece. So you can pick any chapter anywhere in the book, read it, and get something meaningful out of it. If you read the book from beginning to end in order, you'll get a more in-depth and complex feel for my life story. But it's not necessary to read it chronologically.

I've formatted the book this way so it's friendly for busy people and anyone with ADHD. Also, I don't write chronologically, or linearly; I write in circular time. Writing this way is very much an exercise in time travelling all over my memory universe.

Some of the chapters are darker and others lighter. Some chapters are shorter and others longer. Some are more polished and others far rougher. I've also included some poetry and odds and ends.

I've paired each chapter with a list of music that helped me get through those events or that period of my life—or reflect musically what I felt during that time. Had it not been for music, I wouldn't have survived until I finally got to therapy at age twenty-nine.

Show, Don't Tell

This book is not an autobiography; it's a memoir. According to my definition, the difference between the two is that a memoir is a story (or stories) *from* a life and an autobiography is an account *of* a life. Or put another way, a memoir does more showing and an autobiography does more telling. Just what is that difference? What is "showing" versus "telling" anyway? Here's how I understand it: Showing lets you, the reader, decide for yourself what you want to accept as truth. Telling doesn't let you, the reader, decide for yourself what you want to accept as truth. Showing says, "This is how I felt." Telling says, "This is how it factually was."

I've written, or attempted to write, mostly in the style of creative nonfiction so that the book reads like fiction. Conveying the emotional truth of my experiences is the driving force in telling you my story. Those emotional truths are most effectively demonstrated by showing you what happened through writing scenes (a fiction technique), instead of telling you what happened through writing dry facts. I've tried to show as much as possible and limit the telling as much as possible.

I give huge thanks to Joni B. Cole—the writer's writer extraordinaire—for bringing out the scared and traumatized writer in me, for her tireless encouragement and guidance, for teaching me methods that cut through the overwhelm, and for not letting me quit. This book wouldn't exist without her. She's been the best consultant, coach, mentor, teacher, author, and editor in the universe for me. All my sentences and paragraphs and sections that are crafted well owe their thanks to her and, of course, all the less-than-stellar content is due to my inability to meet writing deadlines and having had to forego her wise insight and editorial eye.

I also give big thanks to Michelle Witman-Blumenfeld—educational and learning disabilities consultant—for giving me the tools to manage my ADHD during my last year at Columbia, for teaching me how to break down my writing effectively, for giving her wisdom and advice and support unconditionally all the way back in the very beginning of this book over eight years ago, and for believing in me throughout all this time.

I finally now understand why writers thank their editors and coaches so profusely. It's crucial to the success of a book to have good people supporting and encouraging one throughout the long, often despairing and lonely, journey, especially when reliving traumatic memories. I wanted to give up countless times, too many times to remember. During those times, I thought I wouldn't be able to pick the pen back up and find my groove again.

Amish Words

Some chapters have endnotes. Please read the notes for explanations about Amish words, terms, definitions, or concepts.

It should be noted that I don't use the term "ex-Amish." There are complex problems with that label. We need to come up with terminology that accurately represents those of us who are outside the Church. We need a term that's useful, productive, and not cumbersome (for example, "nonpracticing," "nonconforming," and "cultural Amish" are better terms, but still pose certain problems). "Ex-Amish" implies that we're no longer Amish, and that is false. A change of clothes doesn't erase our Amish identity.

CHAPTER 1

Escape from the Amish: My Basic Story

When I was eleven, I made the conscious decision to leave the Amish. I planned my escape for four years. I literally escaped in the middle of the night at age fifteen without telling a single person goodbye.

My Failed First Attempt

(Amish House Arrest)

Nine months earlier, I'd been placed under Amish house arrest for a failed first attempt. My father Henry Bontrager considered me a "flight risk" and subjected me to severe physical and psychological interrogation techniques that included sleep deprivation, isolation from my friends, and confinement within controlled environments. "You're going to hell," he'd tell me over and over, while forcing me to stay awake for hours into the night listening to his rhetoric. (He decided it was okay for him to resign from the Amish Church about five years after my escape. But I will still go to hell because I disobeyed him by escaping, and because I don't subscribe to his born-again, right-wing, fundamentalist Christianity.)

The night I left the second time, I didn't know if I'd ever see any of my siblings, family, or community members again. My decision to escape was final. Returning to the Amish world was not an option. I left with only what I could carry: the clothes on my back, $170 and a small satchel.

Why I Wanted to Escape

For as long as I can remember, I'd envisioned a life that I later realized was not compatible with the Amish religion and lifestyle. But my efforts to escape were driven by an innate desire to be free and happy. As an Amish child, I was deprived of personal freedom and happiness.

I loved learning, and I cried when I couldn't go back to school the fall after graduating from Amish eighth grade. I was thirteen years old and denied further academic learning, based on Amish Church rules and beliefs. I wanted to continue school so badly that I taught myself algebra out of the back of the eighth grade math books we had, so I'd be better prepared for when I escaped and entered high school. Amish aren't taught algebra, because our education ends after eight years. For forever. We'd never use that useless *x* and *y* stuff.

Years later when I was a student at Columbia, I discovered that those particular math books that had prepped me for a higher education were published by Columbia University Press. Not every Amish school uses those textbooks. The coincidence of that is interesting to me. I'd never heard of Columbia until I applied to attend when I was in my early twenties, but all along I'd been learning directly from Columbia via its math lessons. In 1972, the Amish won a Supreme Court case, *Wisconsin v. Yoder* (www.law.cornell.edu/supremecourt/text/406/205), that allowed them to pull their children out of public schools on the grounds of religious freedom and put them into Amish-only schools taught by Amish teachers who themselves hadn't gone to school beyond the Amish eighth grade. The curriculum administered by the Amish is rudimentary—reading, writing and arithmetic— and not current with modern events and advances. No science or sex education is allowed either. I didn't know what "H_2O" meant until my first year of high school post-escape.

I understood, at age eleven, that according to US law, I wasn't considered an adult until I was eighteen and that, until then, the police could send me back to my parents or put me into a foster home. I didn't want to wait until I was that old to go to high school, so for four years, I tried to come up with a way that I could leave earlier but not be forced back to my parents.

My Current Educational and Familial Status

In 2007, at age twenty-six, I graduated from Columbia University with a BA in Philosophy and a focus on Tibetan Buddhism under the guidance of Professor Robert Thurman. To my knowledge, I'm the first first-generation Amish[1] person to graduate

3

from an Ivy League school, not to mention having been a first-generation college student. This is a big deal, and I hope that whoever reads this book is inspired and pursues their dreams of going to college, too. We need well-educated Amish people, so please reach out to me for advice and help on how to navigate the higher educational system. You can do it the hard way or you can do it the smart way by learning from the few of us Amish who have earned our degrees.

I have a very colorful work history. I'm a full-blooded entrepreneur, with professional experience as a marketing consultant and diplomatic liaison.

I'm the oldest of eleven children. Three of my siblings were born after I escaped. My parents resigned from the Amish Church around five years after I did. However, that didn't change anything and, in fact, things became progressively worse over the years to such an extent that the only way I could stop my father from harassing me was to get the police involved. My father has always ostracized me, and during the rare times I did visit my family (in order to see my siblings), he'd attempt to convert me to his religion, get me to come back and resume his psychological torture methods (for example, religious brainwashing, gaslighting, manipulation, and preying upon my vulnerabilities). My mother, Ida Bontrager, faithfully defends her abusive, criminal husband.

As of today, I have zero contact with my birth parents and siblings. They've all turned against me. None of them believe—or they deny it—that our nonpracticing Amish paternal uncles raped me, despite the fact that my oldest brother Al (Alvin) originally supported me when I told him what happened. At some point, for reasons unknown to me, Al decided that I'm a liar. One of my youngest brothers, Lewis, told me that I'm a shame and disgrace to the family for having been raped, and to "fuck off." My sister Rachel Coblentz demands that one of my friends (who's also nonpracticing Amish) remove from her Facebook page the posted news articles about my uncle Enos Bontrager's rape charges. My brother Al is also against the postings and public disclosure of the crimes. My sister Regina Miller says the uncles would never do anything like that. My parents, to date, have not once expressed empathy for me nor acknowledged the crimes. I haven't heard a word from them about the rapes, even after Al—when he'd first supported me—told them the story over six years ago.

My father did, however, write me several years later when my then-fiancé died: "I heard your boyfriend died. If you were a Christian, bad things wouldn't happen to you."

My father and my mother are fanatical proselytizers. There are religions worse than the Amish. One of the things I appreciate about the Amish religion is that proselytizing (attempting to convert others to one's belief system) is not allowed. The Amish Church actively discourages non-Amish people from converting into the religion. The last I heard, my father owns/runs an orphanage called God's Little Children in Guatemala (for the purposes of proselytizing) and operates a mini storage barn business called BC Barns located in Ovid, Michigan (just outside of Lansing), and may do other construction work under the name Bontrager Construction.

I was born and raised traditional Amish[2] in the Midwest in small communities, not large ones like Ohio, Pennsylvania, and Indiana. My knowledge about my own people is restricted and based on the experiences and conversations I've personally had. There are so many variations and there is so much privatization of knowledge within the Amish Church as a whole that no single Amish person knows everything about all or perhaps even most Amish. Very few universal rules apply to all Amish communities. There's no credible body of Amish literature to consult or learn from about the many differences, complexities, and nuances. That's something that I hope to change, so future genera-tions of Amish—as well as non-Amish—can access factual and credible information about our heritage.

Common Misconceptions or Myths About the Amish

Myth: The Amish speak English as a native language.

Fact: We speak Amish. It's its own language but non-Amish etymologists refuse to recognize that and insist that it's only a German dialect. That's not true. The Amish language has evolved over the past three hundred-plus years in the United States and Canada and meets the sociopolitical criteria for qualifying as a language. In addition, we Amish neither speak nor understand conversational High German (or modern-day German). Our Amish language has at least three distinct dialects: Pennsylvania Amish, Midwestern Amish, and Swiss Amish. Amish was an oral-only language until I was around fifteen years old, at which point someone translated the Bible into the Pennsylvania dialect of Amish (which is very different from the Midwestern dialect that I speak). In practical terms, Amish is still only a spoken language.

I still speak Amish fluently, and I speak English with an accent. I've retained my native tongue despite having very little interaction with fellow Amish over the past twenty-plus years.

Myth: All the Amish are the same.

Fact: In terms of the religion, there are traditional Amish, New Order Amish, Beachy Amish, and so forth. "Traditional Amish" is what the general public understands as simply "Amish"—or most often thinks of when they hear or see things about the Amish. I use the terms "traditional Amish" or "Amish" to define those who prohibit electricity, cameras, and cars.

Some outsiders—particularly self-proclaimed experts—call us "Old Order Amish." The Old Order label is not used by us in our language; neither did we invent that label. We refer to ourselves in our language as just Amish (unless we are part of a subset of traditional Amish, in which case the label "Old Order" is still not used).

There are many groups who spun off from the Amish who include an adjective with the word "Amish" as part of their group's identity, and to separate themselves from traditional Amish. Such spin-off groups include Beachy Amish and New Order Amish, who are more materialistically modern than traditional Amish. To make things even more confusing, there are groups within the category of traditional Amish who also identify themselves as "[adjective]" Amish. For example, the Swartzentruber Amish are even less materialistically modern than the rest of the traditional Amish. There's a third subset, Swiss Amish, who are not more or less modern than the range of traditional Amish, and who speak a different dialect—so different that I couldn't understand it as a kid.

Traditional Amish range from extremely strict in terms of material conveniences (for example, no indoor bathrooms and no running hot water) to "modern" (for example, indoor bathrooms and phones in the barns). The prohibition to use electricity, drive cars, and have cameras distinguishes traditional Amish from more materialistically modern spin-off groups who identify themselves as "[adjective]" Amish.

I was born into a very strict traditional Amish community in Iowa and then my parents moved to a similarly strict community in Wisconsin. When I was around ten, my parents moved to a community in Michigan on the "modern" end of the spectrum.

Myth: The Amish are ruled by a central governing authority similar to the pope (of the Catholic Church).

Fact: There's no central governing authority that determines and dictates all the rules that apply equally to all Amish churches or communities. There are some universal rules or laws that apply to all versions of Amish, such as the prohibition of electricity, cameras, cars, English clothes, TV, radio, musical instruments (except the harmonica in some communities), and education beyond the eighth grade. The rules differ from community to community as to what is allowed in terms of indoor bathrooms, phones in the barns, cell phones, bicycles, the length of women's dresses, the colors of clothes (dark versus lighter), the styles of the home-sewn clothes, air-powered tools, types of occupations, and so forth.

It is a mystery to me who exactly lobbies on behalf of the autonomy that the Amish enjoy and makes it possible for the Amish to live exempt from the laws of the United States, which apply to every other citizen, such as paying Social Security tax and being held accountable for violating civil, constitutional, human, child, and animal rights. I hear that there's a secret delegation of Amish that meets with the president of the United States in Washington, DC, every year. I'd like to know who the members of that delegation are and when those meetings occur.

Myth: The Amish are baptized as infants.

Fact: The Amish aren't allowed to get baptized until between age sixteen and when they marry within the Amish Church. I wasn't baptized as a member of the Amish Church. That means that officially I can't be excommunicated. However, I can be shunned—or ostracized. Only baptized members are allowed to participate in communion and foot washing services. You can't get married within the Amish Church before first being baptized.

Myth: Amish teens have a choice as to whether they want to remain inside the Church; that's what *rumspringa* is for.

Fact: The Amish do their best to coerce their children into becoming baptized members of the Church. We're neither encouraged nor supported to look into alternatives to the Amish Church. One of the baptismal vows is to remain a practicing member until your death. It's more sacred than your marriage vow, which says a lot, because the Amish don't allow divorce.

Rumspringa absolutely does *not* mean that we are given a choice. *Rumspringa* is only this: a period of time from age sixteen or seventeen until marriage inside the Amish Church. *That's it. Nothing more.* I cannot emphasize this definition enough, due to the fact that reality TV, some documentary films, and self-proclaimed academic experts outright lie about what rumspringa really is.

What happens during rumspringa varies from

community to community. In large communities—just as in major cities—where there are hundreds of teens, the parents have less control over whether or how their children break the rules. In small communities, such as the ones I grew up in, the number of families is limited to around thirty and the distance to another community is outside the driving range of a horse and buggy, precisely so the teens can't band together to drink and party. In either setting—large community or small—it's understood that a teen or adult is not allowed to actually exit the Church; that's an unspoken line that one is not to cross no matter how much drinking and partying goes on during rumspringa.

Myth: If you resign or escape from within the Amish Church, you're no longer Amish.

Fact: Amish isn't only a religion. It's a culture, language, ethnicity, and minority group. Just because I no longer wear Amish clothes doesn't mean I'm no longer Amish.

Myth: The Amish are Mormons or Mennonites or pilgrims.

Myth: Amish men have more than one wife.

Myth: The Amish put all their income into the same pot, like a communist or socialist banking system.

Myth: The Amish have arranged marriages.

Fact: Not exactly, or it depends on the girl's father. If he doesn't approve of the boy you want to marry, then you're in a situation in which you're forced to marry someone he does approve of, not get married at all, or go against his wishes (and that carries negative consequences). The Amish aren't allowed to marry outside the Church, so there are very limited marriage options.

Myth: Amish are "peaceful, gentle folk."

Fact: To the outside world, the Amish are peaceful, quaint, nonviolent, gentle folk. This is thanks to the genius of Amish marketing. And to the lobbying by non-Amish special interest groups such as the so-called academic experts on the Amish, and Pennsylvania politicians (governors, senators, representatives, and so forth). And to the maintaining of strict control by the Amish patriarchy over the churches and communities, which keeps us isolated and disengaged from the rest of the world.

At one time, I was determined to destroy the entire Amish culture as it stands today. I saw nothing good in my people. I'd experienced so much trauma, abuse, abandonment, rejection, betrayal, and attack by the hands of the Amish (my parents, relatives, siblings, and community/society as a whole) that I really didn't feel that there was anything worth saving. I felt that the percentage of negativity outweighed the good, and that there was nothing of value that couldn't already be found in other societies.

The Positives of Growing Up Amish

One of the best things about the Amish is their integrity and pride in their work. Whether it's building a handcrafted piece of furniture or canning fruit and growing vegetables, things get done right. In the plastic world and fast-food economy we live in today, solid integrity is hard to find. That's one of the things I appreciate the most about my Amish heritage.

Becoming bilingual at age six is another positive I'm very grateful for. Knowing how to communicate in more than one language is a huge asset. I didn't become fluent in English until after I escaped, and I was very self-conscious about my command of the English language until after I got to Columbia. But my ability to speak more than one language bridged so many cultural gaps for me and made it much easier for me to navigate the globe. Everyone should be bilingual at a minimum.

I like the Amish emphasis on the importance of the extended family unit. Knowing that you always have family and support to fall back on if you need help is such a security blanket that it keeps most Amish kids from leaving—or makes them return if they do venture outside. Coming to terms with the loss of family was something that I battled for over fifteen years.

I like the Amish emphasis on being hospitable to strangers and helping those in need, whether Amish or English (anyone who's not Amish or Anabaptist is "English," no matter what language or culture they represent). I just wish that that practice would be extended to those of us who are outside the Church.

I like knowing that I know how to build my own house, grow my own food, sew my own clothes, and live without electricity, internet, and cars. The self-reliance and self-preservation skills I learned as an Amish child are truly invaluable.

Growing up Amish also gave me the ability to relate to non-American and non-Western cultures much better than I would have otherwise.

The Negatives of Growing Up Amish

The overarching negatives within the Amish are the rape culture (rape, incest, molestation, and other sexual abuse runs rampant throughout the majority of communities); rudimentary education; physical and verbal abuse in the name of discipline; denial and violations of women's (and children's) rights; religion—and its accompanying fear-mongering and brainwashing—as a means of control (and an extremely effective means at that); and animal abuse.

I used to consider these negatives as personal positives in a somewhat perverted or distorted way. Without having experienced what I did, I wouldn't be the person I am today. While that's true, I'm against suffering. One doesn't need to suffer in order to appreciate beauty, enjoy life, and be a good person. The idea that suffering is a virtue or makes you a better person is designed to keep you subjugated to whomever is in control or making the rules (whether those are the rules of a church, club, or country). There's no honor in suffering.

I tell people that I'm thankful for having grown up Amish because of the positive aspects of the things I learned, but I'd never wish it upon anyone else. You can learn basic positive values and skills in any culture.

The Myth of the "Peaceful, Gentle Folk"

Outsiders (non-Amish) tend to have a nostalgic image of the Amish, but the reality is that the volume of human rights violations that take place in Amish communities is overwhelming. Domestic violence is a huge problem, but it's recognized neither by the Church nor by Amish parents as violence. Abuse in the name of discipline is the mark of being a good Amish person upholding the beliefs of the Church.

The Amish take the Bible verse "spare the rod and spoil the child" in a literal sense. Parents routinely beat their children with anything from fly swatters, to leather belt straps (the most typical weapon), to horse whips (those are the most excruciating), to pieces of wood, to furniture or cookware.

After I turned eleven, my mother would make me run down to the cellar to retrieve a piece of wood to get beaten with. I'd choose the thinner ones because I thought they'd hurt less. One day I couldn't find a thin piece so I had to get a thicker one. Luckily, I discovered that the thick ones hurt less. Every time after that, I'd pick a heavier stick or chunk of firewood. It made her think that she was hurting me more, and I'd scream harder just to make sure she didn't catch on that it actually hurt less.

One of my acquaintances stuttered when he was little. Because of that, his dad made him put his toe under the rocking chair. His father then sat in the chair, rocked over the toe and said, "That's what you get for stuttering."

Even little babies are abused for crying too much during church or otherwise "misbehaving." I've heard women beating their babies—less than a year old—so much that it made me cringe. Thinking of the pain those helpless little babies endured makes me cringe even now as I write this.

My First Suicide Attempt

My father was a hunter and taught me how to shoot. I grew up with rifles, shotguns, pistols (hand guns), bows and arrows, and ammunition in the house. Owning guns for the purposes of hunting and for killing livestock raised for meat is normal within the Amish. Around age eleven, I started practicing with a .22 rifle and later moved on to live targets—the rabbits we'd raised from birth that we released to hop around in the barnyard. "Set the rifle on top of the fence post and shoot," my father said. I learned to become a good shot very quickly because my father got angry if I missed and wasted bullets.

(Today I enjoy target shooting. It's a form of meditation for me. I'm also very much an advocate for growing one's own food, raising one's own meat, and living as cleanly and toxic- and chemical-free as possible. I don't enjoy seeing beautiful wild animals die, but I'd rather hunt or raise and shoot them myself and know where my meat is coming from than buy from nebulous or unethical sources. I *do not* condone factory farming and I avoid buying factory-farmed meats and other products. That stuff is highly toxic and poisonous and should not be labeled fit for consumption.)

One evening when I was fourteen, after having graduated from the eighth grade, I walked back from target practice in our field. The sun was setting and I paused for a moment on a little knoll below the house to enjoy the view. My shooting session had gone well. Suddenly a thought struck me: Today would be a good day to die.

I hadn't gotten beaten by my mother that day and, unlike the usual routine, we hadn't had any significant arguments over anything. I thought, If I die, I want to die without being mad at my mom. I might as well take the opportunity to do so before I get back to the house. Who knows whether there'll be another fight or a beating before the day ends.

I put a bullet in the chamber and raised the rifle. The closer it got to my head, the faster my heart beat. I was taught that people who killed themselves went to hell. But I was so miserable being trapped in the Amish Church and in an abusive home that I believed God would understand and let me get into heaven.

Despite my intentions, I didn't have the guts to point the barrel straight at my head. Okay, I thought, I'll just put the gun next to my cheek to see what it feels like. The instant I felt the cold hard steel, I realized that I wanted to live. I'd never had that thought before in my life. I'd always thought, I want to die.

I don't know where the idea came from that I wanted to live, but it completely changed the possibilities I saw for myself and my future. It was an infinitesimal, fleeting blip from out of the blue, but in that moment, I realized that I truly wanted to be alive, that someday I'd be happy, and that I must be destined for something better in life. That thought gave me the enduring strength and self-belief that I needed in order to keep trying to figure out a way to set myself free and hold on to the vision of peace and happiness I had for myself.

I branded that thought and feeling into my psyche. I told myself to never forget it, no matter how depressed I got or how much I might want to kill myself in the future. Even if I didn't have that same feeling again about wanting to live, I told myself that I shouldn't kill myself because there was a better life in store for me.

Not too long after that, I stumbled across an article that let me know how I could attain independence and legal protection before I turned eighteen, as an emancipated minor.

Searching for an Escape Plan

I have three paternal uncles who left the Amish Church when they were young. One of them, Harvey Bell, lived in Montana. I'd only met him once, when I was eleven, but I somehow knew that he'd help me escape.

We were allowed to have phones in the barn but not in the house—I never understood why it was against the rules to have a phone in the house but that, apparently, God was totally cool with it being in the barn. One day when I was fourteen, I sneaked into my father's desk when my mother was taking her afternoon nap, memorized Harv's number, and called him collect. I knew that a long-distance number would show up on the phone bill unless I called collect. This isn't common knowledge among Amish kids. It's something I picked up by being around my father so much and observing and absorbing everything he did and said.

For about a year, I'd wait until everyone in the house was asleep and then I'd sneak down the stairs. I became intimate with every creak and groan in the staircase and how to avoid each one. During the day, I'd spray WD-40 on the bathroom door hinges and the window. Then I'd crawl out the window after flushing the toilet to cover the sound and run to the barn. I made many nighttime trips out to call my uncle and talk. He was the only person I could talk to about my trapped situation. Of course, it never occurred to me that when I'd finally make it out of that frying pan of abuse, I'd land in the fires of his repeated rapes.

"You can come stay with me," he said, "but if you leave before you turn eighteen, you can't go to high school. You need parental consent for that."

My father subscribed to the local rural daily newspaper, so I read it to learn more about the world outside in order to prepare myself better for the transition. When my mother caught me reading it, she beat me for what she deemed an open sign of rebellion: reading about the evil outside. After that I'd wait until she took her nap. Then I'd read the paper from cover to cover. My favorites were the comic strips and the Dear Abby column. I couldn't understand most of the situations I read about in Dear Abby. Daily English life sounded so exotic and surreal. Is that what my life will be like when I finally leave? I wondered. Most of the problems sounded so insignificant compared to mine. I couldn't wait to have a pleasant life like that.

When I was fourteen or fifteen, a front-page article covered the case of a sixteen-year-old boy who divorced his parents. He'd been awarded limited emancipation in the state of Michigan on the grounds of abuse by his parents. The article stated that anyone who was younger than eighteen but at least sixteen could become emancipated based on physical, verbal, or sexual abuse, educational deprivation, and a few other conditions. Emancipation gave one all the rights of an eighteen-year-old.

Ah! This is how I can leave before I'm eighteen and go to high school, I thought.

I called Harv that night. He hadn't heard of the law, but he called his attorney and, luckily, Montana was one of the handful of states where the new law was in effect. Finally, I could leave Michigan and live free in Montana.

My Successful Escape in the Middle of the Night

My parents moved to a new Amish community in Ovid, Michigan, after my failed first escape attempt in Ludington, Michigan. The solution to all Amish problems is to move. It certainly threw a wrench into my plans for a second attempt. I was stuck in a brand new part of the state with no knowledge of how to access the Amtrak train or Greyhound bus to get to Montana.

One early evening on my way home from my job at the Amish bakery, I called my Wisconsin uncle, Enos Bontrager, from the phone in the Amish schoolhouse. Enos had left the Amish Church when he was around eighteen.

"I can't stand being Amish anymore. I don't know the geography around here and I have no escape options. If I could, I'd leave tonight."

"If I drove over tonight to pick you up, would you go?"

I hadn't expected that response from him. I called Harv immediately afterward to tell him that I'd be leaving that night. Before bed, I retrieved my birth certificate, Social Security card, and vaccination record from my father's safe. Harv had told me I'd need those documents in order to attend high school. I'd located the items long before, so I'd know exactly where to get them when the day of my departure arrived. Not all Amish children have Social Security numbers and vaccination records. Some don't even have birth certificates, and many don't know where or how to get documentation of themselves. I was lucky to have mine.

Several weeks earlier, I'd packed two small boxes to take with me in case of a last-minute escape opportunity. Those boxes contained all the worldly possessions dear to me at the time. But at the last minute, I made the heartbreaking decision to leave the boxes behind. I couldn't take the risk of getting caught with them if my parents woke up and saw me. Without the boxes, I could say I was going to the bathroom.

That night when everyone was sound asleep, I crept down the old house's god-awful creaky stairs—even the mightiness of WD-40 had lost the battle against that ancient staircase—crossed the god-awful creaky dining room floor, and slipped through the god-awful creaky back kitchen door. During all that time, I did everything I could to restrain myself from making a "screw it" dash for the door.

Before my exit out the back door, however, I found myself trapped in the kitchen. Fortunately the fridge—we were allowed propane gas fridges—kicked in and covered the noise of the creaky kitchen door, another failed WD-40 job. The only thing I could think of during those last few moments still in the house was that freedom lay on the other side of that door. Only several yards away. All I had to do was just get outside. So close and yet… so. far. away. My heart thundered. Enos was waiting for me down the road, and no one was going to stop me this time. Even if my father saw me in the kitchen, I'd make a run for it and make it outside—on the freedom side of the door.

Once my feet finally hit the grass, after creeping

through a final last door, the screen door, I felt an uncontrollable hit of adrenaline rush through my blood. I tore across the yard, heading straight for the road. I ran about a quarter mile down the road until I reached the creek where Enos had been designated to wait for me.

On the way I stopped only once, for just a second, to look back. I debated whether I wanted to do that. *What if I jinx myself if I look?* But then I thought, This is a huge moment in my life and I want to take just one more look at the homestead and remember this. My life will never be the same after I get into that car.

I stopped on the concrete road and turned around. Everything was quiet. No movement, no noise, no lights on in the house, nothing. I was safe. No one knew I wasn't up in my room sound asleep.

I took off again as fast as I could to where Enos' car was supposed to be parked. At first I thought he wasn't there. My heart almost stopped. He must have come and gone without me! What was I going to do now?

Just before despair over another failed escape attempt set in, I saw a light coming from inside a car as the door opened; Enos had parked further off the road. An eight-hour drive later, we arrived in Wisconsin where he and his family lived.

I spent two days with them. Barb, his wife, took me shopping for English clothes. I'll never forget the first time I tried on a pair of jeans. Levi's from Kohl's. I couldn't believe how comfortable they were. I also got my picture taken, which is the only photo I have of me in Amish clothes. That photo is on the cover of my book, and those are the clothes I wore on the night of my escape.

On the second day, Enos and Barb put me on the Amtrak train to Montana to stay with Harv. I got a ticket under a pseudonym in case my parents called Amtrak to try to hunt me down. Two days later, I was in Montana.

I felt free at last. I'd worked so long and so hard to make it through the abuses of my home life and environment, past suicide, through Amish interrogation and torture routines because of the failed first attempt, and finally, I had made it. Finally I'd have the happiness I deserved.

Then the rapes began.

What Lies Ahead

2018 marks the twenty-two-year anniversary of my new life. After travelling to roughly thirty countries and educating myself on "the ways of the world" (good and bad), my focus is now on facilitating positive change within the Amish, starting by releasing my memoir.

My big vision is to rebrand and transform the Amish, a largely autonomous nation of people in the United States of America whose ancestors migrated from Europe in the sixteen-hundreds and who shun the use of electricity, speak their own language (Amish), and isolate themselves from mainstream America and the modern world.

There are many serious problems within the Amish that need to be addressed: How do you successfully transform an entire society to experience real love, fulfillment, and meaning, both personally and collectively? How do you successfully transform an entire society to operate on love, rather than fear? How do you successfully transform an entire society to contribute their talents, gifts, and potential to the planet instead of remaining paralyzed and stuck in isolationist mode? How do you help those who've left the Church, or want to leave, to successfully make the transition to the outside world and integrate into mainstream American society? And how do you help those who are still inside the Church who are unhappy but don't want to leave and don't know who to turn to for help?

How to effectively understand and deal with these issues requires looking at the Amish as the immigrant population they are, with all the challenges that an immigrant group faces. I need your help to do this work. I can't do it alone.

Notes

1. I use the term "first-generation Amish" to refer to those of us who were born and raised traditional Amish and personally escaped, left, or resigned from the Church. This distinction is different from a child whose parent/guardian escaped, left, or resigned. Such a child could be a first-generation college student or an Amish first-generation college student, but not a "first-generation Amish" college student.

"Amish first-generation" refers to anyone of Amish heritage, whether or not they practice the religion. "First-generation Amish" refers only to someone who was born and raised in the Church and subsequently escaped, left, or resigned from the Church.

2. In terms of the religion, there are traditional Amish, New Order Amish, Beachy Amish, and so forth. "Traditional Amish" is what the general public understands as simply "Amish"—or most often thinks of when they hear or see things about the Amish. I use the terms "traditional Amish" or "Amish" to define those who prohibit electricity, cameras, and cars.

Some outsiders—particularly self-proclaimed experts—call us "Old Order Amish." The Old Order label is not used by us in our language; neither did we invent that label. We refer to ourselves in our language as just Amish (unless we are part of a subset of traditional Amish, in which case the label "Old Order" is still not used).

There are many groups who spun off from the Amish who include an adjective with the word "Amish" as part of their group's identity, and to separate themselves from traditional Amish. Such spin-off groups include Beachy Amish and New Order Amish, who are more materialistically modern than traditional Amish. To make things even more confusing, there are groups within the category of traditional Amish who also identify themselves as "[adjective]" Amish. For example, the Swartzentruber Amish are even less materialistically modern than the rest of the traditional Amish. There's a third subset, Swiss Amish, who are not more or less modern than the range of traditional Amish, and who speak a different dialect—so different that I couldn't understand it as a kid.

Traditional Amish range from extremely strict in terms of material conveniences (for example, no indoor bathrooms and no running hot water) to "modern" (for example, indoor bathrooms and phones in the barns). The prohibition to use electricity, drive cars, and have cameras distinguishes traditional Amish from more materialistically modern spin-off groups who identify themselves as "[adjective]" Amish.

Music for the Soul

---

*Here are several selections that helped me get through the
events or period of this chapter, or reflect musically what I
felt during this time. I understood very little of most
lyrics—even today my ears don't process most words—but
the melodies and instruments fed my soul. Had it not been
for music, I wouldn't have survived until I finally got to
therapy at age twenty-nine.*

- "Weird Al" Yankovic. "Amish Paradise."
  Bad Hair Day, 1996.

- Billy Idol. "Rebel Yell." *Rebel Yell*, 1983.

- Billy Idol. "Flesh for Fantasy." *Rebel Yell*,
  1983.

- Billy Idol. "Catch My Fall." *Rebel Yell*, 1983.

- John Prine. "Dear Abby." *Prime Prine*,
  1971.

- John Prine. "Souvenirs." *Prime Prine*, 1971.

CHAPTER 2

Held Hostage in Montana . . . and Wisconsin

Or, On the Need for an Amish Underground Railroad

M ay 1996. I was free at last. And then it began.
. . .

What follows is an edited and expanded version of the original interview article "Survivor Speaks Out Against Amish Rape Culture Ahead of Sentencing," by Mary Simms,[1] that first appeared on *The Huffington Post* on November 6, 2016.

The article explains why we need an underground railroad for the Amish, and shares my journey of breaking the rules to steal back my freedom.

Mary Simms' Introduction to Torah's Story

Torah Bontrager's betrayal by those closest to her began as early as age three. In the shielded-from-view world of her Amish community, her ordeal started with severe parental physical and verbal abuse followed by uncles' serial rapes. At fifteen, Torah fled to the false safety of a divorced paternal uncle, Harvey Bell, in Montana, who, shortly after her arrival, raped her more times than she can remember over the course of seven months.

To Torah's knowledge, Harvey Bell, approximately age sixty-two and five feet two with dark brown hair, still resides in Alder, Montana, or in one of the tiny towns in the Ruby Valley, a popular tourist destination in Madison County, Montana. He may also live or work in Alaska at times. Anyone reading this should be duly warned and spread the word that there is a sexual predator roaming free within their community.

Montana's laws are so unjust that by the time Torah was able to report the crimes, the statute of limitations had already expired. There is no hope for restitution under criminal law. Bell will never be held accountable for his crimes. He will never serve time behind bars. He will not even be investigated for the allegations against him.

Bell threatened Torah with death if she ever revealed to anyone that he raped her (and that bought her silence for over thirteen years). Fearing for her life, she managed to escape to, once again, the false safety of . . . yet another paternal uncle, Enos Bontrager, in Friesland, Wisconsin, who is also a blatant, serial rapist and child molester. Enos raped Torah during the first and subsequent opportunities he got: when his wife Barb went out of town on overnight business trips—while his three children, aged approximately seven, six, and four, slept in the next room.

In September 2016, Enos Bontrager, forty-eight, was arrested and charged with four counts of sexual assault of a child under thirteen years old, two counts of second-degree sexual assault of a child, and one count of sexual assault of a child under sixteen. These charges were for only one of his many other victims, not Torah. During the same time period that Enos had been molesting and raping that victim, he had also been molesting and raping Torah.

Torah's case against Enos Bontrager's repeated rapes has not been taken into consideration in those proceedings because neither the District Attorney nor the detective, Detective Sgt. Michael Haverley, Jr., assigned to handle Torah's reports have helped her. Detective Sgt. Michael Haverley, Jr., of Columbia County, Wisconsin, refused to conduct a proper and due investigation (he would not even conduct an interview with her uncle, the suspect). Detective Haverley sat on the case until he deemed that the statute of limitations had expired—on his watch—and then he closed out her case without even notifying Torah that he had done so.

To date, neither he nor his superior, Detective Lt. Roger Brandner of Columbia County, nor the District Attorney have bothered to inform Torah about the status of her case. Torah learned of the status indirectly months after it had been closed out. She has since learned that the statute of limitations in her particular circumstances never expire under Wisconsin law. She will take all legal action available to rectify these acts of negligence and obstruction of justice, and hold her uncle and all accomplices accountable for their actions.

To Torah's knowledge, Enos and his wife Barb

have relocated to the Fond du Lac area of Wisconsin, but Enos may still work from his furniture shop Pride Originals in Cambria, Wisconsin. Anyone reading this should be duly warned and spread the word that there is a sexual predator roaming free within their community.

Torah, the author of the forthcoming book *An Amish Girl in Manhattan* (a memoir), and I discussed her nightmarish but all too common experience against a backdrop of a national discussion of sexual assault that became a part of the conversation and debate in the 2016 presidential election.

Interview Questions and Answers

Mary Simms: When I think of Amish culture, I think of minimalism, growing vegetables from heirloom seeds, raising animals, hunting deer, and foraging for mushrooms, berries, and plants in the wild. But, after speaking with you, I also think of rape. And the sad reality of Amish rape culture is that so many young girls fall victim and can't escape. What do you think it is about the Amish culture that makes it so prone to rape?

Torah Bontrager: It's a culture that, from the get-go, from the day you're born, especially as a female, you're groomed to be a victim. The patriarchal structure, the hierarchy, is one huge problem. That's the foundation of the problem. God is number one, then it's the husband, then it's the wife, then it's the children, then the animals. The wife literally has to promise on her wedding day to obey her husband for the rest of her life. She, as a female, has no individual or independent rights except for perhaps a brief time between the age of twenty or twenty-one and before she gets married, if she isn't already married by twenty or twenty-one. In general, the only way a woman can make any independent decisions for herself—or direct her own life, within the confines of the Amish Church of course—is by remaining single. I didn't know that there was such a thing as human and constitutional rights, or that I was entitled to the basics of those rights such as life, liberty, and the pursuit of happiness simply by virtue of being a US citizen or human. I was taught that as a female, I had no rights. I was less than, inferior to, males. But somehow I just knew that how I was being treated was wrong.

Reading about Harriet Tubman who escaped slavery and led other slaves to freedom via the Underground Railroad gave me the belief and knowhow that I needed to set myself free, too. She was my role model. I learned how to go about thinking and planning my escape by paying attention to what she did in the books I read about her. That was my blueprint for freedom from the Amish.

I later learned from taking political science and ethics classes at Columbia University that precisely which human rights one is entitled to varies from country to country and that as a US citizen, I'm entitled to the rights in The Bill of Rights and other amendments. That includes freedom of religion; freedom of speech or expression; freedom of the press; protection against unreasonable search and seizure; protection against cruel and unusual punishment—freedom from torture; I can't be forced to testify against myself and I can't be punished without due process of law; I have a right to a speedy trial, to legal counsel, and to confront my accusers; and that women and children have certain further rights. I was denied all of these rights as an Amish child and female. And these rights are routinely violated within the Amish Church. The Church does not recognize them, especially as they pertain to women and children.

The biblical commandment "honor your parents" is interpreted as a literal "obey your parents no matter what" and is constantly enforced. It's one of the first things I learned as a child—before I could probably even talk. You're not ever supposed to say no to your parents or no to adults, certainly not adults in positions of authority such as aunts, uncles, grandparents, teachers, and preachers. If you say no, you get reprimanded and shamed at best and usually physically punished. Spanked, hit, beaten, whipped—depending on the perceived severity of the crime and disposition of the adult.

What that level of continual enforcement does is groom women and children, especially female children, to be victims. Of course, then, when an authority figure, especially a male, approaches you, you've already been trained and pre-conditioned to say yes to whatever that adult demands of you. At the very least, you don't resist and you don't protest out of fear of getting a severe beating, getting sent to bed hungry, or punished in whatever other ways in which you've already experienced. Boys are raped, molested, and assaulted, too. I don't want to overlook or diminish that fact. Part of my work is to investigate and uncover the real statistics of sexual assault against both females *and* males within the Amish and committed by *both* adult Amish men and women.

The Amish refuse to educate their children about even the basics of sex, so you're also not taught to recognize the signs of sexual advances and predatory characteristics. They won't even warn their children of known child molesters and rapists within the community. For example, my siblings, parents, and most cousins actively defend Enos Bontrager and do their best to keep his crimes from being publicized. My parents refused to tell my younger siblings (both sisters and brothers) about the rapes when they were informed over six years ago, and they continue to associate with Enos. My sister Rachel Coblentz, currently living in North Dakota with a daughter who herself could become Enos' next victim (if not already), demanded that one of my friends (who's also nonpracticing Amish) remove the news articles about Enos' rape charges; my friend had re-posted the articles on Facebook.

The Amish pretend that the rampant sexual assault found in almost every community doesn't exist. The attitude toward sexual assault is so bad that when a female is raped, she is punished for "being too tempting" to the male and is required to ask the male attacker's forgiveness for having tempted him.

Mary: You were raped multiple times in this culture by your uncles. Can you share a little bit about that?

Torah: Yes. I was molested when I was around six years old but I didn't understand what was going on. I didn't think in terms of "Oh, I'm being molested." I just knew that something really bad had happened. There was something very wrong. This was the Wisconsin uncle, Enos Bontrager, whom the article is about. That was the first time he assaulted me.

[To find the above-mentioned article, do a search online for "Survivor Speaks Out Against Amish Rape Culture Ahead of Sentencing" or go directly to www.huffingtonpost.com/entry/survivor-speaks-out-against-amish-rape-culture-ahead_us_581e7b02e4b0334571e09cfd and scroll through to find the information.

That article is titled "Friesland man charged with sexual assault of child relative in 1990s," by Jonathan Stefonek, and first appeared on *Portage Daily Register* on September 8, 2016. The direct link is www.wiscnews.com/portagedailyregister/news/article_553ed135-f223-5de2-be9f-4327c1663956.html and it includes a mug shot of Enos Bontrager taken when he was first arrested and jailed before being released on bail. He and his wife Barb have since moved to the Fond du Lac area of Wisconsin—or to my knowledge, away from Friesland. Please be warned that he is a lifelong, serial rapist and child molester.

I have reason to believe that he continues to

assault and rape other victims. If you are one of them, please contact me for help to bring a case against him.]

I escaped from my Amish parents, Henry and Ida Bontrager, in the middle of the night because of how severely they both abused me. I thought I'd be safe with my Montana uncle Harvey Bell, my father's older brother. I trusted Harvey completely and without question. He was the only person I knew who understood me, I thought, because he had also escaped from his father—my paternal grandfather—when he was young. Never once did it occur to me that he would rape me, or that I wouldn't be safe with him. It was a beyond heinous situation of jumping out of the frying pan and into the fire. And then into the fire again when I escaped from him and went to his younger brother Enos Bontrager in Wisconsin. Enos had helped me the night I escaped from my parents when I was fifteen. He picked me up in Michigan—he'd been waiting for me a quarter mile down the road from my parents' house—drove me across state lines into Wisconsin, and then put me on a train out to the Montana uncle. I had repressed the memories of Enos molesting me and my younger sister when I was little, so I had no idea that he wasn't safe either.

By the time you're preyed upon, you're already trained to never say no to your parents. The consequence for saying no is a severe physical beating or worse. So, of course you're not going to say no. You're taught that you must always obey your parents and if you don't, you'll go to hell. By the time you're an adolescent, you have long been acutely aware of the imminent threat of severe punishment or going to hell to burn alive for eternity for being a bad, disobedient child.

Mary: Do you think that the physical abuse lent itself to you being victim to sexual abuse?

Torah: Of course. What child is going to say no, after getting beaten and abused in various other ways so many times? Especially a female, where you're a second-class citizen, and an older male, especially male authority figures like my uncles, comes and demands something from you.

I didn't even know what was happening the first time until it had already started and then the shock of it and the confusion. . . . I didn't want that. But I couldn't say no because he demanded it, forced himself, and then threatened me with death the next day if I told anyone. At that point, saying no meant death, getting killed.

Mary: Unlike many victims of physical and sexual abuse, you were able to escape. And you almost did so by means of a bullet. Can you please tell me about that and what it was within you that gave you the fortitude within yourself to be able to escape?

Torah: I was determined to have a happy life. My home life was so abusive, it was so bad, and I didn't know when I'd ever figure out a way to escape. When I was eleven years old, I made the conscious decision to leave, and by the time I turned fifteen, I could barely make it through each day. I had always had a very bad relationship with my mother—from age twelve to fifteen, she beat me almost every day unless I was out of the house to work jobs elsewhere—and my father turned increasingly more sadistic and tyrannical the older I got. He's a bona fide psychopath. So because I still hadn't figured out a way to get out of there, I tried to kill myself. I talk about this incident in my book.

Before I pulled the trigger, I had this thought that ran through my head: I want to live. And I realized in that moment that that was the first time that I had ever thought in terms of "I want to live" instead of "I want to die."

Mary: Would you say you escaped into an even more abusive situation?

Torah: I have suffered from almost every kind of abuse that exists, essentially from birth. That includes verbal, physical, emotional, mental or psychological, spiritual, educational, and so forth. My early childhood years were fraught with routine, daily abuse, and the repeated rapes put the icing on the cake. I only recently learned from one of my doctors that I actually suffer from stunted neuronal maturation,[2] a direct result of how both of my Amish parents treated me during my developmental years and then further solidified by my rapist uncles. It was a one-two punch situation. My parents set it up and my uncles finished it off. The second blow—the rapes—I will never fully recover from. I was robbed of my virginity and sexual sovereignty and murdered alive; I call it a murder of the soul. Which is worse? The frying pan or the fire? They're both heinous; they will both kill you.

What added to the rape torture was being threatened with my life if I ever spoke out. My Montana uncle, Harvey Bell, threatened to kill me if I ever said anything. I knew that if he suspected I would report him or tell anyone, he'd kill me and that the only way to stop him from raping me was to get away from him without raising his suspicions that I'd speak out. He was divorced, and after the summer was over and his kids weren't visiting, I was all alone in the house with him, isolated in a small Montana town, with nowhere to go. I was completely dependent on him for my survival: I had no job after the summer was over, I barely had any money (several hundred dollars at most) and I had no vehicle. I had one adult female friend, Jodi, whom I would've asked for help, but she seemed to think highly of my uncle so I couldn't trust her to help me escape.

Finally I thought of making the reason to leave an economic one. There were no jobs for high school students in Montana during the winter, so I told Harv that I was going to move to Wisconsin during the winter break to work for Enos in his furniture shop. I made the decision to leave Montana about wanting to be independent and self-reliant and supporting myself. I told Harv that Enos had said okay, I could live with them and work in the shop after school so I could earn some money. In hindsight, I wonder if Harv knew that his broth-

er was a rapist, too, and if so, of course he wasn't
threatened if I went there.

I thought the worst of my life was over and that
I'd finally be in a safe place and be able to live as a
free person. Because Enos was married, had a wife,
and kids, right?

The first time his wife Barb went on an overnight business trip, the same thing happened. He
did the same thing that the Montana uncle did. At
that point, I felt "This is just what uncles do. . .
." That I couldn't ever be alone around any of my
uncles again. It was. . . . I don't know how to describe it. . . . It was like, here I did all this work to
get away from the Montana uncle, and now it's the
exact same thing, again, in Wisconsin. And these
things happened immediately and nonstop, after I
had finally figured out how to successfully escape
from my parents after planning that for four years
with a failed first attempt that put me under Amish
house arrest and interrogation routines for the
next nine months. Why was God letting these bad
things happen to me? I'm a good person and I left
the Amish for valid reasons, not because I was a
bad, disobedient child who didn't obey her parents.
Why would a loving God let these vile, evil things
happen? I didn't deserve getting raped over and
over and fearing assassination if I spoke out and
reported the crimes.

I wasn't afraid of Enos Bontrager as much as
I was of his brother, Harvey Bell. Had it just been
Enos, at that point I would have reported him to
the police. But I was afraid of Harv because of his
death threat. I was afraid that if I reported Enos,

that would threaten Harv and he'd have me killed, come after me himself, or send someone after me.

Mary: We live in a society where we tell girls they can grow up to be anything they want. They can grow up to be the president of the United States. Right here in America, you see Hillary Clinton. But for many of these girls, that isn't an option and they don't have a way out. What's the solution for them?

Torah: The solution is that there is a way out. If you're reading this or hearing this, you have a way out. There is support here for you. You're not alone and you're not crazy. Find a sexual assault or domestic violence shelter or organization and they will help you; and then of course, email or call me. I have a list of resources in my book and that list is also posted on my website.

In terms of the girls—and boys—who are lost in the Amish system, who don't know about me or how to get out, that's something I'm on a mission to change. Most of the kids are unhappy. The majority of teens, I would say, are unhappy Amish teens. There are also lots of unhappy women. And men, too. Especially younger married families. They don't leave, because they don't know how to make it on the outside. They don't have the resources, or they don't know how to integrate into a foreign culture. They don't know who to trust and how to make friends with foreigners.

It's best to think of the Amish as an independent country: they don't know how to immigrate to the US. They don't how to get out, how to leave their situation, what the laws of the US are, what their human and civil rights are—they don't know they even have any human rights! They don't speak English fluently, either. English is not our first language and is used only when conversing with non-Amish people.

To make things even more difficult, the US government doesn't recognize the Amish as a minority and, hence, despite the fact that we Amish are indeed a minority group, there are no legal or other advocacy groups working on our behalf. It makes it next to impossible to make the transition away from this heavily closed Amish society into mainstream US society that has no awareness or experience or understanding of the depths of the problems and challenges facing us Amish immigrants.

The solution is to create a support system and a grassroots movement inside and outside. This is what I want to do with the book and everything, with all the publicity. Here's the support system. You have me now, you can come to me; I have resources and people who want to help but don't know how to reach you. I want to connect people and resources to each other. One of the projects is to set up a nonprofit[3] and start identifying places where they can go, like safe houses and jobs and trustworthy people around the country to help make the transition easier for them than it was for me. They need places to go outside of the Amish where it's safe, with a supportive community to plug into and legal and financial assistance and education to live their versions of the American dream. Education is a big part of this effort. Practical life skills, street smarts, money management, reclaiming a sense of meaning, fulfillment, self-worth, self-empowerment, and self-love.

And of course learning when *not* to trust people, because they've been taught to obey and never question. The kids have no discernment skills. They get into drugs, they can't read people, they get taken advantage of. There are all sorts of cases where they've gotten caught in human trafficking, sex slavery, drug addictions, criminal pursuits, things like that, because they just. . . . They don't know how to assess people nor how to protect themselves. And having been deprived of education means that they're automatically on the bottom rung of society and usually stay there, no upward mobility.

These are all things that I want to offer through the nonprofit, The Amish Heritage Foundation (www.AmishHeritage.org).[3] Creating this support system has been one of my dreams from way back when I was a young teenage Amish girl who vowed that someday if she made it, she would help the ones left behind. She would create an underground railroad, like Harriet Tubman did.

Mary: What do you want people to take away from your book?

Torah: Ultimately I want people to get it that yes, you can have the life of your dreams. If you really want to be happy, then—unless you have a debilitating situation—take back your power and set yourself free. It's okay to be afraid but it's not okay to let fear control your happiness, or lack of happiness. All brave people feel fear. All the time. I didn't escape because I wasn't afraid. I escaped because I valued myself and my personal dream of happiness more. I was determined to one day be free or die trying.

I hope that one of the things that people get from my book is how to turn their tragedies into assets and what I call stealing back their freedom, by breaking all the rules. No matter whether you're Amish or not, most people are unhappy with their lives or businesses or other situations. There is always a way to turn the worst of what happens into a payoff, but it often means breaking the rules of whatever culture or society or family that you're part of. It's not necessarily easy to go against whatever everyone else says and follow your heart, but I hope that I can offer tools and different ways of thinking that make it a little bit easier and, at the least, let you know that you're not alone.

Believe in yourself and look for people who are positive and supportive and encouraging and non-judgmental. Surround yourself with kind people and avoid people who use fear to scare you or control you. The unknown is not nearly as terrible as the preachers and politicians make it out to be. By far, the very worst things—the most heinous acts committed against me—were done by my very own people, the Amish. Not anyone on the outside.

So take personal responsibility for your life. If you're not happy, do something about it. You are not powerless. If you're reading or hearing this, then you definitely are not powerless.

I've been through the worst of hells a million times and back. I've wanted to kill myself at least six times over the past twenty years. I have no shame in saying that. I know what it feels like to be all alone and not see a way out. Some of the very hard lessons I've had to learn are that no one can save me and I can save no one else but me. I can't do anyone else's work for them. Everyone has to walk their own path—do their own work— but there are good people in this world who will support you and encourage you along your path of personal freedom. Keep believing in yourself and your right to be happy and free.

Mary: After everything you've been through, do you still believe in God?

Torah: God is love, kindness, compassion, and wisdom. What's true for me is that despite all the evil on this planet, love is still a far more powerful force in the universe. The bad things that happened to me are examples of humans taking religion and perverting it for their own nefarious purposes. If it doesn't come from love, it's not from God.

Notes

1. Mary is the founder of The Mary Simms Public Relations Agency. Formerly an NBC television news reporter, US Army Veteran and war correspondent, and past spokeswoman for the US Environmental Protection Agency, she uses her 15+ years of experience as a media insider to help high-profile clients favorably influence media coverage, embrace their expertise, and land favorable features on top tier media outlets, blogs, and podcasts that lead to increased revenue and exposure. Follow her on Twitter @marysimms or visit www.marysimms.com. Please give her your business. She's a badass.

2. I am alive today only because of regular ketamine infusions. For more details about PTS/PTSD and ketamine, read chapter 25 or watch this episode in which I interview my doctor, Dr. Glen Brooks: "What Ketamine Is + How It Helps with PTSD, Depression, and Pain." *Amish Entrepreneur Show with Torah Bontrager*, season 3, episode 8, www.amishheritage.org/what-ketamine-is-how-it-helps-with-ptsd-depression-pain. I also share more details about how I found ketamine in this article: Bontrager, Torah. "PTSD and the Designer Drug That Saves Me From Suicide." *Our Stories Untold*, 10 Apr. 2018, www.ourstoriesuntold.com/ptsd-designer-drug-saves-suicide. Accessed 25 Mar. 2019.

3. I founded The Amish Heritage Foundation (AHF) in 2018. According to my research, AHF is the first 501(c)(3) organization in history that advocates for Amish people without a religious price tag, promotes compassionate secular values and nonsectarian harmony, and empowers those who leave the Church. No other nonsectarian organization does what we strive

to do on behalf of Amish women and children, both inside and outside the Church.

If you need help (whether you're inside or outside the Church), call 212.634.4255 and leave a message with your contact information. That's also the number to call if you need help escaping.

You can text to that number as well.

AHF's website is www.AmishHeritage.org and you can send a message to me via the Contact page. You can also reach me directly via email: torah@AmishHeritage.org or torah@TorahBontrager.com

Music for the Soul

Here are several selections that helped me get through the events or period of this chapter, or reflect musically what I felt during this time. I understood very little of most lyrics—even today my ears don't process most words—but the melodies and instruments fed my soul. Had it not been for music, I wouldn't have survived until I finally got to therapy at age twenty-nine.

- Stephen Foster. "Gwine to Run All Night." 1850.

- Stephen Foster. "Old Folks at Home." 1851.

- Stephen Foster. "My Old Kentucky Home, Good-Night!" 1852.

CHAPTER 3

Second Breakfast

I reached up, stretching on tiptoes, my fingers just long enough to curl over the edge of the door-knob.

"Cli-iii-ccck!"

The door squeaked open, into a hallway that connected my parents' little house with my grand-parents' big house on the farm. The hallway looked like a long tunnel. Books filled the built-in shelves on the left side. All the way at the end to the right was a bedroom. Opposite that was another door, which led into the kitchen where I often watched my grandma cook.

I'd already eaten at 6 AM, before my father left for work with the construction crew.

"Good morning," he'd said, carrying me to the dining table in our little house. On the way, he'd stopped at his desk to get the latest issue of *Outdoor Life*. I sat on his lap and played with his suspenders while he read.

"Ask Mom when breakfast is ready," he said, drumming his fingers against the table. He slid me down to the floor and took a sip of coffee. My mother had brewed a pot before he woke up.

I ran toward the kitchen stove. "Mommy, Daddy wants breakfast."

"It's ready now." She flipped the last pancake

out of the skillet. "Here, take the sugar to Dad."
She followed me to the table.

"Thank you." My father took the bowl and
strapped me into a highchair next to him.

"Hungry." I reached for homemade toast.

"Here." He smiled and broke off a corner.

"We have to pray first." My mother grabbed my
hands. "Put your *pattehs* together and close your
eyes."

My parents didn't speak to each other while
they ate. My mother paid no attention to me. My
father indulged my chattering.

Before breakfast was over, a truck pulled up
outside.

"The driver is here." My mother left the table
and brought back a lunchbox and thermos.

My father took them from her and patted me on
the head. "I have to go to work now." He didn't say
goodbye to her. The screen door slammed behind
him.

I ran to the window and waved until the vehicle's headlights disappeared in the dark.

My mother went back to sleep and I played in
the living room. My father had built a toy box for
me that was shaped like a barn and painted red. I
liked opening and closing the hinged roof and pulling out wood numbers and books.

Two hours later, I didn't know what to do. The
house was still quiet and the blue curtains still
closed. I looked at the door that went to Grandpa's.
Maybe I could twist the knob far enough.

The door led into a dark tunnel. But a crack of
light came through an opening all the way at the

end. I heard voices and banging silverware coming
from it, too. I followed the sounds, past the rows
of books in the shadows. The noises got louder as
I went through the door at the end and around the
corner.

"Morning! Morning! Morning!"

Everyone looked up. Grandpa at the head of the
table. Perry, twenty-two, and Daniel, twenty, at the
far end. Vera, fourteen, Samuel, twelve, and Alice,
ten, sitting in the middle. Grandma at the stove.
Lena, seventeen, helping Grandma.

"Torah! How did you get here?" Alice asked.
She was my playmate and second mother.

I smelled butter sizzling in a pan where Grandma and Lena stood.

"Come," Daniel said, putting down his spoon.
He lifted me up and swung me into a chair.

Alice tied a bib around my neck and Perry's elbow hit a plate. It fell to the floor. Perry didn't talk
much but he smiled at me. I was his favorite niece
and he loved to take me with him around the farm.

Grandma sat down. She was short and had very
curly brown-gray hair that curled up even more
from the heat when she cooked. As soon as she
started to eat, Daniel said, "More cocoa and toast."
And Vera said, "More oatmeal, please." Grandma
left her bowl of Grape-Nuts and went back to the
stove.

"Hurry up and eat, boys. We gotta get out to
the fields," Grandpa said. He passed the eggs, gath-
ered from the hen house that morning, to the end
of the table.

"Where's the milk?" Perry asked, spoon in one

hand and a mug in the other.

"What?"

"Milk!"

Lena dropped a cast iron skillet on the stove and it made a loud bang.

"I can't hear you." Grandpa squished the eggs in his plate with a fork and put them on a piece of toast. Yellow oozed out, dripping down his fingers and onto his long beard.

Alice and Vera talked.

"Girls, stop yakking," Daniel said. "Perry wants milk."

"Here." Alice made a face and pushed the pitcher.

"Awww." A stack of toast had gone around the table and arrived at Samuel's spot empty. "Why don't I ever get any?"

"Patience," Lena said. "More's coming."

"Almost done," Grandma said. She threw another piece of wood in the stove and picked up slices of bread from the hot surface with her bare hands.

The teakettle whistled and Vera covered her ears.

"More eggs." Grandpa's chair scraped the wood floor. He leaned forward.

Grandma put some on his plate. She carried a pot in her other hand.

"Cocoa and toast, please." I held out my pink sippy cup. It had two handles and a picture of a baby deer on one side. Great-aunt Edna had given it to me when I was born.

Grandma filled it and wiped the sweat off her forehead.

Years later, that stark difference between the households still remains: my parents not communicating during meals, my father often angry, and my mother sullen; my grandparents friendly, warm, and loud. After that first solo trip through the hallway, I'd go to Grandpa's even on the mornings that my mother didn't nap. I didn't go because I was hungry, but because I felt welcome there. When they ate, I wanted to eat, too. It made me feel like I belonged. My parents moved away from the farm when I was three, so I couldn't run to my grandparents anymore. From then on, I'd go to the next closest thing: food.

"Yummy, Granma." I took a piece of toast from her and dipped it in my cup.

NOTE: Some names and details have been changed to protect certain identities.

Music for the Soul

———

Here are several selections that helped me get through the events or period of this chapter, or reflect musically what I felt during this time. I understood very little of most lyrics—even today my ears don't process most words—but the melodies and instruments fed my soul. Had it not been for music, I wouldn't have survived until I finally got to therapy at age twenty-nine.

- The Beatles. "Yellow Submarine." *Yellow Submarine*, 1969.

- The Beatles. "Octopus's Garden." *Abbey Road*, 1969.

- Tripping Daisy. "Human Contact." *Jesus Hits Like the Atom Bomb*, 1998.

CHAPTER 4

Look at Me

"**M**om, Mom, look at me!" I inched as close to the edge of the boulder as I dared. The gully below looked so far away that it felt as if I were standing on a towery cliff jutting over a ravine. I tingled. Goosebumps.

"Look at me, Mom!"

The dark green woods where I was playing touched our back yard. Across the fence, my mother kept her head down. The garden needed her attention. She hoed beans, pulled up carrots, and yanked out weeds. A fat, gray cutworm fell out of the soil as she shook a clump of cockleburs. She threw the clump on a growing pile in the wheelbarrow and crushed the worm on a rock with the flat side of her hoe. Juice sprayed out. It left a fresh stain and quickly dried in the summer sun.

The cat got in her way.

"Out, Tigger!" My mother swung the hoe at him.

Tigger yawned and took his time.

Back at the weeds, bent over, my mother seemed engrossed in a different world from mine. Hers was one of heating up water, washing dishes by hand, and producing children until menopause. Mine was of freedom, exploring the woods, and breathing in nature. Sweat dripped down her face.

She'd exchanged her white cap with strings for a dark blue, triangle-folded *kopp duch* (headscarf) twisted in a knot behind her ears and under her bun of curly brown hair. Sometimes she put the hoe down and used the pointy fabric corners to wipe little beads out of her eyes. The heat from the sun dried up the soil, and every so often she'd moisten the ground with a watering can so the veggies and weeds would come out more easily.

I loved to dance across the rocks and logs. I pretended I was a Native and the forest was my home. My mother had told me about *Caddie Woodlawn*. Caddie was a tomboy from the pioneer days who loved the outdoors and had Native friends. I liked the story because I felt that I was like her, preferring adventure to being stuck indoors. I liked it even more because the story was true and set in Wisconsin where we lived.

"Yes, this really happened," my mother would say, "and when you're old enough to go to school, you'll get to read the book for yourself."

I couldn't wait to learn how to read. My mother never had enough time to tell me stories. My favorites were ones about people from the past, like Caddie and Laura Ingalls Wilder, because they let me peek into the world outside. Through real-life stories, I sensed what was possible beyond my Amish confines—beyond the rules that I was born into and bound by.

"Mommmmm!"

"Be careful." She still didn't look up. Another handful of weeds landed on the pile. She tossed a stack of string beans into a plastic ice cream pail.

"And stop pestering me."

Barefoot, I climbed up even bigger boulders and jumped across the gully to another rock. One of my knees hit a ridge and blood seeped out.

My mother saw me. "Get down from there! What did I tell you about falling?"

The possibility of breaking an arm or leg didn't occur to me. I wanted her to acknowledge the successful leaps I made. But she didn't see. All she saw was danger, that I was pushing against the safe boundaries of her familiar domestic yard and into the shadows of a landscape that to her were frightening. She didn't see that I was safe and loved by the rocks and the trees and the plants and the birds. That I was part of the material universe. She saw only the unknown. The darkness of the woodlands. The hidden sunlight. The forbidden. Nothing good could come from there.

"Ouch. . . . Mom, it won't stop bleeding. Can I have a Band-Aid?"

My mother sighed and put the hoe down. Now she'd have to tend to me. Why couldn't her oldest child leave her alone for once before the baby woke up? She walked into the house to fetch a jar of homemade drawing salve and a roll of Johnson & Johnson waterproof tape.

I hopped down from my castles and back into the yard. The mounds of unwashed veggies that my mother had left, scattered around in the garden, looked good. I ate as much as I could before she returned.

"Stop eating the carrots!" I heard the screen door slam. My mother was on her way back. A big crease sunk between her brows. She never liked it when I ate from the garden.

She cut off a piece of tape and jerked my hand away. "*'Sis net genunk fer supper.*" ("There's not enough for supper.")

Music for the Soul

Here are several selections that helped me get through the events or period of this chapter, or reflect musically what I felt during this time. I understood very little of most lyrics—even today my ears don't process most words—but the melodies and instruments fed my soul. Had it not been for music, I wouldn't have survived until I finally got to therapy at age twenty-nine.

- Jefferson Starship & Paul Kantner. "Have You Seen the Stars Tonight?" _Blows Against the Empire_, 1970.

- Hank Williams. "(I Heard That) Lonesome Whistle." Released as a single, 1951.

- Unknown origin [British?]. "Three Blind Mice." Circa 1609.

CHAPTER 5

The Cat Knew the Way (Part I of a Trilogy)

O ur destination was a tree in the middle of the blackberries in the woods across the cornfields. The tree had a long, thick, curved limb that stretched out low above the ground. The oversized knots jutting out from the trunk looked like built-in steps and the limb was just wide enough for us to sit on and swing our feet. We'd never been there without adults, usually with our mother on a weekday or both parents on a Sunday.

"I wanna go to the blackberry patch and play on the tree," my four-year-old sister Rachel had said. Curly light brown hair stuck out from under her home-sewn cap, and streaks of mud and grass stained her blue hand-me-down dress.

"I don't know the way," I said.

Rachel pinched her mouth and crossed her arms. "But I'm bored!"

Earlier that day, our mother had made it clear that she was not to be disturbed during her nap.

"Stay out and play," she'd ordered.

I knew from past experience that my mother wouldn't be in a good mood for the rest of the day if we woke her up and asked her what to do. She expected me to watch my siblings because I was six years old already and the oldest. I had to figure out how to keep my sister and baby brother amused. My father often praised me for being smart. I was his favorite child and wanted to be just like him. He'd know how to get to the tree. Maybe I could find it, too.

"First we have to go up the hill behind the house to the fence along that field," I pointed, the other hand shading my eyes from the hot summer sun.

Rachel picked up her faceless doll. "Ready. C'mon."

"Take Al's other hand." I helped him up from the grass.

Together, with two-year-old Al between us, we began the slow walk up the hill toward the English neighbor's property. Snoopy, our brown dachshund, tagged along.

The tree was half a mile away but we were hardy children who were used to walking, even Al. Our lane was a quarter mile long, and I'd often go with my mother to get the mail. As long as I could see the house, I'd know how to get back.

I knew how to get to the woods. But I didn't know which part of the woods was the right way in that led to the blackberries. The English farmer's tractor tracks had clearly marked a path along the fields, but they faded before reaching the trees. I wasn't sure if I'd remember which clumps of bushes at the end of the corn rows were the right ones to walk past.

Tigger, the orange-colored cat, caught up with

us at the top of the field and trotted ahead. Snoopy barked and barked and ran around in circles between our legs, sometimes behind us and sometimes in front of us and sometimes running off to chase butterflies.

"Look, Tigger knows which way it is," Rachel said.

Then I remembered that the last time we'd been in the patch with our mother, Tigger had found us awhile later. He knew how to get there by himself.

"Go home, Snoopy," I yelled, running after him and waving my arms toward the house. I was afraid he'd run away and get lost.

"Shoo, Snoopy, shoo," Rachel and Al yelled, too.

Snoopy went back several yards, turned around, and then raced ahead jumping and yapping. He thought we were playing with him.

"Bad dog! Go home!"

When all three of us shouted and chased and flapped our arms at him enough times, he slunk slowly back down the hill.

We walked as fast as we could without stepping on too many thistles with our bare feet. Avoiding sand burrs was much harder. Soon our clothes were covered in prickly spikelets that grew everywhere along the path.

At last we got to the edge of the woods. The trail that led to the patch began several yards inside the trees. I walked up and down and stared into the underbrush. Nothing looked familiar. All the bushes looked the same.

I hope Tigger remembers how to find it, I thought. If he doesn't, we have to turn around. I didn't want to go home. For what had seemed like many hours, Rachel, Al, and I had entertained ourselves with all sorts of made-up games back at the house. The switches from the big willow tree in the front yard were always a favorite play toy. When we played grown-up, Rachel fought to be the mother so she could spank me with a switch, just like our mother did in real life.

"I wonder where that trail is," I said.

Rachel started running with Al in tow. "It's that way."

"No, get back here. It's somewhere over here."

I noticed a flash of orange. Tigger. Weaving back and forth inside the woods, he moved further and further into the trees.

"Let's follow him," I said. As long as we kept him in sight, I thought we'd be okay. Even if we didn't find the patch, it was fun running around and picking stray clumps of fruit scattered everywhere.

"Oww," Al wailed. He'd stumbled over a sneaky bramble and fallen flat on his face. Blood oozed out from long scratches all over his arms.

"I'm still hungry and I wanna play on the tree." Rachel stamped her foot and blackberry juice dripped down her face. "When will we get there?"

I wiped the blood off Al's arms with my skirt and looked for Tigger. He'd found the narrow pathway. Soon we were walking past oaks, maples, and firs on the well-worn trail dotted with deer tracks. Gradually the path widened and opened up onto a sunlit clearing. There was our beloved play tree, surrounded by bushes hanging low with plump juicy fruit as far as our eyes could see.

It was much cooler here than in the yard at home, and there were many new things to explore. Rachel ran to the tree and climbed up on the limb.

"Get me blackberries," she said, her feet sticking out at me.

Al went to a cluster hanging so low that it touched the ground. When he sat down, he landed in a pile of thorns. But he didn't cry. He pulled berries off one by one and colored his face with purple splotches as he put big handfuls in his mouth.

"Hurry up. Why is it taking so long? I'm hungry," Rachel said. The front of her dress billowed up in the breeze and slapped her face.

"Getting you some." I picked until a heap appeared in my dress. I held the bottom of the dress up with one hand to make a pail for collecting the berries. My mother did it like that with her apron when she took us to the patch.

"Yuck." I backed away from a bush. A little white worm peeked out through a hole on one side of a berry.

"Here, Rachel." I avoided ruts and gnarly brambles hiding in the clearing floor on the way to the tree. Rachel took the whole mound. She didn't leave any for me.

I don't know how long we were playing when I heard a sound coming from far away.

"Torah!!! Torrrraaaaahhhhh! Rachel!!! Raaaaachelllll!"

My mother appeared in the clearing with

Snoopy. She looked upset.

"Why did you come here all by yourself? You could've gotten lost or a bad English man could've kidnapped you." She made it sound as if I had done a terrible thing.

"You said we couldn't wake you up," I said.

"Don't you ever come here again without my permission."

"Okay, Mom." *Now we'll be stuck playing around the house and getting bored whenever she takes her naps. Why can't I go to the woods alone again? I know the way.*

That night when our father came home from work, he dumped his stainless steel coffee thermos and red Igloo cooler on the floor and hurried to his desk. Rachel, Al, and I ran to the cooler to see if there were any leftovers from his lunch. The food our mother packed for him tasted much better than what she made for us.

"Ida, did you bring the mail in today?" he yelled to my mother who was in the kitchen.

The lunchbox was empty so I pestered him for attention. "Dad, guess what happened today?"

My mother frowned. She didn't look excited like I did.

When my father heard the story, he didn't seem bothered that we'd gone off alone. *He thinks I'm smart that I got to the patch by myself,* I thought. But he did agree with my mother that I wasn't allowed to go back again without an adult.

He laughed when he heard that we believed that the cat knew the way. "Tigger didn't know. Cats are stupid. You should've taken Snoopy and made Tigger stay home."

"But he found the trail," I said, tugging the sleeve of his shirt. I was sure I could make him understand.

"You were just lucky," he said, looking down from his chair as he hit the calculator and wrote numbers on a ledger. "Dogs are smart and cats are dumb."

No, they're not.

My father had always given me special treatment and bragged to everyone about how smart I was. He was God to me; I worshipped him, and before that day, I never questioned his judgment. Today he was wrong. His laughter and derision stung. *Why didn't he believe me? Why did he say I was stupid for trusting the cat?*

Silent, I walked away.

My father continued punching numbers.

Music for the Soul

Here are several selections that helped me get through the events or period of this chapter, or reflect musically what I felt during this time. I understood very little of most lyrics—even today my ears don't process most words—but the melodies and instruments fed my soul. Had it not been for music, I wouldn't have survived until I finally got to therapy at age twenty-nine.

- Crosby, Stills, Nash & Young. "Teach the Children." *Deja Vu*, 1970.

- Unknown French origin. "Frère Jacques." Circa 1780.

- Gorillaz. "Every Planet We Reach Is Dead." *Demon Days*, 2005.

CHAPTER 6

Aborted Snowflakes and a Wheelbarrow for Christmas

"Tomorrow is Christmas," my mother said, casting a purple stitch. A partial mitten appeared under her knitting needles. Long cracks spidered her hands from the cold temperatures and never-ending daily household chores. Each night, she moisturized with Vaseline—a petroleum jelly— but her hands remained dry and rough. I didn't like it when she touched my arms or washed my face. Her hands scratched my sensitive skin.

Everyone sat around the living room stove after supper. Joseph slept in a baby basket next to my mother, his pacifier hanging from a string pinned to his homemade dress. In our particular Wisconsin community, little boys wore dresses like the girls until they started walking. Al stacked a pile of wood blocks on the floor. His blond hair, cut in the shape of an upside-down soup bowl, needed another trim; the curls were too long and got into his eyes. Rachel pretend-fed milk to her twin faceless Amish dolls dressed in matching dark blue clothes.

"What's Christmas?" I asked. A picture book slid off my lap and fell on the floor.

"It's a very special day," my father said. "We're

going to surprise you."

"What's the surprise?"

"Go to sleep. When you wake up, you'll find out." He swiveled back in his chair and flipped to the next page of the Amish newspaper *The Budget*.[1]

My mother took me to my bed. I was six years old and in school, old enough to be alone upstairs. My second brother had just been born that month. There was no room for me in the downstairs bedroom anymore. Rachel had rotated to the top bunk in my parents' room, Al to the bottom, and the new baby in the crib.

"You're a big girl now. Sleep upstairs," my father had said.

I wanted to be a big girl. I wanted to please my father.

Tonight like every night, my mother led me up, carrying a clunky black kerosene heater lit with a wick like a candle. The fumes smelled awful, acrid, and gave me a nauseous buzz. My head hurt. But I was cold and crept close for warmth.

My mother set the heater on the floor and tucked me into bed. The upstairs was drafty and bare. Most of the old farmhouse felt like a hollow freezer. It was as cold inside as it was outside. The warmth from the downstairs stove avoided me and fled through the window frames and cracks in the drywall.

"Say your prayers."

"It's sooooo cold." I curled up in a ball under the blankets, hugging my shoulders. "Please leave the heater up here."

"I can't. It might catch on fire and burn the

house down. Now say your prayers." I recited the German—not Amish—bedtime prayer my mother had begun to teach me as soon as I started talking:

Müde bin ich, geh' zur Ruh',
Schließe beide Äuglein zu;
Vater, laß die Augen dein
Über meinem Bette sein!

When I was two, I thought the 1817 poem—"Müde bin ich" by Luise Hensel—was about me. *Ruh'* meant "rest" but it sounded like my birth name "Ruth." When my mother realized that I thought I was praying to myself, she devoted all her efforts to correcting my understanding. I was to pray to God and Jesus, not myself, or I'd go to hell. *"Hab' ich. . . . Hab' ich?"* I couldn't remember the next line. My teeth chattered and my head ached. I smelled kerosene but I didn't feel warmer. The room stayed cold. *"Hab' ich Unrecht heut' gethan."* My mother looked irritated that I still hadn't memorized the second verse:

Hab' ich Unrecht heut' gethan,
Sieh' es, lieber Gott, nicht an!
Deine Gnad' und Jesu Blut
Macht ja allen Schaden gut.

"Good. Here's your water." She set the glass on the nightstand, turned to pick up the heater, and left the room.

In the morning, the glass of water had morphed into a block of ice. My toes and fingers were numb. I stood over the register in the floor next to the chimney, but the fire below me had died. I walked over to a window and peeked out. Today was Christmas. Would it look any different? The single glass panes frosted over with aborted snowflakes shrouded my view. Tiny drifts of snow lodged in the corners of the frames. Some of the snowbanks had made their way through inside and dusted the sills with layers of white.

I touched an icy panel, blew warm puffs so the crystals would melt, and scratched a peephole through the glass. It was still pitch-dark outside. I shivered. The pink cotton nightgown and nightcap that my mother had made for me couldn't shield me from the below-zero Wisconsin cold.

I pulled a blanket off the lumpy mattress, wrapped it around my body, and fumbled toward the stairs. It was a long flight in the dark. I'd fallen all the way down countless times—in daylight. With one hand glued onto the banister to keep from tripping, I tugged the cumbersome blanket trailing behind me. Determined to keep it from slipping away, I descended, one foot planted on a creaky wooden step, the other sticking out in space and waving about until I felt another board.

A big door at the bottom of the staircase led into the summer kitchen. I crossed it to get to the next door, which opened up into the living room. That was where the stove—and warmth—was.

No one woke up when I walked in. I curled up by the chimney to get warm. On the other side of the stove, an odd shape appeared in the dark. It hadn't been there the night before.

What is it? I stared at the mysterious glob.

I heard a noise behind me. My mother.

"What's that, Mom?"

"Today is Christmas. It's the surprise." Her figure emerged from the shadows with a dim kerosene lamp. The shape turned a blurry red.

"I want to see it!" I ran to the thing.

"Wait until Dad wakes up. This is for all you children."

"Dad! Dad!"

"Sh! He's still sleeping." My mother put her finger over her mouth.

My father heard me from the bedroom and came out.

"What is it, Dad? Can I see it?"

"Sure." He smiled, picked up the thing, and placed it on the kitchen table. My mother lit a bright gas lantern and I crawled up on a chair. The object had wooden handles.

"It's a red toy wheelbarrow full of presents for you kids." My father seemed pleased with the work tool he had gotten us.

"A *schupkay*! Can I play with it?" I felt grown-up. Now I had a wheelbarrow just like my father.

"After breakfast."

Rachel and Al woke up and my mother made homemade cocoa and toast and eggs. After the table was cleared and the dishes were done, my father handed us each our own present from the wheelbarrow.

"Look inside," he pointed to the bottom.

"There's more."

I leaned closer.

"Candy!"

Striped red-and-white candy canes, root beer barrels, pink saltwater taffy, hard butterscotch buttons, and gumdrops in all the colors of the rainbow covered the bottom. I had never seen so much candy in our house before.

"Today is a special day so you can have as much as you want."

Rachel snatched up two fistfuls and Al tipped the wheelbarrow to make a candy cane slide out. My mother watched while breastfeeding Joseph.

"That's enough for now," my father said. "Open your presents."

I picked up the box next to me and tore the holiday wrapping.

"Don't ruin it," my mother said. "We need to save it for next year."

Rachel and Al had already gone into the living room and ripped their boxes open. Paper wreckage littered the floor. They chased each other on all fours with their brand new toys. I was old enough to be more careful. My mother expected me to behave like an adult and not leave behind wasted pieces of wrapping.

"Use the scissors."

I slowly cut along the edges, past the pictures of Santa Claus and through the reindeer, wreathes, and snowmen. A flashlight in the shape of a van with wheels tumbled out. It was yellow. Al's was red and Rachel's was blue.

"Here, let me put the batteries in," my father

said. "Now slide this switch." He pointed to a button on top of the vehicle.

A bright beam shot out through the van's headlights.

"Wooooow!" we said.

Lights on, lights off. Red, yellow, and blue. Laughter and happy screams. I pushed the flashlight van around the floor. *From now on, Christmas is the best time of year.*

Seventeen years later, I spent my first Christmas morning in New York City alone. This time the room I'd slept in was toasty warm. The stairs I descended were marble and all the hallways lit. I stood in an empty, massive drawing room, graced with a towering Christmas tree, and looked out across Riverside Drive, beyond the park, and over the icy Hudson River. The view through the thick, floor-to-ceiling, stained glass windows—the freshly fallen snow not yet disturbed by pedestrians and their dogs, the highway empty of traffic, the absence of taxis and honking busses—conveyed a feeling of the entire city sleeping in: a city of twenty-two million people engulfed in peace and calm. Except me. I'd come to dread Christmas.

The building I lived in housed around seven hundred students, but this morning it was empty. No one walked the halls. The administrative offices were locked. The cafeteria was closed for a week. Most students had left as soon as finals were over to be with their family and friends. Everyone had someone who loved them. Except me. I spent Christmases alone.

After my escape from the Amish, Christmas seasons had become suicidal marathons to get through—the only time of year that brought back happy memories of my childhood. Christmas had been the one time of year that I'd been allowed to be a child, free of responsibilities, free to just play. Christmas was the one day that I knew for sure that my parents wouldn't fight and that my mother would treat me nice. Everyone was happy.

Now I'd barely make it through the winter holidays. I'd get no presents, no signs of affection, no calls to say that I was loved and cherished. The memories of what a family was supposed to be like—of parents who were supposed to love me—would eat away at me, growing more powerful and turning me more suicidal as Thanksgiving came and went, shops—this year on Fifth Avenue—dressed up their windows with festive scenes, the weeks counted down to the big day, and my classmates asked, "Where are you going for winter break?" Maybe this year will be different, I thought each year. But nothing changed.

"Why don't you come home for Christmas?" my mother asked one time, several years before my move to New York.

"I can't. I don't have the money."

"I'll pay for your ticket," my father said.

My heart soared. I cried after I hung up the phone. *He's giving me a present. He loves me after all.* He'd said I was going to hell for leaving, and whenever I visited—my effort to let my siblings know that there was a way out—he'd verbally waterboard me for hours and hours, quoting Bible verses and attacking my self-worth, in the hopes that I'd crack and return under his rule. *Things are finally changing.* When I called the transportation company to verify the details, customer service informed me that the ticket was for one way only. Good thing I checked, I thought. I dialed my parents' Michigan number.

"The confirmation you gave me is for only getting into Lansing. What's the info for the return?"

"Wait until you get here," my father said.

What? I'd meticulously gone over the dates with him and he hadn't said anything about not booking the return. *What was going on?* "What do you mean?"

"You don't have to go back so soon. Didn't you say you're off from school until after New Year's? Stay longer. I'll get the ticket when you know which day you'll be leaving."

Something didn't feel right. "Thanks, Dad, but I really need to be back by Monday. I have to work. I can't stay for the whole break."

Silence.

"Dad?"

"I'm not buying you a return." His voice punctuated the other end of the line. Hard. Cold. In a matter of minutes, he'd changed completely, not the friendly, loving father into which I'd thought he'd evolved.

"What? What do you mean?" My voice cracked. Surely I hadn't just heard what I heard. Was, was he. . . ? Had he really just tried to trick me?

"You need to come back home where you belong. I'm not buying a round-trip. If you're not gonna stay, you can pay for the return yourself."

The full weight of what my father had tried to do sunk in. He'd intended to hold me hostage. He knew I had no money.

"But you *said* you'd buy my ticket," I screamed into the phone. "You lied. You lied! You said you'd buy my ticket!"

I slammed the phone down, dropped into a heap on the floor, and sobbed. *How could he lie to me like that? He hasn't changed. He doesn't love me. He deliberately planned to trick me.* If I'd just believed him and gotten on that bus without verifying the details, I'd be a prisoner again in his house.

Snowflakes swirled down outside the tall glass panes, and someone walked a dog through the park. I lived in a building owned by the Rockefellers, one of the wealthiest families in the world. I attended Columbia University, one of the most elite schools in the world. And I'd finally found my home, in one of the most expensive cities in the world. I was happy—throughout the rest of the year.

But when Christmas came, I couldn't deny the cold, brutal reality that I was financially destitute, and that my parents actually didn't care. I was alone in the world. Too poor to buy a ticket to spend the holidays with my school friends and too ashamed to tell them that it was because I had no money. My friends were trust fund kids and kids who had parents who loved them; they didn't understand what it was like to be poor—so poor that even a fast-food meal was unaffordable. No one comprehended my situation. After all, I spoke

English. I was born a US citizen. And I looked white. I must not be disadvantaged or wanting for anything. *I used to wonder how anyone could be suicidal during Christmas. Now I understand. It's the worst time of year.* I turned away from the window, away from the happy people outside, and took the elevator back up to my room. Maybe I could make myself fall asleep so I'd forget the gnawing hunger in my stomach.

Note

1. *The Budget* is a weekly print newspaper that's sort of the Amish equivalent of social media. Except only one designated person from each Church district is allowed to send in a report of the happenings in their community that week or month.

Music for the Soul

Here are several selections that helped me get through the events or period of this chapter, or reflect musically what I felt during this time. I understood very little of most lyrics—even today my ears don't process most words—but the melodies and instruments fed my soul. Had it not been for music, I wouldn't have survived until I finally got to therapy at age twenty-nine.

- Traditional Christmas carol. "O Holy Night." Composed by Adolphe Adam, 1847.

- Santana. "Dom." *Shape Shifter*, 2012.

- John Cale. "Antarctica Starts Here." *Paris 1919*, 1973.

CHAPTER 7

Grandmother, the Light in My Life

Grandma laughed a lot and wore her hair in braids. She was the only grown woman I knew who wore her hair like a young girl. Amish women didn't do that. They put their hair up in buns, fastened in place with long straight hairpins, and hid them underneath a white or black Amish-style cap with strings.

I couldn't wait until I was ten years old so I could wear my hair in a bun, too. That meant that I'd finally be a grown-up. The bun went hand-in-hand with an upgrade in the style of clothes. Instead of wearing a dress that buttoned up in the back, I'd wear one that was closed up in the front with straight sewing pins, like the pins that tailors use when marking alterations. When I did turn ten, those pins pricked me all the time. Often they fell into the bowl when I was stirring cookie dough, or onto the floor throughout my work day.

"Why don't you make a bun, Grandma?" I asked her when I was little. I stood by her side on an Amish-built oak dining chair at the kitchen sink where she'd just washed her hair.

"I don't like buns. Braids stay up and buns fall down. And the pins hurt me."

Grandma had filled a stainless steel bowl full

of hot water from the whistling tea kettle on her wood-burning stove. After she shampooed, she dumped the water down the drain and filled the bowl again for rinsing.

The bottle of conditioner slipped in my hands, but I caught it before it fell. It made me feel like a big girl to help Grandma.

"I'm ready for the conditioner now."

Grandma dried her hair with a towel and we both sat down. I watched as her hands quickly pushed her gray hair into two piles, one on each side of her head. Then her fingers zipped through the piles and divided them into three strands each. Soon a braid emerged, like magic. At the end of each braid, she inserted a piece of brightly colored yarn—sometimes pink or yellow or variegated— that extended about six inches from beyond the last twist of hair. She arranged the braids into a pretzel against the back of her head and tied the shape in place with the yarn.

"How can you braid your own hair, Grandma?" Mesmerized, glued, I tried to figure out how she did it. My mother always braided mine.

"I taught myself when I was a girl." Grandma's smile anticipated my next question before I could ask "How?" again. "Many, many years of practice. It's easy."

When I got older, I noticed that Grandma was different from everyone else in my Amish world. When we visited her from out of state, she bounded out of the farmhouse and down the cement sidewalk. Pretty, colorful beds of flowers

lined each side of the walkway, like a receiving line
to welcome us. As we tumbled out of the passen-
ger van one by one after the twelve-hour trip from
Michigan, she wrapped each of us in a fluffy hug.
Amish people didn't hug. But Grandma did.

When birthday time came around, she sent
each of her forty-plus grandchildren a card smoth-
ered in stickers. Hers was the highlight of all the
ones I got. Grandma left barely enough room to
write a note. Even her handwriting was unlike
anyone else's. It looked like a hen had scratched
the words, like the patterns I saw on the ground by
the coop where the chickens ran free. Even though
I couldn't read her writing, I always knew from the
stickers that this one was from Grandma Bontrager.

"'Dear Torah,'" my mother would read out loud
after I opened the envelope. "'Happy Birthday.
From *Doddy* and *Mummy*.'" That was my grandma's
Amish language phonetic translation for "Grandpa"
and "Grandma."

I was around eight years old when I learned
that Grandma was partly Native. From the time my
mother first told me stories from *Caddie Woodlawn*,
I wanted to be a Native. I loved the outdoors and I
didn't like being a girl stuck inside the house with
my mother. I thought the Natives were fascinating
and exciting. I wanted to live in teepees like they
did in Caddie's time, hunt wild animals, pick wild
berries, and walk in the woods with moccasins that
didn't make any sounds. I wanted to be different
from everyone else.

I felt different, not Amish, and I lived in the
worlds I travelled to in books. I dreamed about

driving fast red cars, living on the ocean, and sailing hundred-foot yachts. On many Sunday afternoons I'd lie on the grass and watch tiny dots of planes with little trails of gray pass over our house. How can heavy things stay in the air? I wondered. Who are the people inside those planes all the way up there? Where are they going? Do they know how lucky they are that they're allowed to ride in a plane?

One day a letter from Grandma arrived. "The son of a Winnebago chief married an Amish girl in the eighteen hundreds," she wrote, "and took the girl's last name." Now I finally had proof that I was indeed different and unique and not only like every other Amish person.

My grandmother and her mother's skin were slightly darker than most of the Amish from Europe. Many of my relatives on that side looked a little different, too: the skin color, the shape of their eyes, and some other features. I hadn't inherited any of those physical traits, but from that time onward, I identified as Native—and even before, never as white. I saw myself as wild and free, belonging to nature and not to the domesticated prison of Amish life. Even the life of *die Englische*—the Amish term for everyone on the planet who isn't Amish or Anabaptist—seemed dull compared to the Natives'. Today, I still know nothing about the customs and culture of my Winnebago lineage, but my connections to Earth, herbs, plant medicine, nature, planets, galaxies, and the hidden and unseen are deeply a part of who I am. Humans' nefarious ways and destruction—really, a raping—of our planet infuriate me.

Even though Grandma wasn't Native enough to qualify as a member of the tribe, fragments of Winnebago influences seeped down through the generations. Her personality—nonjudgmental, unconditionally loving, accepting of one's choices even if they differed from hers, not buying into the Amish mentality of martyrdom—came from that heritage. Even her food tasted different from typical Amish dishes. The whole house smelled delicious, with exotic spices and flavors floating from room to room when she cooked.

"What are you making, Grandma?" I asked when she got done with her hair. I followed her from stove to countertop to table to sink and back to the stove with nonstop questions:

"What's that?"

"Why are you putting this in?"

"Can I stir it?"

"When's it gonna be done?"

"Why do you do it that way?"

"Why doesn't mine look like yours?"

"I wanna taste it. Can I?"

"Here." She picked up a ladle and scooped some liquid from a simmering pot. "Try it."

"Yummm. Can I have more?"

Grandma laughed and filled a bowl for me. Short, with stooped shoulders and twinkly eyes, her whole body bounced when she laughed. I sat at the kitchen table, ate as fast as I could without burning my tongue, and asked for more. I was always hungry and Grandma never told me I'd spoil

my dinner if I ate before everyone else.
When I was around eleven, Grandma taught
me how to make hominy, a Native dish, and lefse,
a Norwegian flatbread. Those were some of her
special holiday treats during Christmas or Thanksgiving at her house. The highlight of Christmas by
far was helping her make homemade candy: miles
and mounds and heaps and piles of sugary bliss.
Square-shaped. Rectangle-shaped. Rounds. Globs.
Chocolate-covered. White-covered. Coconut- and
rainbow-sprinkled. Maple, vanilla, and fruit-fla-
vored creams. Caramel turtles and peanut butter
brittle. Cashews, almonds, pretzels, and graham
cracker pieces. All dipped in chocolate melted
from ten-pound bulk slabs on the wood-burning
stove. Grandma had mastered the art and science
of tempering chocolate without the precision of gas
or electric heat. She knew just when to throw in
another log or move the pan to a cooler section.

My favorite candies were the rectangle-shaped
chocolate-covered mints and perfectly round peanut butter balls. The peanut butter balls were easy
to tell apart from other round shapes: I just looked
for the indent left by the toothpick Grandma had
used to dunk the ball in chocolate. The mints were
more difficult to distinguish. Eventually my guess-
es became pretty accurate: I looked for a slightly
unique rectangular shape and volume. I'm sure that
that was how Grandma designed them so she could
tell them apart herself. She'd make hundreds of
pounds of a dozen or more varieties of near-iden-
tical shapes, each one coated with the same shade
of chocolate—like little uniformed Amish children,

who all looked the same on the outside. Grandma could tell what was different on the inside—just like she could tell what was different about each of her grandchildren.

After my escape at age fifteen, Grandma was the only person who didn't say anything negative about me. She neither questioned my decision nor judged me, unlike my parents and other family members. She didn't say or insinuate that I'd go to hell, or that I'd disobeyed my parents. She sent me handwritten chicken-scratch letters regularly and a sticker-loaded card every birthday. I had to learn how to read her writing so I could stay in touch with her.

My friend Yanik believes that there's a special connection that occurs between the hand and the heart when someone writes with a pen instead of on the computer. He encourages all his friends and fellow entrepreneurs to send handwritten notes to their clients and business associates on a regular basis. Yanik also campaigns tirelessly on the merits of keeping a journal. Not a computer-written journal. A handwritten journal. And not just any notebook, but one that has been selected with care. When Yanik shared his view about the heart connection in handwriting, I finally understood why my grandmother had insisted that I send her written letters, not typed.

"Typing isn't personal," she'd penned more and more frequently. "Please *write* me. I don't want something printed from a computer."

I'd get upset because I felt she should be happy

that I made the time to write her at all. I had to juggle a full-time class load at Columbia and two energy-draining jobs in order to pay my tuition and keep a roof over my head, with barely enough left over from each paycheck to eat. Didn't she understand how hard I worked? How much I struggled each day to survive?

I never told her about my poverty-stricken life. I was afraid that if I revealed my destitute situation, she'd stop loving me and respond with psychological manipulation tactics and extortion attempts like my father—her son—did every time I asked for money or mentioned that I didn't have enough for food or tuition: "God's punishing you for disobeying your parents and leaving the Church. If you come back, I'll give you money. You wouldn't be poor if you just repented and came back."

One day I got a letter from her that said, "You need to come back and get baptized. You're going to go to hell if you don't." My head reeled. *After all these years, why is she saying this?*

I tried to forget that part of the letter, but later ones became more and more condemnatory. I didn't understand why she said that after all the years. Deeply hurt and feeling deeply betrayed, I stopped writing her back. Eventually her letters stopped coming, too. When she died during my late twenties, I didn't go to her funeral. I was angry at her for saying that I was a bad person.

In recent years, my uncle—not one of the rapists—who had also escaped when he was young helped me to see things differently. "Any judgmental things she said were dictated by Grandpa. He'd censor her letters at times and force her to write such things." My uncle had been close to Grandma, and she'd stayed in regular contact with him, too.

I'm so sorry, Grandma. I didn't know, I wanted to tell her, and give her a hug and feel her hugging me close like she used to when I was a child. But I couldn't because she was gone.

"What are you making, Grandma?" I asked over and over, shadowing her from stove to countertop to table to sink and back to the stove. I was twelve years old, clutching a college-ruled notepad and pencil, doing my best to keep up with Grandma as she flurried about the kitchen. Our religion forbade cameras so I had to take copious notes and memorize Grandma's every move. I'd rifle through her recipe boxes, cookbooks, and spice jars to get a visual and document my favorite dishes.

"Jelly rolls," she said, beating the egg whites and egg yolks separately. "Here's the recipe. Watch. There's a secret to making the dough. If you don't do it right, it'll turn out hard instead of soft."

Grandma Bontrager's Original Chocolate-Covered Peanut Butter Balls

(by Torah Bontrager's Grandmother)

Several years ago, I got ahold of Grandma's original peanut butter candy recipe. It's the same recipe I refer to in this chapter. Beginning around age thirteen, I'd consult her instructions to make these for the holidays.

> *2 cups peanut butter*
> *3/4 stick margarine*
> *1 cup powdered sugar*
> *1/4 teaspoon salt*
>
> *Mix peanut butter and margarine. Add powdered sugar and salt; mix well.*
>
> *Put layer of melted chocolate in baking cups.*
>
> *When set, add 1 teaspoon in center of chocolate. Cover with melted chocolate. Hide, if you want to keep them. [This is classic Grandma humor.]*

My mother hated cooking and wouldn't teach me how to make flavorful dishes, so I tried to crack the code by myself—with no success because we lived too far away from Grandma for me to get her help outside the once-a-year or less visits. Looking at her recipe today, I understand why I'd gotten so frustrated as a child when I tried to learn on my own. Grandma's formulas aren't scientific, logical, and complete. At least not on paper. Nowhere in the ingredients list is there any mention of chocolate. Nor are there instructions on how to melt the chocolate when it finally is mentioned later. In addition, the recipe says to make peanut butter cups, not balls.

During the short journey thus far in my culinary education as an adult, I've come to learn that recipes really are just guides. This got pounded into my head by *The Next Iron Chef* runner-up Chef Jehangir Mehta when he stressed that point over and over while teaching me how to make Lemongrass Panna Cotta with Tangerine-Star Anise Tartare. I kept running to him every microsecond for explanations about the ingredients and unclear, discrepant instructions.

"These recipes are guides," he'd repeat patiently. "They don't have to be followed rigidly."

If food really is life, then maybe this is what life is all about: a set of general instructions that aren't meant to limit us but to allow us the freedom to create whatever it is that's truly an expression of us. Maybe life, and cooking, is about finding one's own voice. And then stepping back to proudly and happily acknowledge our creations, one dish at a time.

Thanks to Chef Mehta, I now appreciate Grandma's vague guidance and what she was trying to convey to me, as well as to all her loved ones. We're not meant to exist contained in a box. We're meant to spill out and *live*, with no apologies.

Music for the Soul

———

Here are several selections that helped me get through the events or period of this chapter, or reflect musically what I felt during this time. I understood very little of most lyrics—even today my ears don't process most words—but the melodies and instruments fed my soul. Had it not been for music, I wouldn't have survived until I finally got to therapy at age twenty-nine.

- Rob Thomas. "A New York Christmas." *A New York Christmas*, 2002.

- Roxy Music. "Love Is the Drug." *The Best of Roxy Music*, 2001.

- Santana. "No One to Depend On." *Ultimate Santana*, 2007.

CHAPTER 8

The School Bus and the Shack in the Ditch

My father had built a little shack at the end of our quarter-mile long lane. In later years, my mother said that she'd felt sorry for me having to walk that far every day to get to the school bus. I didn't care. I was happy. I'd waited for eons until I was old enough to go to school and learn how to read and speak English.

"Mom, read me a story. I want *Peter Goes to School*." I'd push the worn picture book in her face when she sat in the rocking chair putting the baby to sleep.

"Again?" She'd exhale a weighted sigh and switch the baby to her other side. "'Every day Peter woke up and said, 'Is this the day that I go to school?' 'No,' his mother said. 'Not today.' 'Finally the day came. . . .'"

"When can I go to school, Mom?" I'd ask every day, just like Peter.

"When you're six."

Every school day I'd walk the quarter mile back and forth through sun and wind. I wore rubber boots over my shoes on the days that it rained and snowed and green mittens over my hands during the winter. My mother knitted a new pair for me each year. I carried a tin, red-checkered lunch box packed with store-bought white bread, bologna, and mayonnaise; a banana, apple, or orange; cherry Kool-Aid; Jell-O with cottage cheese; and church or oatmeal cookies, or on rare occasions, chocolate chip cookies—my favorite.

When winter came that first year of school, my father installed a little hut in the ditch to protect me from the weather while I waited for the bus. The shack was an A-frame bare-bones structure with a scrap sheet metal roof nailed onto two by fours. No insulation. No heat. No floor. Just set on top of bare ground and dead weeds.

One rickety, old, backless chair that had been headed for firewood decorated the interior. The ground was uneven, so whenever I sat on the chair, it wobbled and I had to balance myself against the side of the shack. A metal flap opening toward the road let me peek outside.

In this particular Wisconsin community, the public school system transported us Amish children on the same rural route as the non-Amish children. Instead of taking us into town, however, we got dropped off at our one-room Amish-only schoolhouse. I worried that the school bus driver wouldn't stop for me when I sat hidden inside the hut. How would the driver know I was there?

"Dad, I'm very afraid the bus won't stop for me," I said.

"I told Joan that you're in the shack. She'll honk when she gets there."

"What if she forgets? I don't want to miss

school."

I wanted a perfect attendance record. My mother promised me a reward at the end of the year if I didn't miss school. That was something her teacher, Mrs. Nolan, had done. My mother was from the generation prior to the 1971–72 Supreme Court case, *Wisconsin v. Yoder,* and had received a public school education. She hadn't gone to the schools in town with non-Amish kids but to one-room country schoolhouses in Iowa, restricted to Amish kids but taught by non-Amish teachers assigned by the Iowa State Board of Education.

My mother often spoke about Mrs. Nolan playing the piano at school. That's where she learned secular and patriotic American songs, read classic American and British literature, and studied basic health and hygiene. I was allowed to leisure read during school hours after I finished my assignments. Amish children weren't given homework; our lessons were completed at school. By the time I was in the second and third grades, I was gobbling up titles that my mother handed down to me from her education, such as *Anne of Green Gables, Nancy Drew Mystery Stories, The Hardy Boys, The Boxcar Children, Caddie Woodlawn, Where the Red Fern Grows,* and *The Secret Garden.*

Books became my passport to the universe. I lived in exotic worlds, each story a new experience. Words captivated me. Artistic words. Rhythmic words. Pretty words. Creative words. Colors. Objects. Sights. Sounds. Smells. Aliveness. People and places that weren't Amish. I read anything that could take me away from the drab and unhappy existence that was my homelife. Being old enough to go to school meant that I was also old enough to take on adult responsibilities. My mother saddled me with chores and caring for my younger siblings. Getting away from her and the drudgery were the reasons I didn't want to miss school, but getting a prize for earning a perfect attendance record was further motivation.

Every morning I worried that the bus would forget to stop for me. My father finally did something about it. "Okay, I'll make a flag for you." He always knew how to fix my problems. He knocked a pole into the ground and tied one of his torn red handkerchiefs onto it. If the flag was up, Joan knew I was there.

Still anxious, I couldn't stay put on the stool. I'd run in and out of the shack to check for the yellow flash coming down the road. What if it was a substitute driver who didn't know what the flag meant and they flew on by? The thought of missing one day of learning and getting stuck with my mother was too much to bear.

On the bus rides home, I'd hear Paul Harvey on the radio. His *The Rest of the Story* newscasts always ended with "This is Paul Harvey. And now you know the rest of the story."

I'd sit toward the front of the bus in the mornings, but on the way home, I moved further and further to the seats in the back as the older kids got off. My stop was one of the last on the route. Empty of schoolmates to talk to, I had nothing to do but listen to Paul Harvey's voice. He sounded so authoritative. People listen to him, I thought.

That's what I'll do when I grow up to make people listen to me, too.

I dreaded recess because Amos Borntreger, the school bully, picked on me every day. He was mean to all of the lower graders, but until I arrived, no one fought back. Everyone was too afraid of him. It's wrong that he's mean to the little kids, I thought when I watched him. At lunch he grabbed whatever food he wanted from the younger children when we sat outside on the grass to eat. The kids cried, but no one stopped him. No one made him give it back, so I ran after him.

I was fat and slow and Amos was skinny and fast. He ran just slow enough to make me think I'd catch up with him. Just as I was about to grab the stolen piece of candy or sandwich out of his hand, he sped up, laughed, and ran around me in circles, holding the food just out of my arm's reach. I huffed and puffed and got red in the face from running. Sometimes I tripped and fell because I didn't watch where I was going. He laughed even harder when that happened.

The teacher, Andy Wengerd, was never in the schoolyard to supervise. He stayed inside to smoke his tobacco pipe. In that particular community, the men—but not the women—were allowed to smoke. But only pipes. Cigarettes would send you to hell. When I complained to Andy about Amos, he said, "Don't be a tattletale." Amos kept bullying us.

Sometimes the upper grade girls noticed what was happening and made Amos behave. But most of the time we lower graders played in a separate

part of the schoolyard. By the time my first year
was over, Amos rarely picked on anyone but me.
I thought I was successfully protecting the rest of
the kids but he probably just had more fun picking
on me: I was so hopelessly fat with no chance of
ever beating him.

"You have to tell me everything that happens
in school," my mother said. As soon as I got home,
she wanted a report. After a few years, I quit telling her because it didn't do any good. When I had
complained about the injustices, nothing changed.
But then, when my mother heard about the scraps
I'd gotten into from her best friend Orpha or one of
the other mothers, she'd yell at me, "Why did you
disobey me? I told you you have to tell me everything!" She'd beat me, and often made me do extra
chores. Or go without an after-school snack. Or
carry the chamber pot outside and dump it in the
garden. If it was full—or too heavy for me to carry—urine would slosh out and down along the side
of the bucket. I loathed seeing the feces, urine, and
toilet paper swirling inside the bucket, so I'd walk
too fast to try to get it over with. Then the urine
would splash onto my legs.

Neither the teacher, nor Amos' parents, nor
my parents, nor any of the other children's parents did anything to make the playground safe and
bully-free. So I kept fighting. I didn't care if the
odds were stacked against me. I became smarter.
I couldn't catch up with Amos physically, but I
discovered that I could ambush him and that once
he was on the ground, I could pummel him. I used
his own tactics against him. In the schoolroom

during class time, he'd stick his foot out to trip me as I walked past on my way to the back of the room to get a book; so during recess when we played tag, I'd hide on one side of the schoolhouse, and when he rounded the corner, I'd jump out, kick his leg hard enough to make him fall, ball my hands up into fists, and beat him as fast and as hard as I could. My weight served me well when he was on the ground and I was on top pinning him down.

We moved to Michigan when I was around ten. That community allowed more modern conveniences, such as phones in the barn. As long as they weren't in the house, God wouldn't send us to hell for having a phone. But the bullying on the playground was no different. This time the resident bully was a boy in my grade named Marlin Troyer. When I fought back, the entire community denounced my actions.

"Such shameful behavior!" The women of the Church wagged their heads.

"Your daughter is the problem," the bully's parents said.

"Torah is a troublemaker," the teacher said.

"Why aren't you turning the other cheek?" my mother yelled.

My father said nothing. I was his favorite child, but he didn't stick up for me or do anything to fix the problems in school. He left me to the mercy of my mother, who beat me regularly for protesting injustices and fighting back when the teachers looked the other way or took the side of the perpetrator.

"Bend over on that chair." My mother would

point, her eyes firing out flames at me. Her mouth
would turn hard, her posture ruthless, as she
hustled to the cabinet where the leather belt was
stored.

Rachel, two years younger than me, would
snicker from across the room. My mother's favorite, she tattled on me about school happenings or
made up lies when we came home whenever she
didn't want to do the chores that my mother had
assigned to her. My mother believed her, not me,
so I'd get a lashing as well as all of Rachel's chores
that night.

For the rest of my four years in the Michigan
school—until my graduation from the eighth
grade—I didn't back down despite my father's
refusal to create a safe environment for me, my
mother's punishments, and the community's
vindictiveness. I couldn't look the other way when
I saw that something needed to change. It wasn't
right that just by virtue of being a male, Marlin was
allowed to get away with bullying, but because I
was a female, I was targeted and made out to be
the bad person.

"When are you going to learn to be submissive?" My mother struck the belt across my back
and bare legs in alternating fashion until my skin
was blood red and I screamed hard enough from
the pain to satisfy her.

Music for the Soul

———

Here are several selections that helped me get through the events or period of this chapter, or reflect musically what I felt during this time. I understood very little of most lyrics—even today my ears don't process most words—but the melodies and instruments fed my soul. Had it not been for music, I wouldn't have survived until I finally got to therapy at age twenty-nine.

- The Beatles. "Here Comes the Sun." *Abbey Road*, 1969.

- Gnarls Barkley. "Crazy." *St. Elsewhere*, 2006.

- Nick Drake. "Magic." *Made to Love Magic*, 2004.

CHAPTER 9

A Car Crash and My First Funeral

"If you forsake the Amish, God will punish you and send you to hell," the bishop said. He stood before around eight hundred people seated in a barn. Everyone was dressed in black.

Hard wooden benches with no backs lined the width of the barn and divided it down the middle. Men and boys, their black wide-brimmed hats removed, sat on one side and women and girls, wearing white or black caps with strings knotted below their chins, sat on the other. I was in the women's section with my mother, my sister just younger than me—six-year-old Rachel—and two-year-old baby Joseph. My father and four-year-old brother Al sat across the aisle with the rest of the men.

Earlier that week, members of the two Amish Church districts in our Wisconsin community had gotten together to prepare for the funeral. They'd moved the bales of hay into a corner and swept the floor clean. But bits of straw floated around from the breeze coming through the open barn door. When the pieces landed, the men and boys leaned down to pick them up. They chewed on the stems—and spit them out—during the long, three-hour service.

A teenage boy lay in the open casket next to

the bishop. During *rumspringa*—a period of time
from age sixteen or seventeen until marriage—he'd
bought a car and, after a night of drinking and
partying, ended up killed in a crash. This shook the
community up.

"He was a very bad boy," my mother had told
me when we got the news of the death. She looked
grim. "He disobeyed his parents and now he's going to hell."

Our religion prohibited us from owning and
driving cars—but not from paying a non-Amish
person to chauffeur us when the destination was
too far away for a horse and buggy. In a lot of the
communities, some of the *junge*—youth from age
sixteen or seventeen until marriage—broke the
rules until they got baptized. They had radios
and cameras, drank, smoked, partied on week-
ends, didn't wear suspenders, and wore dresses
that were shorter than they were supposed to be.
Some, mostly boys and far less often girls, even
bought cars—one of the worst of sins—or left the
Amish Church for good, which was the worst sin
of all. That week, at eight years old, I learned that
getting killed in a car accident was a direct punishment from God for disobeying the rules. Such a
death was proof of how evil and sinful it was for an
Amish person to drive.

I didn't know who the boy was because he belonged to a family in the other Church district, not
the one we attended on a regular basis. I'd been to
funerals when I was younger but none that I could
remember, and none that stirred up such angst
within the community. I was excited and curious

to see this infamous boy. What would a bad, dead person look like?

"The world is the devil's playground," the preacher said. "This is what happens if you get a car."

Two women sitting on a bench near the casket cried out loud. Their sobs travelled all the way down through the barn to where I sat. I'd never heard a grown-up cry before. It was even more startling because not even children were allowed to cry during church services. If a child cried or made too much noise, the parents shushed them, or removed them from the service and spanked them. If babies fussed too loudly, the women took them to the bedroom.[1]

"Who's crying?" I whispered, tugging my mother's sleeve. It sounded different from a child and no one got up to make it stop.

"Sh!" My mother looked annoyed that my whisper blared. Joseph slept in her lap and Rachel leaned against her other side. "It's the English[2] women."

"Why are those *fremde leht* crying?"

I squirmed around on the bench to get a better look. Unlike regular church services, Mennonites and other non-Amish relatives and friends attended. All I could see between the spaces in the crowd were the backs of the two women's uncovered heads. At funerals, people were seated in relation to the deceased. Because we weren't related to the family, we sat too far away for me to see their faces.

"They're his friends. One of them was his girlfriend. Now sit still. No more wiggling, no more questions. Listen to the preacher."

I couldn't understand most of what the ministers said because they spoke in German instead of Amish. But unlike during normal services, it was easy for me to remain facing forward toward the preacher for three hours because of the strange sobbing. Didn't they know they should be quiet? When the sermon, hymns, and prayers were over, the final preacher sat down. Row after row, people in the barn filed past the casket and returned to their seat. The adults held their small children up and pointed when they got to the dead boy.

"Mom. Mom! Why are people walking around like that?"

"That's what we do at funerals. Everyone goes up to see the person who died."

When it was our turn, I walked behind my mother, who carried Joseph. I was tall enough to see inside the casket. It looked like the boy was sleeping. He was dressed in Amish clothes and he didn't look English—not like someone who drove a car. *Is he really in hell now?*

"Don't stop," my mother said, looking back at me while holding onto Rachel's hand.

I wanted to stay longer, but there were so many people that no one was allowed to slow down. So I stared at the English women as we walked past them on the way back. They kept dabbing their eyes with Kleenex, their faces puffy and blotched with tears. They wore pretty hair, bright makeup, and short tailored dresses that exposed their legs. The hundreds of Amish women all wore ankle-length, frumpy outfits, hair stuck underneath caps, and no makeup.

None of the Amish people in the front rows had tears on their faces. The longer I inspected their behavior, the more it seemed to me that the boy's English friends really loved him and that maybe his Amish relatives didn't care for him quite as much. Was he that bad if he had friends who cried so much in front of all the people? They seemed very sad that he was dead.

After everyone returned to their seat, the funeral ended and people started mingling. Funerals were like reunions, with friends and family coming from all over the Midwestern and Eastern states. The sun shone brightly, puffy clouds floated in the sky, and a mixture of hay and cow manure perfumed the air. It was the perfect day for a gathering and making new friends.

"Want to play tag?" I collected a group of girls. Some were my classmates in school, others from far away who became new friends for the day. The freshly mown grass felt good underneath my bare feet as we ran around, zigzagging between clusters of adults scattered throughout the front yard.

An old man with a long white beard pulled up next to the barn. He drove an odd-looking wagon. Six men, three on each side of the casket, slowly moved out of the barn and put the casket in the wagon.

"What are they doing?" I ran over to my mother, who was visiting with a group of women on benches in the grass.

"They're going to bury the boy now."

"Giddy-up," the old man said. He guided the horse and wagon toward the road.

A long line of buggies followed him out the driveway and onto the blacktop toward the Amish cemetery. Several vans carrying out-of-state relatives trailed behind.

"When are we going?" I asked.

"Only the boy's parents and relatives go to the graveyard."

"Why? I want to see them put him in the ground."

"Be nice!"

That meant "Stop begging and asking questions."

Disappointed, I watched the procession of buggies disappear from view, the sound of the horses' clip-clops fading in the distance. I felt cheated and excluded.

"Come, it's time to go home." My mother walked toward our buggy where my father and brother Al waited.

Later that week, I kept asking to visit the graveyard. I'd picked up that the boy was buried in an Amish one, not the English one that we passed by on our way into town during shopping trips—for things we didn't make ourselves, like sugar and hardware. Every Memorial Day, lots of English people, dressed up in nice clothes, put little American flags and bunches of flowers on the plots of their loved ones.

"Why do they put flags on them?" I'd asked one time, my bare feet swinging from the back seat of the buggy.

"Those were the people who died in wars," my father said.

"We don't go to war," my mother said. She frowned and tied her cap strings extra tight. "It's wrong to kill people."

"We're conscientious objectors," my father said. "The government doesn't make us fight because it's against our religion. But in the past, we were persecuted for our beliefs."

I'd scrutinize the activities as our horse and buggy slowly drifted by. Some of the headstones were big and ornate and the grass was meticulously manicured. I liked the colorful flowers scattered everywhere—beautiful white lilies and red roses. The English seemed to care a great deal for their dead.

"Stop staring," my mother would say, as if by ignoring—not looking—the evils of the outside world went away.

I assumed that our cemetery was just as beautiful as the English one in town. My parents had made it sound like it was special. "I want to see the Amish graveyard where the bad boy was buried," I begged.

My mother swept up a pile of dirt from the dining room floor. "It's too far. It's in the other Church district."

"But I want to see it!"

My father looked up from The Budget,[3] the weekly Amish newspaper. "We'll take you to the old one by Raymond's."

Raymond Schrock was the bishop of our district and he lived a quarter mile up the road. That

Sunday after church, we went on a walk. My mother had packed a picnic basket with lemonade and homemade popcorn. We munched on the snacks along the way.

"This is how an Amish graveyard looks like?" I asked. It didn't look nice like the English one.

My father laughed when he saw how disappointed I was. "No one gets buried here anymore."

I walked around the tiny, bedraggled grounds. The bishop's sons kept it mowed, but the grass was brown and had bare spots and hurt my feet. Dirt mounds and ruts and stalks of weeds shot up in uneven places. The headstones were small. And some of them were so tiny that they barely appeared above the ground.

"Why aren't there any big ones?" I asked.

"That's *zu hoch*," my mother said. Too prideful, arrogant.

"The English spend all their money on stupid things," my father said. He smirked and stroked his beard. "It's just a corpse that rots in the ground. When you die, you go to heaven or hell. A big stone is like an idol. We don't worship idols."

"This is where Old Alvin Lambright's cousin was buried." My mother pointed out all the names she recognized.

"Who's this?" I asked her. One of the stones was less plain-looking and engraved in pretty lettering.

"I don't know. They died before we moved here."

"Why aren't there any names on these?" I hopped along a row of blank markers all the way in the back by a tree.

"It costs money to put the names on. Maybe they were too poor. Or maybe it's a stillborn baby who had no name. Sometimes it's someone's child like the boy whose funeral we went to. They get buried in the back because they were bad."

"How do they know who's buried here?"

"The preachers keep a record in a book of everyone who dies and where they were put."

"I want to be buried in a nice one. With flowers."

"We don't get buried in English graveyards."

That was when it hit me that even in death, we Amish had to stay separated from the rest of the world. There'd be no crying. No big tombstones. No lilies on Memorial Day. And no name on the concrete slab if I was bad.

"Stop jumping on those stones," my mother said. "There are dead people under there."

Notes

1. Amish families take turns hosting church services in their home. We do not have church buildings.

2. Anyone who isn't Amish is "English," even if they don't speak English—unless they're a member of the Anabaptists, such as the Mennonites and Hutterites, who are religious ancestors of the Amish.

3. *The Budget* is a weekly print newspaper that's sort of the Amish equivalent of social media. Except only one designated person from each Church district is allowed to send in a report of the happenings in their community that week or month.

Music for the Soul

Here are several selections that helped me get through the events or period of this chapter, or reflect musically what I felt during this time. I understood very little of most lyrics—even today my ears don't process most words—but the melodies and instruments fed my soul. Had it not been for music, I wouldn't have survived until I finally got to therapy at age twenty-nine.

- Johnny Cash. "(Ghost) Riders in the Sky." *Silver*, 1978. [A cover of the 1948 original by Stan Jones.]

- Johnny Cash. "Ring of Fire." *Ring of Fire: The Best of Johnny Cash*, 1963.

- Broken Bells. "Trap Doors." *Broken Bells*, 2010.

CHAPTER 10

Freedom in the Skies

Under the Kansas Stars

My flight instructor pulled the carburetor, effectively killing the engine. The prop stopped turning. Our tiny two-seater Cessna 150 stalled. The nose tipped over and we plummeted straight down. I lost several thousand feet before recovering and turning skyward again.

"If you can't leave your problems on the ground, you're never going to learn how to fly." Aaron, my instructor sitting next to me in the copilot seat, didn't look too happy.

I was in my first year of college in Hesston, Kansas, at a two-year liberal arts school with an aviation program. I'd been taking lessons for several weeks, with the goal of earning my pilot's license by semester's end. I couldn't lose more than one hundred feet of altitude in order to pass the Federal Aviation Administration (FAA) exam. The engine could quit at any time—with no warning from my instructor—and I had to respond instantly. If my mind was wandering, losing even just several seconds of response time cost me more than a hundred-foot drop.

What the hell does he mean by saying I have problems that are affecting my flying? I did well in school. Aaron was the problem, not me.

More than anything, I wanted to fly. Flying was the ticket to realizing my Amish childhood dream of visiting every country in the world and exploring all that the globe had to offer. I had no idea why Aaron was upset with me, but I wasn't going to not get my license. Through sheer will and determination, while being pissed at Aaron during most of that time, I learned to turn off my inner turmoil and experience a state of "now." I hadn't yet heard of meditation, but that was what I was practicing.

Flying became the tool that snapped me into a state of being in the present moment. Once I stepped into the plane, nothing outside that moment existed. For one hour, I was truly free. Free from all the pain, suffering, and trauma that dogged me on the ground. For one fleeting hour, I forgot all the horrors of my past; it was as if none of it had ever happened. That was when I began to fly with precision, dance in the sky, play with the elements, and be one with my plane.

Around four months later, Aaron signed me off to fly solo, north to the FAA exam center in Salina, Kansas. I passed. I had finally earned my wings.

That night I returned a real pilot. Just me and my plane humming peacefully under a perfect upside-down bowl of Kansas stars. The lights in the towns four thousand feet below me glowed and twinkled yellow. The empty, silent Kansas plains stretched beneath me for as far as I could see and above me clear skies stretched to infinity. No headwind slowed me down and no crosswind threw me off course. The calm and clear conditions were also metaphors for how I felt about my prospects for the future. I had the piece of paper that said I was free to fly on my own; nothing stood in my way. I'd faced staggering challenges to secure that independent access to the skies. Being in the air had become my high, my therapy, my addiction. My bliss. I thought of the people in the houses below me and I imagined what they were doing. How they had no idea that I was passing overhead. How they didn't know what it was like to have wings. How they'd never tasted the exhilaration of freedom.

That night I scanned my gauges more than usual to make sure that I wasn't dreaming or hallucinating, and that everything was okay with my plane: I was on course, not drifting. Engine running. Fuel levels good. Altimeter functioning. Transmitter working. Wings level. Precisely aligned with the horizon. Everything was so perfect that I dropped altitude, veering off and back several degrees just to make sure my gauges hadn't frozen somehow, that they weren't misleading me.

For the first time in my life, nothing was wrong. Nothing was a struggle. I didn't even have a crosswind to deal with—not normal for Kansas where the wind whipped unobstructed across flat and unpopulated space, often too much for student pilots to handle. There'd always been uncertainty as to whether I'd be cleared to fly on a given day when I arrived at the base for my lesson. Tonight, my world was perfectly perfect. I didn't want to return to the ground. I wanted to stay up forever and never let go of that moment.

And then I had to land.

The beacon at Newton airport got bigger and bigger as I neared my approach. No other plane was out that night—just one of the instructors, Ben, waiting for me on the ground. Everything was quiet and dark except for the lights around the field. I picked a runway and started my descent. The strips of lights outlining my path grew further and further apart the closer I got to the ground. At just the right time, I pulled back on the controls. Just the right amount for a gentle bump.

I radioed my status—"Newton Traffic, Cessna Two Eight Zero Hotel Charlie, clear of runway, Newton"—to the silence around me, into the empty darkness, and taxied to the hangar. It was over. My trip was done.

"Congratulations," Ben said, his smile as wide as the stars overhead. "You passed."

Dharamsala, Home of the Dalai Lama

"What are those huts for?" I asked Arun, my Indian guide. We crawled along a bumpy, narrow dirt road, up the Himalayan Mountains toward Dharamsala, home to the Dalai Lama and the Tibetan government-in-exile. Little mud and straw shacks lined each side of the road.

"Huts? Those are houses."

"Huh?" I was sure I hadn't heard him right.

"Houses. People live in them."

Just a few weeks before, I'd met Arun in a chatroom while searching the internet for information about the Dalai Lama. This was in the era of dial-up and AOL when our version of social media engagement took place in anonymous chatrooms, which were often sleazy. Arun claimed to have worked for Japan Airlines and now be some sort of consultant. My question had been on how to get an audience with the Dalai Lama and Arun just happened to know.

"Anyone can see the Dalai Lama," he said. "He holds open visiting hours every so often. Kind of like a professor's office hours in college. You can walk in without an appointment. Let me look into his schedule and get back to you."

A few days later, Arun confirmed the dates. December 2000. All I needed to do was show up. Skip work, get on a plane, and fly halfway around the globe. But first I had to get my visa for India. I was lucky: Houston, Texas, had an embassy with expedited services.

After a three-day flight by virtue of crossing multitudes of time zones, and with an all-day connection in Frankfurt, I stepped off the plane in New Delhi, the capital, early enough in the morning to see the sun rise. The heavy, humid, monsoon-influenced subtropical climate accompanied by an intense acrid smell in the arrivals hall through customs made breathing hurt. It's a smell that's uniquely India. A cocktail of putrid waste, dust clouds, and dripping, stinking sweat from over a billion people crammed into the size of about a third of the US. Imagine the entire population of the US—around three hundred million—confined to an area from the Northeast to the Midwest, and you'll have the right proportions.

The overwhelming volume of amplified noises, smells, and scenes of India stupefied me. There were endless numbers of people in all directions as far as my eyes could see streaming through the markets, jostling along the sidewalks, and spilling into traffic. People dressed in bright colors and distinctly different types of clothing: saris, burkas, suits, dresses, monk's robes, or nearly naked. Camels, elephants, monkeys, live dancing cobras, rickshaws, motorcycles, honking horns, and cars hurtled by. The ceaseless din and volume swallowed everyone and everything in its wake. I saw a police officer crack a long whip, lashing the backs and bare arms of motorcycle riders to make the drivers obey the lights at a major intersection. But no one stopped. Traffic swirled into what looked like roads from a dozen different directions converging all at once. The officer's whip looked like the horse whips that the Amish used, like the one that my father had flogged me with.

"Whoa! Did you see that?" I asked Arun. I couldn't believe my eyes.

"What? Oh, yeah. That's totally normal. They do that to prevent accidents."

I had learned about the Dalai Lama through one of the clients of the company I worked for who had us handle the private flight arrangements for her trip to Dharamsala.

"This is a very VIP flight," my boss Lisa said when the details showed up on my computer. "Extreme high priority. She's visiting the Dalai Lama."

"Who's that?"

"Where have you been? You really don't know? He's like, only the world's most well-known humanitarian."

Lisa gave me just enough of a background on him for me to say, "He sounds amazing. I'd love to meet him."

"Are you serious? You have to be rich or famous to get time with him." Lisa's platinum blonde hair, blue eyes, and bright red lips enhanced her snobbishness.

"Well, if he's as much of a compassionate person as you say he is, then I should be able to see him, too. Even if I'm not rich and famous."

Lisa acted as if I'd lost all my marbles. She was the married department head's girlfriend. If she wasn't important enough to meet the Dalai Lama, then certainly her underling wasn't.

You really think I'm such a nobody that I can't figure out how to meet this Dalai Lama dude myself? Watch me.

Several months later, I found myself on a ten-day trip, half of those days consumed to just make the flight there and back. Four days on the ground was all I could swing from the remaining of my vacation and sick days at work.

The air became lighter, clearer, colder, less polluted, and actually breathable the further up the mountains we got. I couldn't grasp the concept that people lived in those roadside shacks. They looked like the little shack my father had built for me in the ditch at the end of our quarter-mile drive when I was six years old, and going to school for the first time.

"I'd love to see the inside," I said. "How do

people live like that?" It was a comment, more of a private musing out loud, but Arun, in the role of "Do whatever the rich white American lady wants" tourist guide, took it as a command.

"Stop the car," he told the driver. "Stay here," he told me. "I'll find out if anyone's home."

Arun knocked on the exterior door. A dark-skinned middle-aged woman with ragged clothes cracked it open and poked her head out. I watched from inside the car as Arun motioned toward me and gestured while the woman stood there.

Arun walked back. "She can't understand Hindi or English, but I knew enough words of the local language to tell her that you wanted to see the inside. Come."

The other side of the door revealed an open-air courtyard-style hut, with no interior doors and no floors. A few walls sectioned off several rooms on one side. The rooms had cutouts for windows— no glass or panes—and more dirt floors. An older woman, a grandmother, and several children with bright black eyes and dark brown skin stared at me. They were as curious about me as I was about them.

I looked around, barely able to comprehend what I was seeing. No beds, no furniture, no lights in the rooms where they slept. Tattered, straw mats for beds. This is their home. And I'm being a crazy, white American intruder barging in on them. We can't even communicate with each other.

The only source of heat for cooking came from an open-fire pit in the courtyard. The woman smiled at me and watched me walk around while she heated up some oil in a pan over the fire. When the flat, thin dough turned brown on both sides, she took it out of the pan and let it cool off a little. Then she picked the bread up with both hands and offered it to me. No words, just a smile.

I turned to Arun. "Am I going to get food poisoning from this?"

"No, it's been cooked in oil. This is what they eat, and it's probably the only food they'll have all day."

"Then I really can't eat it. They don't have enough for themselves."

The woman knelt on the ground, still holding the bread. The grandmother, the other woman, and the children crowded closer and watched, silent.

"You need to accept it. They think that you could be a kind person from one of their past lifetimes, and it's an honor to them that you're in their home."

"That's really who they think I am?"

Arun nodded. "Eat it."

"But this is all they have. . . ."

"Then just one bite out of respect."

I took the bread and broke off a small edge. Then I gave it back to the woman. I was glad I didn't have to eat the whole piece and make them go hungrier than they already were.

Arun and I returned to the car parked outside and resumed our trek up to the Dalai Lama's residence. I'd been taught that anyone who worshipped a non-biblical god or statues was doomed—and that included Catholics because they prayed to the Virgin Mary. Surely those people aren't going to hell like the born-again, fundamentalist Christians say, I thought. They invited me, a complete foreigner, into their home and offered me the only food they had. They don't need conversion. They're already practicing what Jesus taught: being kind to strangers.

This marked the definitive end of my struggle with Christianity, which hadn't satisfied me with answers as to why bad things happen to good people if God was a loving and all-powerful God. I'd already quit going to church. I wondered if Eastern religions had the answers. Perhaps there was something to multiple gods. I began studying non-Western beliefs and their enlightenment concepts. Little did I suspect that several years later, I'd become so drawn to Buddhism that I'd learn how to read, and even translate, ancient classical Tibetan texts.

We approached the gate. A sign in English and a strange-looking script—Tibetan—announced our location: the entrance to the Dalai Lama's complex, which included his offices and private house. A guard ushered us through security, beneath prayer flags—blue, white, red, green, and yellow—strung overhead. Monks in crimson robes milled about the open-air temple opposite the entrance. Some chanted with prayer beads. Some looked like they were in debate class. Others spun prayer wheels as they walked by. Cute little baby boy monks dotted the plaza and classrooms. And a flag with a rising sun and a pair of snow lions flapped in the breeze. The flag of Tibet—forbidden to fly in the Land of Snow, its country of origin.

Dubai, a City Built on Sinking Sand

"It's not safe here," one of the Marines told me. "You're travelling alone over here? A female?" "What do you mean it's not safe? That's just American propaganda."

The Marine seemed genuinely nervous. "Something's going down. Something's about to happen. You're not safe here."

I wasn't about to be bullied by political propaganda or misogyny, like I was some helpless female who needed to have a man by her side or be told where she could and could not travel. Americans are so ignorant and brainwashed, I thought. Sheltered, crybaby Americans who never bother to travel to other countries, learn a second language, or educate themselves about other cultures, religions, and belief systems. Who actually believe that the US is the greatest country in the world, the savior of the world, and does no wrong. Who buy into all the fear-mongering and war-mongering from the preachers and the politicians. The outside world is not a scary place; the inside world is.

The worst of the bad shit that happened to me was inflicted by those on the inside, within my own culture. The worst damage, by far, came from my very own people, not strangers. My parents neglected and abused me in the name of discipline. My nonpracticing Amish uncles raped me repeatedly. And my church of origin ostracized me and protected the rapists, not the victims.

"You're just trying to scare me. You're making it up. It's completely safe here for Americans."

"No, you need to get out. Leave."

"What exactly is going to happen?"

"I'm not allowed to say. It's classified."

"You expect me to just believe you, with no proof? That's b.s."

The Marine walked back to his fellow soldiers. I returned to smoking my *shisha*, apple-flavored tobacco. Several days later, I was on a flight back to the dreaded reality of my miserable job and unhappy life in corporate America. Several weeks later, the towers fell.

I watched the second plane hit New York and the words "terrorists," "Islam," "Arabs," and "war" blast across the TV screen. Which city is next? Is this a full-on attack on the US? Is there going to be war on American soil? I was scared. I wanted to return to Dubai. I had felt safe there. If the Arabs really were attacking us, then the safest place in the world for me was to be in an Arab country where I had access to the royal family of Dubai. They'd protect me, even if I was American. Because I wasn't a typical American. And they weren't the stereotypical fanatical Islamists. They were smart, educated, intelligent people.

My plans to escape failed. I couldn't fly away. All the planes were grounded. For who knew how long. . . . But if the worst happened—if a war started—I knew that I'd find a way to get out. The planet was small, accessible, familiar to me.

My miserable corporate job had transformed the world into a radically shrunken sphere for me to easily cover and comb. My prior perception of an expansive and inaccessible Earth had collapsed and disintegrated. I acquired a completely new concept of time and space and a whole new set of reference points by coordinating corporate pilots' flight schedules to around two hundred countries. Access to any of those places felt doable. Seven hours alone got me to a different continent. Only seven hours. I couldn't even drive all the way across Texas in that amount of time.

Each day my superior briefed us on up-to-the-minute, real-time political conditions of the countries our pilots flew to. Those details mattered because we needed to get the pilots their overhead flight clearances, landing slots, and refuelling stops. Our political briefings were flavored differently from what the news stations broadcasted. We got realistic, practical, and factual information. And the pilots I spoke to gave me friendlier reports about the countries they flew to than what the media and State Department advertised.

I'm gonna go into international affairs, I thought, and tell people what these countries really are like. This is how I can bring more peace to the world. One of my first stops to observe a non-Western culture was the United Arab Emirates.

"Why do you go to Dubai? What's it like there?" I asked one of our pilots one day.

"You should visit. You'll like it. It's completely Western-friendly. You can even wear a bikini on the beach."

Dubai turned out to be one of the most inspiring experiences of my travels. If the UAE could build a city on sinking sand, then surely I could build my castles in the sky—my impossible dreams. I was one of the few female Americans—certainly solo female Americans—to visit before Dubai made itself the global destination it is today. I watched the city grow up, taking notes as it evolved. This is how you change a culture. This is how you change an entire religion, country, people. The city became my model and guide for how to create a shift within the Amish.

"If you make too many changes too fast, the people will riot," Prince Ahmed told me one evening during a yacht party. "You have to introduce things slowly. Your vision is too big for the people to understand. You have to *lead* people toward your vision. And be patient. It takes a long time."

I listened intently while enjoying the view of the city lights across the water, Ahmed's figure silhouetted against the backdrop. He wore a traditional *dishdasha*—an ankle-length white robe that represented his royal status—over his clothes; and a *keffiyeh*—a scarf made from a square white cloth folded into a triangle—over his head, held in place with two rings of black coil. The *keffiyeh* flowed down his back, like a Western bride's veil.

"It's good caviar, isn't it?" He nodded toward the plate in my hand. "From Russia. Some of the best."

I have no idea whether it's better than other kinds. I've never had any before. "Yes." I nodded and smiled.

The thought of eating fish eggs made me want to gag. When Ahmed left to chat with other guests, I dumped the caviar over the side of the yacht. The round pieces floated down toward the water, like strings of pearl droplets.

My Sex Life

If guys could have emotionless sex, then so could girls, I figured. So I cut off all my emotions, blocked out my feelings, and just focussed on the physicality of sex. Like exposure therapy. Or what you do when you fall off a bike. If you don't get back on right away, the fear of falling grows stronger and stronger until it incapacitates you, until it freezes you, until it takes you over, until you're paralyzed. You have to get back on again and replace that last memory with a new, less frightening memory.

Intuitively I knew that the only way I'd be able to cope, function, and keep on living was to attempt to replace those rape memories with positive sex experiences. Where I was in control. Where I dictated what happened in the bedroom. Where I overlaid the bad memories and experiences with good experiences that erased, or at least mollified, the bad ones.

But no matter how much I tried, I couldn't forget what happened and I couldn't disconnect from the horror of what happened. It always dripped in the background. Like a leaking faucet that you can't turn off. That's turned all the way off. But still keeps dripping. Drop by drop. Day and night. Night and day. Always dripping. Drop by drop. Drop. By. Drop.

No matter how often and how hard I slammed the valve off, it wouldn't stop. I couldn't make the drip stop. I couldn't fix it. I couldn't make it okay. I couldn't rationalize any scenario that made what happened to me okay. I couldn't pretend that "Well, it really wasn't such a bad thing that happened to me." I couldn't escape. The demons kept following me around, nipping at my heels and ravaging my soul.

Flying away to other countries and immersing myself in other cultures gave me temporary relief. The geographical distances and the completely different cultures, in non-Western settings with no reminders of my American traumas, helped to psychologically separate me from the rapes. Maybe I could forget about what happened. Maybe I could somehow get away from all of that. Maybe it was just a very bad dream.

But then there was always the inevitable return. I had to go back to "the real world," back to the US, back to my job. I was a slave to my work—and a slave to my memories. I needed the paycheck to keep my apartment. There was nowhere else to go. No family. No one who cared. Nothing to live for. Except my dreams.

NOTE: Some names and details have been changed to protect certain identities.

Music for the Soul

———

Here are several selections that helped me get through the events or period of this chapter, or reflect musically what I felt during this time. I understood very little of most lyrics—even today my ears don't process most words—but the melodies and instruments fed my soul. Had it not been for music, I wouldn't have survived until I finally got to therapy at age twenty-nine.

- Pink Floyd. "Learning to Fly." *A Momentary Lapse of Reason*, 1987.

- Enya. "Orinoco Flow (Sail Away)." *Watermark*, 1988.

- Enya. "Wild Child." *A Day Without Rain*, 2000.

- Enya. "Only Time." *A Day Without Rain*, 2000.

CHAPTER 11

How to Snort Cocaine Like a Rock Star: Encounters with Alice Cooper, the Godfather of Shock Rock

Michael Bruce. Washed-up seventies rock star, strung out on coke whenever his royalty check came in, holed up in a hotel room with a woman of the night. Until all the cash burned through and he needed to pawn his guitars again to make the rent.

That's how I came by his double-neck acoustic guitar. I was nineteen years old, living in Houston, Texas, working a full-time job and going to flight school.

Greg called me one day. "Hey, you wanna buy a guitar from an original member of the Alice Cooper band?"

Alice Cooper, I'd learned, was the godfather of shock rock, or heavy metal theatrics. Greg had taken great pleasure in "corrupting" this unschooled Amish kid. He educated me on the history of the band's stage acts, which ranged from horror-film-inspired costumes, black eye makeup, mutilated heads of baby dolls, fake guillotine executions, and sadistic nurses, to live boa constrictors. The Alice Cooper band members had been greatly influenced by The Beatles. But they'd rebranded themselves into the antithesis of the peace and love scene, departing from the psychedelic rock sound of their 1969 debut album *Pretties for You.*

"Are you crazy? You know I can't afford a guitar, for sure not a celebrity's."

"Yeah, you can." Greg's sardonic laugh on the other end of the phone didn't make sense to me.

What the hell is he up to?

"You can pick it up for seventy bucks. Go to the pawn shop on Wertheimer and Benson. Go now. Get it before someone else steals it. I'll meet you there."

Greg gave me the address, I got into my car, and twenty minutes later, I pulled into a lot in a shitty part of town with faded parking spot lines, broken concrete, potholes everywhere waiting to tear off a low-hanging muffler under a speeding car, and crooked signage dangling lopsided off abandoned storefronts. A shady-feeling character smoking something in a corner further down the sidewalk eyed me as I got out of my vehicle. Greg, dressed in combat boots and an Alice Cooper shirt, stood outside the door under an awning that said "Big Daddy's Pawn & Guns, Fast Cash." Iron bars covered the windows of the shop and entrance. I'd never seen iron frames over windows and doors before. The place gave me the creeps.

That year I learned what *not* to do with fame and money. I saw firsthand what drug addiction did to incredible talent and potential. Michael was a gifted vocalist and lyricist who had written or co-written many of the original Alice Cooper band's hit songs and often the music or melodies, too. He played rhythm guitar and keyboards and, despite his coke habit, still looked attractive, easily recognizable in his old age as the hot-looking young rocker who had played around the world on stages for tens of thousands of raving fans. But the addiction killed his opportunities to remain a steady employable musician. None of the fame-by-name and none of the residual income had the power to reclaim the glory of his youth.

"He thinks he's still living in the seventies," Greg often said, frustrated when Michael went MIA during royalty payday and refused to emerge from his dungeons.

Greg had become Michael's de facto manager. For Greg, this was a dream come true, to be involved at that level with one of his childhood heroes. He believed he could rehabilitate Michael's career, despite the previous manager's warnings. Greg poured a ton of his own money into securing gigs and covering travel expenses. In the process, I got a front seat and insider's education on the politics and pitfalls of celebrityhood. I learned to spot eight-balls hidden in music gear, pat down equipment before a flight, and never carry or check in anything that was Michael's.

"Don't get caught with his magic marbles," Greg showed me the round, black leather coke ball pouches.

"Why is it called an 'eight-ball'?"

"Because it weighs an eighth of an ounce. That's 3.5 grams."

Greg didn't do coke and neither did I. But he showed me how it was done. Lay out thin white lines on a coffee table with a razor blade or credit card, roll up a dollar bill, stick one end in your nostril, and snort it up.

"People snort powder into their noses?! What the fuck. Doesn't that hurt?"

I wanted to try it but I was too scared of getting addicted. I hadn't planned my escape for four years, failed at my first attempt, finally made it out, and worked my ass off ever since for whatever little I'd gotten in life just to get addicted to drugs and never become somebody. One day I'd be a musician. A famous one. I'd be rich and popular and happy. I wasn't going to let drugs steal my freedom.

Ten years later, in the pits of hell, after graduating from an Ivy League school, at the lowest point of my life—if it's possible to go through a hell worse than repeat rape—I was snorting heavy lines off gold-etched glass table tops in a New York City Soho penthouse. Long, perfectly symmetric lines in double rows.

"Damn, girl, you're a pro," Nick said, sprawled on a brown leather sofa, pants down, a coke-laced joint tucked in his fingers.

I gave him blow jobs and he gave me blow.

NOTE: Some names and details have been changed to protect certain identities.

Music for the Soul

Here are several selections that helped me get through the events or period of this chapter, or reflect musically what I felt during this time. I understood very little of most lyrics—even today my ears don't process most words—but the melodies and instruments fed my soul. Had it not been for music, I wouldn't have survived until I finally got to therapy at age twenty-nine.

- Alice Cooper. "School's Out." *School's Out,* 1972.

- Alice Cooper. "Welcome to My Nightmare." *Welcome to My Nightmare,* 1975.

- The Velvet Underground & Nico. "Femme Fatale." *The Velvet Underground & Nico,* 1967.

CHAPTER 12

Love Is Not Safe (Ethan, the NASA Engineer)

Instead of rings, we got matching tattoos. I told myself I didn't want a ring because it was an imposed institutional symbol of ownership. No man owned me. I was a free woman and of equal status to males. I'd fought hard for my freedom, and I'd never give that up. But the truth, which I didn't want to acknowledge and feel, was that I was deeply hurt. Hurt that Ethan asked me to marry him and didn't bother to consider how I felt about engagement and wedding rings.

"I don't believe in rings," he announced when I said yes. The way he said it made me feel that I had no choice in the matter. It didn't matter what I wanted. So I sucked up the hurt, stuffed my feelings down, and pretended I agreed with him.

"It's American commercialization and consumerism," he said. Ethan took great pride in being a liberal half-European and anti-establishment. He was against Valentine's Day, too.

"It's Hallmark propaganda," he said, flicking his hand through his hair and pointing his nose just a bit higher than usual.

That year with him I was given no romantic

gifts, no birthday gifts, no Christmas gifts, no random gifts—nothing to celebrate love and intimacy. Even Amish girlfriends and some wives were recognized more than Ethan acknowledged me. In my particular Amish family, Valentine's Day, Mother's Day, Father's Day, birthdays, and Christmases were all approved of with at least a card and often more depending on the occasion. Granted, the acknowledgment was a token gesture by my father, an emotional, verbal, psychological, and physical abuser. Over the years, rather than actual snippets of caring, these events seemed to be opportunities he took to make himself look like he was a good person, to feed his delusion or project upon us that he was a good guy. In reality, he was a manipulative, truly evil psychopath who enjoyed torturing his wife and children.

For this pending marriage that I thought was going to last a lifetime, I wanted something to symbolize our commitment to each other. I mustered up the courage to suggest something radical that might appeal to Ethan, something that was definitely not "commercial": "Let's get matching tattoos and put them over our hearts."

He went for it. It was my second tattoo and his first.

When I met Ethan, I was twenty years old, and it would be another ten years before I started my journey of self-development and personal growth, in which I'd learn to value myself, love myself, and not settle for anything less than what I truly wanted and deserved. But at that time, I just felt lucky. Lucky that Ethan "loved" me.

Ethan was thirty-two, and we ran across each other in the early days of online dating, on Match. com, dinosaur years before apps like Bumble. I thought he was my dream man: tall, dark, and handsome with long black hair, educated, worldly, well-travelled, book smart, multicultural (half Italian), and multilingual. Born into a socioeconomic and intellectual status that I'd never belong to naturally, he came from the world I wanted entry into. I thought getting engaged to him signified a permanent turning point out of the fires and turmoil of my past and into an infinitely soaring future of happiness.

Later, as the relationship waned and I picked up on the social cues, mannerisms, and expectations of the educated class, I wondered what had attracted him to me, because he hadn't recognized my academic smarts—something that he placed an extremely high value on—nor expressed any interest in my Amish heritage and experiences. I battled crippling body image issues and was never sure if I was actually pretty. Ethan didn't say or do anything that encouraged me to think or feel that I was attractive. Or beautiful. Or sexy. So I believed that it must not have been physical looks either that had made him want to be with me. We did, however, have some things in common: his things that I was also interested in and wanted to learn more about.

I soaked up a vast library of knowledge from Ethan, information I hadn't been exposed to before. He taught me an appreciation for European and indie filmmaking, and what made a film a good film as opposed to mindless, cookie-cutter blockbusters or flicks. I learned that an educated person used the word "film" and not "movie" and that when I was asked what my favorite films were, I was to respond with the names of my favorite directors, not titles of movies. We spent many Sunday afternoons lounging in the bedroom watching Ingmar Bergman, Roberto Rossellini, Stanley Kubrick, Quentin Tarantino, and Cannes Film Festival selections while eating Ben & Jerry's ice cream. Ethan's choices were cerebrally engaging and emotionally compelling narratives.

"I'd like to become a filmmaker," I said after we watched Bergman's black-and-white classic *The Seventh Seal*. Intrigued by this method of storytelling and beginning to understand how the pieces of filmmaking fit together—thanks to Ethan's deconstructing—I felt that that would be the most powerful medium for me to get my Amish story into the world. I could reach far more people through a well-made film than I could through a book. The mass population watched movies. They didn't read. Via my education from Ethan, I understood I'd need to make a film of my story, not just a book, if I wanted to market my message effectively on a mass scale.

Ethan laughed so hard that some of the ice cream spilled out of his mouth. "You'll never be a filmmaker. Real filmmaking takes talent."

What? I was surprised, and angry, that he laughed at me. *Fuck you. Who are you to tell me I can't become a filmmaker? I can do anything I make up my mind to do.* But I didn't say anything. Because I was just happy that, at last, someone "loved" me.

Ethan introduced me to the blues and classic science fiction, too. He pointed me in the direction toward developing a deep love for Buddy Guy, who stirs my soul and makes me smile whenever I need a mood lift. Before Ethan, I'd thought that the blues were a sub-genre of R&B. I didn't like R&B. I liked rock.

"All the great rock musicians learned from the blues," Ethan said.

Because of my love of flying but unviable aviation career aspirations, I played with the idea of becoming an astrophysicist—something that would get me closer to the stars and in better touch with all that was out there beyond the visible eye. What lay on the other side of the moon? What was on Mars? I wanted to travel to those places and see for myself.

After not being able to figure out how to pay for the astronomical costs of flight training beyond my private pilot certification (a license to fly a small plane), I'd dropped out of school to reassess my future. I didn't know what to study or what I really wanted to be. Ethan was a junior engineer at NASA (National Aeronautics and Space Administration), responsible for helping to calculate the payload of the Space Shuttle before it launched into orbit to dock at the International Space Station. That put me one degree closer to exiting Planet Earth, or at least becoming connected to astronauts.

During the first week we met, he bought me two science fiction books, *Stranger in a Strange Land* by Robert Heinlein and *Brave New World* by Aldous Huxley—the only physical gifts he ever gave me.

Those books opened up my world beyond the limits of ordinary human imagination, into the outer space regions of what I, as an isolated Amish child, dreamed of, believed possible, wondered about, and wanted to explore.

Our conversations centered around physics and astronomy, science fiction, and NASA's latest discoveries and initiatives. Ethan often talked to me about the multiple PhDs so many of the NASA people had, how difficult and competitive it was to land a job there, and how underpaid everyone was relative to their geniuses, accomplishments, and responsibilities. But how people took the jobs because of their love for and belief in the future of space exploration and adventure, and how he himself had been lucky to land a position only because of a personal connection.

"I shouldn't have been interviewed or hired," he said, "because I don't have a degree."

Ethan had secured the interview based on his family's network, and he was hired based on his intellectual talents—but on the specially-made-for-him condition that he re-enrolled in school. He worked full-time during the day and took night classes in a dual computer engineering and physics degree program.

This revelation—knowing the right people— was one of many lessons about life that I learned from Ethan. My dream from as early as eight years old was to go to Harvard. Somehow Elvis Presley and Harvard had seeped into my consciousness, likely from overhearing conversations my father had with non-Amish clients. "Only the very smartest people in the world can go to Harvard" was the message I absorbed.

Someday I'll go, little me thought. I'm the smartest pupil in my grade.

Through Ethan's connections—from his Switzerland boarding school and his parents' friends to NASA—I learned that smartness alone wouldn't be enough to get me the life I wanted. I saw that power resided in having the right names and networks. That power was an element of street smarts, not book smarts. For someone like me, with no fame, money, family, trust fund, or academic pedigree, I had only one shot to make it in the world: I needed to get into an Ivy League school. Those lifelong connections were what the $35,000- to $40,000-per-year price tag was for.

I applied to Harvard despite the unbearable possibility of rejection. I didn't want to go through life with any regrets and what-ifs, wondering whether Harvard would've accepted me if I'd had the courage to risk finding out. But until that moment of insight—that opportunities came from being connected in the right way—I'd been too afraid of the potential denial. My self-value was based solely on my grades and academic achievements. If Harvard rejected me, that would mean I was worth nothing at all. One hundred percent worthless, with nothing more to live for.

The only things I had absolute confidence in about myself were my intellectual abilities and that I could often figure things out alone. I'd routinely work ahead in my textbooks in Amish school. I loved learning, I learned things extremely quickly, and I couldn't learn fast enough—enough, period—to satisfy my hunger for knowledge and answers about the world around me. I wanted to learn how to equip myself with the tools to get the answers I was seeking, because the adults—my parents, teachers, and others—never had enough time for all my questions. I read everything I could get my hands on. As soon as I learned the alphabet, I advanced to reading several grades ahead, going through books I barely understood but wanted to read anyway because I knew how to sound out the words. I looked up every word in the dictionary that I didn't understand, and that was how I built up my English vocabulary. By the time I was eleven, I'd hide books in the front pocket of my dress, underneath my apron, stealing every second I could to read one more sentence or page before my mother realized I'd disappeared again and yelled at me.

"Get back to work! Stop reading! You're such a bookworm!"

"Where are you? You always have your nose in a book."

"Why did it take you so long in the toilet? Were you reading a book again?"

The one non-self-serving interest my mother took in me was my educational progress, and when she saw I wasn't getting the grades I should on my report card, she stepped in. Maybe it was because she'd gotten a public school education and she subscribed to a higher standard of learning than the poor levels at the Amish Wisconsin school I attended. Many years later when I was a student at Columbia, I learned that my mother had had a genuine interest in education and that her father, my grandfather, had been opposed to the Amish pulling their children out of the public system in the seventies and putting them into private Amish-only schools. My father, on the other hand, whom I had believed to be smarter than my mother, turned out to not value education at all. The only thing he cared about was making money. And controlling people into making money for him. Such as his eleven kids. We were his free slave labor. And who knows what other illicit or criminal dealings he was—and still is—involved in.

"You're not going to get your own money until you turn twenty-one," he'd say. "I took care of you all these years. Now it's time for you to pay back what you owe."

When I was eleven, I challenged my father's orders once. The one and only time. He roared to the barn, brought back a long, heavy, black horse whip, dragged me out of the house, and cracked the whip across my back and bare legs for what seemed like an eternity. He made me bend over with my hands on the side of the house and beat me like I was a dead object, as if I couldn't feel. The more I jumped from the burning lashes, the harder he beat me. The louder I screamed, the worse he flogged me. When my hands slipped off the siding, he cracked the whip across my arms. When my back, butt, and legs hurt so much that I couldn't stand up anymore and I started falling down on the grass, he beat me harder and yelled at me to get back up. I thought it would never end. My father was a muscular, heavy-set manual laborer. I was an adolescent girl with wrists as tiny as a ballerina's.

I could barely walk afterward. He kicked me back into the house when he was done. I don't remember what I had questioned him about. It was insignificant. All I remember is thinking over and over during the beating, How could he do this to me? How? I don't deserve this.

I never forgot that incident. I knew that if I wanted to escape successfully, I had to be smarter than he was and never let him suspect my intentions. I had to play the obedient, good girl.

I was his favorite child and got special treatment from him. I thought he loved me. But from that point on, I saw that he was not the nice father I had believed him to be. He'd turn on me in an instant if I said or did anything he didn't like, despite that I was his favorite. I'd been groomed from birth to be his loyal little foot soldier, and he wouldn't hesitate to use me in any way that asserted his authority if I dared to defy him. We children were commodities, our worth measured only in terms of how much we did his bidding and made him money.

You don't have the right to force me to be a slave, I'd think, seething and wanting to fight back. I wasn't the one who chose to have kids. That was you. It's not my fault I was born.

But I had no alternative but to submit under his rule. At least working for him on his construction jobs got me out of the house and away from my mother, who by then had turned increasingly hostile toward and violent with me. Every day she seemed to be on a mission to break me because I questioned her orders and the Church's rules. "Stop talking back! You're not being submissive. Your will needs to be broken," she'd scream while beating me with a leather belt. Or wood logs that she made me retrieve from the stack of firewood in the cellar if she couldn't locate the belt quickly enough. Or sometimes a dining room chair that she grabbed on the fly to slam across my back.

So by age twelve, I didn't mind the long fourteen-hour days working in the hot un-air-conditioned Amish bakery during the summers in Michigan. Or in the open fields under the burning sun, picking asparagus from dawn to dusk with clammy rubber gloves, the repulsive smell of slimy juice beating up my nostrils and making me want to puke. To this day, I want to vomit when I smell asparagus.

By some luck or fortune, I'd consistently received positive reinforcement as a child about how smart I was in school. My aunt Esther says that I was an unusually precocious child. "Not even any of my own fourteen children demonstrated the abilities that you did," she says. Luckily for me, my gifts were recognized and praised—until I got too old and kept asking questions about the religion, refusing to be satisfied with nonsensical and illogical beliefs such as why we'd go to hell if we drove our own car but it was okay to pay someone else to drive us around in a car. Didn't that mean that the driver of the car was going to go to hell? And if not, why would I go to hell if I drove the car? Why were there different rules for different people?

When I was younger, my questions were cute. When I reached adolescence, my questions were disobedient and insubmissive. I wasn't the golden child anymore. I became the outcast and scapegoat, made into a symbol of all the ills of the Ludington, Michigan, community we lived in at the time. The only thing I had going for me was my unwavering belief in myself, that I was smart. I'd figure out a way to escape. And some day I'd be happy.

That year, after getting engaged to Ethan, I retook the ACT and SAT tests and applied to both Harvard and Columbia. I now joke that the response from Harvard was so fast that I received their rejection letter before they got my application. I cried all summer long. "I'll never make it in the world. I'm not smart. I'll never have the life of my dreams."

Becoming a musician—my first childhood dream—hadn't materialized. I'd had to give up my passion for flying—and hence travelling all over the world—because I couldn't afford the training. And now this. My last shot at getting anywhere, destroyed. If Harvard told me I wasn't good enough, wasn't smart enough, then I really wasn't. I cried so much that I couldn't even enjoy and appreciate the big fat package that arrived from Columbia a bit later.

Why are they sending me all their junk? I wondered. The top left corner of the thick envelope said Columbia University in blue ink. I threw it on the floor next to my desk.

"What's this?" Ethan asked that night when he came home from work and saw the package on the floor.

"I don't know. Something from Columbia."

"Did you apply there, too?"

"Yeah."

"You should probably open it."

"It's just junk."

Ethan seemed to think that the package might be about something else. His strange behavior annoyed me. *Why was he taking an interest in my affairs all of a sudden?*

"Did you ask for material from Columbia?"

"I already got stuff from them."

"Maybe it's a yes." The look on his face as he stared at the envelope oscillated between curiosity and disbelief.

I shrugged and ripped open the top. The only thing on my mind was Harvard. Second-rate Columbia didn't matter. They'd been my backup school. I'd never heard of Columbia until I applied to Harvard and looked up the names of the other Ivies. I chose a second Ivy, not because I believed I needed it but because I was practical and gave myself options. Columbia was in New York City, which was where I wanted to live. I hadn't actually wanted to live in Boston.

I pulled out a sheet of paper that said "Welcome. . . .."

"Huh, I guess I'll be going to Columbia." I held the letter in my hand.

"What?!" Ethan's mouth fell open. He couldn't hide his shock. "Give me that. Did you really get in? They took you?"

"Of course." Columbia had had the good sense to do so, unlike Harvard. "Why did you think it was an acceptance letter?"

"Because they would've sent a rejection in a small, thin envelope."

Despite our intellectual conversations, Ethan hadn't believed I was academically competent until that moment. When I saw his reaction, I realized that he'd simply been humoring me when I'd told him that I was applying to Harvard as a transfer student. I'd gotten into the University of Houston's Industrial Design program as well, my third and last option. Before then, he'd expressed that even U of H was a colossal stretch for me and that I should have a backup. I thought he'd only said that because the ID program was one of the best in the country at the time.

Because of Columbia's approval, Ethan started bragging to all his friends about me, his smart girlfriend who'd be going to an Ivy. I was pissed that he'd treated me as intellectually inferior before then. I'd worked my ass off for everything I'd accomplished in life. He didn't grasp what it had taken for me to escape: the planning that had gone into that, the brainwashing and abuse I'd been subjected to—and still battled to overcome—the Amish interrogation and torture I'd endured from a failed first escape attempt, the implications of the lack of familial support, and all the challenges I faced as a stranger in a strange new world, with no one to guide me.

He's never made an effort to get to know the

real me, I fumed inside. It's always been only about him. His life. His hobbies. His films. His food. Someday I'm gonna be a star and he'll be a nobody.

"I think he might still be married," his mother told me during the Christmas holidays. She sat in an armchair with a glass of white wine by the crackling fireplace, swiped a fake blond lock of hair across her face, and watched my response. Caterina had been a gorgeous model in her younger years.

I felt like I'd been hit by a bus. Ethan married? Is that why he keeps putting off our wedding date? "Who?" I tried to keep my voice from shaking.

"I think it's that woman who was in the news this summer."

That's why Ethan was so worried about that article, I thought. All the bits and pieces of the story he'd told me rushed together to form a picture of the whole truth. He'd told me the woman was someone he'd dated in the past and that his attorney had told him not to worry. It made no sense to me why he was concerned about being implicated in her crime, why he'd call a lawyer. But I trusted him. When we first met, I'd asked him if he was married. "No," he'd said. I had believed him.

I didn't confront Ethan with his mother's information. He was off in Europe alone that Christmas to visit his Italian cousins. "I need my space," he'd told me. When I had asked him point-blank if he wanted to end our relationship, he had said no, he just needed his own vacation away. Liberal, understanding me took him at his word, even though it stung that he'd picked Christmas to do it.

Ethan had called earlier that day to wish his mother a "Merry Christmas." When she hung up, I asked, "Did he know I was here?"

"He said he doesn't want to talk to you." Caterina seemed bothered by her son's behavior. The confused look on my face must have made her open up. "I heard girls in the background."

Caterina's ex-husband had cheated on her with Ethan's babysitter and she'd never married again. We'd always gotten along well. She didn't hold a particularly high regard for her son, frequently complaining that he blew through the money in his trust fund and that he was irresponsible. Perhaps it was that combination and his disregard toward me that made her finally tell me about his marriage.

Instead of talking to Ethan, I ran an online database check. Sure enough, he was married. To that woman. He and I had lived together for over a year and I hadn't suspected anything. I didn't tell him I had discovered the truth. Our relationship had already deteriorated, and it was progressively getting worse. I'd initiated conversations several times about what was going on and whether he wanted to continue or end it. He always said he wanted to stay together and blamed the lack of intimacy—the emotional drifting apart—on his depression. "It's just a phase," he said. I didn't know anything about how depression worked, and he refused to go to therapy.

"I don't want kids ever." I'd made it very clear to him, from the beginning.

Because of my Amish upbringing and having been the oldest, I'd been treated as the second mother, saddled with undue responsibilities such as caring for my siblings. Raising kids was hard. I didn't feel that I'd be a good mother—and I also didn't want my hard-fought freedom infringed upon. Kids took away one's personal independence.

"Neither do I," he'd said. "I don't want kids with my depression. But if I did have one, I'd name the girl Sabrina."

Why are you so adamant about not having kids but you've already picked out a name? I wondered. I hated that name. It sounded revolting, but I didn't say anything.

He married the woman he met shortly after me; they had a daughter and named her Sabrina.

I started my year at Columbia in January 2003, right after that Christmas. It took me four years to get over Ethan. His betrayal seared my heart, smashed open the wounds from repeat rape and childhood abuse that had begun to ever so slightly heal. All the trust I'd felt I could give someone I loved disappeared, the ability to trust a man in romance shattered, destroyed. The knight in shining armor, the fairy tale of love—those were delusions, imaginations, not real. They'd never happen for me.

If guys can have sex without feeling, then so can girls, I told myself. I'll never get married. I'll never trust a guy again. Love is too hard.

For the next seven years, I was too afraid of love to form a serious romantic relationship. Scarred and scared, I felt even more worthless than I had before Ethan. I was just a doll, a feelingless rape doll. A doll with no face, like the Amish dolls from my childhood. A disposable toy that my uncles had ravaged to satisfy their perverseness. An object they'd decided they owned, to do with whatever their depravities craved.

Maybe that's why it took so many guys. I'd stopped keeping track of how many I'd slept with after I passed the sixty mark. One day I woke up to realize that the pain from Ethan was completely—magically, finally—gone.

I still hadn't told a single soul that I'd been raped. I still hadn't started therapy. I still didn't think I could ever have a healthy, trusting romantic life. But at least the wound from Ethan no longer held its grip on me.

NOTE: The names of these characters have been changed.

Music for the Soul

———

Here are several selections that helped me get through the events or period of this chapter, or reflect musically what I felt during this time. I understood very little of most lyrics—even today my ears don't process most words—but the melodies and instruments fed my soul. Had it not been for music, I wouldn't have survived until I finally got to therapy at age twenty-nine.

- Leisure Cruise. "Ragged Dawn." *Leisure Cruise*, 2014.

- Bob Marley & The Wailers. "Waiting In Vain." *Legend, the best of*, 2002.

- Angela McCluskey. "Not Crying Anymore." *The Roxy Sessions*, 2016.

CHAPTER 13

Young and Stupid in Karachi, Land of Bullets and Blood

Karachi made my blood crack. The only country—out of around thirty countries I visited—where I genuinely feared for my life, was Pakistan just before 9/11. I was there for only two days and couldn't wait to get the hell back out of there. For me to feel that way was an indication that something bad was brewing. It was dangerous, genuinely dangerous, for a white American female, travelling solo, to be there.

I didn't blend in in Karachi. Despite wearing a local-style headscarf and being accompanied by a male Pakistani for precautionary protection, I couldn't shake the feeling that bullets were trained on me. I could feel eyes on me, every step I took, everywhere I went. Unfriendly eyes. One wrong move and I'd be shot, nabbed, or otherwise disappeared off the planet. Something in the air was just waiting for someone to poke it. With an innocent remark or nuke gone off course. Any excuse would make the bubbles boiling under the surface—underneath the crowded, stinking, sweaty, dirty, putrid, gasoline fume-filled streets—snap. And then explode in clouds of rage, hostility, violence, and vengeance.

+971-50-000-1234, I repeated into memory the cell phone number that my mysterious benefactor had given me.

"If you run into any trouble, call me," he'd said. And then he'd melted into the endless bumping, yelling, jostling spill of crowd exiting customs into the thick envelope of humid, unbreathable air off the shores of the Arabian Sea.

I was twenty years old and had somehow convinced the young male airline agent back in Dubai that the visa laws for American business travellers had changed.

"I don't need a visa," I said when he scrolled through my passport looking for the stamp. After some insistent back and forth, he and all the checkpoints to the boarding gate let me through.

Young and stupid me figured that if I got on the plane, I'd automatically get into Pakistan. Wrong.

"Passport!" the bearded customs official barked, sticking his hand at me. Not even a ghost of a smile anywhere on his soul. I wasn't welcome in Pakistan.

I'd made sure to clothe myself in near-Amish fashion: no cleavage or hints of boobs, no pertinent bare ankles, long sleeves, layers upon layers to hide my inferior, less-than-second-class female shape. I'd even wrapped a scarf around my head. My hair was soaking wet from the river of sweat running down my face while standing in a parking lot of a line for hours, waiting to clear customs. No wonder Karachi stank, especially during its deadly heat waves.

"Visa! Where's your visa?" He brandished open my passport, a sneer carved across his face.

Using my feminine wiles didn't work this time. I quickly learned that just because the airline flew me in, it didn't mean I'd get outside the gates without Pakistani authorization.

"No, the laws haven't changed. How did you even get on this plane?"

I am not *going to* not *make it out of this damn airport, damn it.* I took a deep breath in, made time stop for a moment, blurred out the angry authority figure still yelling at me, and took a long look around.

Signs in English and Urdu, an Arabic-looking script and the national language of Pakistan. According to what my guidebook had said, Urdu was a mixture of Persian, Arabic, and other regional languages. The green and white colors of Pakistan, a flag with a crescent-shaped moon and a single star on a field of green—and a tiny white vertical strip on one side. Currency exchange booths on the other side of this bastard customs guy. The other side that represented freedom. Freedom for me to explore yet another country not normally on the adventure list of a single, white, US female.

Who can help me? Who will *help me?* That's when I caught the eye of the man going through the diplomat line next to me. He was a native of the United Arab Emirates, a member of one of the royal families. I'd learned about the style of dress that indicated this status during my time in Dubai. He overheard the argument I was having with the customs guy, said something to him in Arabic or Urdu, and waved me over.

"You're American?" he asked.

"Yes."

"Why did you come to Karachi?"

"Business."

He smiled and shook his head. He didn't buy my story but he didn't ask any further questions. After a very brief exchange with the official in the diplomat line, my passport got stamped with a thirty-day visa. I couldn't understand what was said, but from the body language, the Pakistani had no choice but to do as ordered by the UAE diplomat.

"*Shukran*," I said as I watched him go. "Thank you" in Arabic.

I looked at the note he'd given me and photographed the information into my brain. I had a feeling this wasn't something I'd want to risk losing.

"This is a hotel that's safe for American women." He'd scrawled the name of the place and his mobile number on a piece of paper. "Call me if you have more problems."

To this day I don't know why he rescued me. We'd been on the same plane, and I'd first noticed him when I was sitting in the boarding area waiting for departure. He was seated in first class and I was in economy. What made him help me? And, why hadn't he been through the diplomat line long before I got to the checkpoint? I was in that ungodly slow immigration line. He should've been out of the airport hours before.

Two days later I was safely back in Dubai on a connecting return to the States.

"Have you been to any of the following countries?" The customs guy at the Canadian border rattled off a list while simultaneously flipping through my thick, amended passport and observing the expressions on my face as he spoke.

Fucking business of terror, I thought, as I listened to the Muslim-populated countries he named. Fifteen years later and nothing has changed in all these years. Not a thing. When are the masses going to wake up and steal back their freedom?

"Pakistan."

His flipping froze and he looked startled. "What took you there?"

"Research. But fifteen years ago. Karachi is a fucking hell hole. I couldn't wait to get out of there."

A tiny smile erased his suspicions. He approved of my descriptive report.

Thank god you're one of us, I could feel him thinking as I passed through and back onto US soil.

If you only knew, I thought back.

Music for the Soul

———

Here are several selections that helped me get through the events or period of this chapter, or reflect musically what I felt during this time. I understood very little of most lyrics—even today my ears don't process most words—but the melodies and instruments fed my soul. Had it not been for music, I wouldn't have survived until I finally got to therapy at age twenty-nine.

- Salif Keita. "Folon." *"Folon".....The Past,* 1995.

- The Polyphonic Spree. "You Don't Know Me." *Yes, It's True.,* 2013.

- Madonna. "American Life." *American Life,* 2003.

CHAPTER 14

The Buddha Showed the Way (Part II of a Trilogy)

"Jesus said, 'Follow me. I am the way' and the Buddha said, 'Follow me. I'll show you the way.' In one sentence, that's the difference between Christianity and Buddhism." Professor Robert Thurman, over six feet tall, sixty-two years old, with wavy blonde hair that hadn't yet grayed and electric blue eyes that struck through his audience, stood at a podium with an entourage that included a co-professor and graduate teaching assistants (TAS) flanking him on both sides. Not your average professor, even for Columbia University.

Everything about him was different: from the way he carried himself and how he wore his clothes—the clothes themselves tailored designer-quality and not the usual menial academic attire—to his accent (not Midwestern American, Northeastern American, gruff New Yorker, any regional sound of the United States, yet clearly inexplicably spoken by a hundred percent US American). His eyes, gleaming and dancing, were as incisive and piercing and bold as the radical un-American statements he made in class.

"Someone asked Gandhi what he thought about

Western civilization. Gandhi said, 'That would be a good idea.'" Thurman chuckled and adjusted his glasses. His TAs snickered. Later I learned that this was a stock line in Thurman's lectures, teachings, and dialogues. To the white American who'd been fed with the attitude that modern Americans are the most advanced civilization in the history of Earth, this was a shocking, irreverent, and sacrilegious assertion. Kind of like Jimi Hendrix's rendition of "The Star Spangled Banner" at Woodstock in 1969.

"I'm a WASP from Harvard but I consider us quite barbaric," Thurman said.

I could feel the room hold its breath. Especially so soon after 9/11. If thoughts had materialized aloud, accusations such as "Traitor!" and "Unpatriotic asshole!" would've filled the air.

I like this guy, I thought. Finally I'm meeting a white US American who hasn't drunk the Kool-Aid. But what the hell does "wasp" mean? I scribbled down the word in all lowercase letters in my notebook.

I could tell that the rest of the students in that room knew what it meant. I wasn't in on it. I felt the intensity of not belonging, how foreign I was, how different I was. Like when I hadn't known what "H_2O" meant in my first year of high school in chemistry class. When I raised my hand and asked the teacher, he almost sent me to the principal's office for being impertinent. All the other students laughed out loud, first because they thought I was being funny. They kept laughing—at me—when they realized that I was serious.

I had that same feeling with "WASP." I wasn't going to raise my hand this time and get laughed at again. I'd find out some other way. Discreetly. No one would know that I wasn't a prep school student and didn't belong at Columbia. As long as I didn't open my mouth, everyone would assume I was a White Anglo-Saxon Protestant, too.

Seated high up in an auditorium-style classroom in Pupin Hall, a building that was home to the physics and astronomy departments and not usually assigned to classes from the religion department, I watched Thurman's hand gestures and attempted—unsuccessfully—to place his unusual American English accent. Later that semester, I picked up that the accent came from speaking classical and modern Tibetan, Sanskrit, Mandarin Chinese, and a few other languages. The room was packed with around a hundred undergraduate students and the volume and distance dwarfed Thurman's larger-than-life personality. From my vantage point, he looked ant-size, like the view four thousand feet below when I'd flown my plane during flight training. Thurman was hard of hearing and, fortunately for me, spoke loudly enough that his voice covered the chasm.

As the semester wore on, I sat at the front and to his right so he'd see my hand sooner when I had questions. It was hard to get his attention from the left because he wore a glass eye on that side. One day he popped it out in class while telling us the story of how losing the original set him on the path of Buddhism.

I appreciated the distinction Thurman made

between Christianity and Buddhism that first day. Wow, I thought, as I wrote in my notebook. Put that way, I definitely like the Buddha far better. I liked Jesus, or what I interpreted to be his actual teachings, such as treating others kindly and not being hypocritical. I was a little let down to realize that, compared with the Buddha's statement, Jesus' statement was pretty patronizing. Over time, as I studied and worked closely with Thurman, I learned about the origins of a variety of ancient cultures and religions, such as the Egyptians. The life and resurrection story of Jesus appeared to me to be a remake of the far older Egyptian stories of Osiris or Horus. Was Jesus an actual historical figure? If so, how many of the facts about him were skewed or embellished by the men who wrote the stories? Men who were motivated by political agendas. And stories that weren't written until around seventy years after Jesus' death. Even as only an eleven-year-old, I'd noticed the many glaring discrepancies in the New Testament, too many for me to blindly believe everything in the book. I'd read it, looking for answers that I'd been told were in the Bible to the questions I had about why, for example, I couldn't have a yellow dress. If God made the flowers, why did he allow them to be yellow and pink and orange, but if I wore those colors, I'd go to hell? The Bible couldn't be one hundred percent true: blatant contradictions filled its pages and I wanted solid, logical answers.

Thurman added another impressive point to the lecture that day: "The Buddha said to not take him for his word but to examine what he says to see if it's actually true."

I felt that I might have found my religion, the ultimate Truth that I'd searched for for so long. The Amish forbade questioning anything. I'd been taught that the Bible was wholly and literally true and that the preachers and parents were always right. Questioning the religion, especially from adolescence onward, was deemed an act of rebellion, or disobedience, and grounds for punishment. Being told by an authority figure to examine and challenge their words was revolutionary. If a leader could say that about their own work, then it was definitely worth exploring their beliefs further.

Several years before, while living in Houston, Texas, in a part of the country that bred an overpopulation of super-mega, fundamentalist, rightwing Christian churches, I'd taken the frightening leap of doubting the notion that the Judeo-Christian god was real. I began to seriously explore other religions for answers. The hypocrisy, fear-mongering, and manipulation within those fundamentalist churches were just as bad as—or worse than—the Amish. If I'd wanted to be evil, I would've started my own fundamentalist establishment. It was so easy to capitalize on people's fears of death and the unknown. I'd never be poor if I raked in money through a religious brainwashing business. But I couldn't in good conscience rip people off. I couldn't affiliate with so-called Christian churches anymore either. None of them practiced what I understood of Jesus' actual teachings.

My then-boyfriend Ethan's mom, Caterina, was into Tibetan Buddhism and brought up Thurman when I told her I'd gotten into Columbia. "If you're interested in learning more about Buddhism, take a class from Prof. Thurman. If they're offered to undergrads," she said.

"Who's he?"

"The first Westerner ordained a Tibetan Buddhist monk. He's a credible authority on Buddhism."

Daring to doubt the existence of the God of the Bible had been petrifying. It was petrifying because if I ended up being wrong, burning in hell for eternity would be my punishment when I died. I resonated with what I felt was the core of Jesus' genuine teachings, but after having read the Old and New Testaments—at age eleven—I couldn't connect with the character of God. Unlike Jesus, who seemed like a good being at heart and perhaps an actual figure, God was a vindictive, temperamental personality concerned with revenge, control, and totalitarianism, very much like my Amish father and the Amish patriarchy. I couldn't find any evidence that God actually existed, neither historically nor by personally feeling a connection. But until my early twenties, I was too terrified to renounce God. My trip to India—my first exposure to a non-Western civilization—dissolved that fear. I became agnostic: open to the possibility of the existence of that kind of a monotheistic deity but not convinced without proof.

By the time I entered Columbia, Buddhism was the last major religion on my list to look into for an answer on whether God was real. I wanted to learn about it from an authentic source, ideally a Tibetan and not a Westerner who'd likely distort what the original texts said. Having read the English Bible as an Amish kid, I'd discovered that what I'd been taught orally in the Church before I had learned how to read was wrong. I also noticed some differences between the English and German Bibles. I couldn't trust anyone's word that they were giving me the facts about a text written in a language I couldn't read. I certainly couldn't trust an outsider's opinions, someone who wasn't born inside the culture. Having learned post-escape about the outside world's myths about the Amish, I understood the necessity of getting as close as possible to the source of a belief system for definitive answers. I wasn't about to blindly believe countless iterations of erroneous translations or interpretations of texts first written hundreds, or thousands, of years ago. Texts likely whitewashed according to people's personal agendas and wishful thinking. Thurman had been friends with the Dalai Lama, the leader of Tibet, for over thirty years and had studied with the same teachers in India who'd taught the Dalai Lama. Given that friendship and history, I figured his credentials were good enough to check out his *Introduction to Indo-Tibetan Buddhism* class and get an overview of what Buddhism was really about.

I'd already visited around twenty countries when I sat in Thurman's class for the first time, in the fall of 2003 and my second semester at Columbia. His syllabus enumerated one of the longest lists of books I would ever see during my years as an undergrad. Among the twenty or so titles, Thurman's *Inner Revolution: Life, Liberty, and the Pursuit of Real Happiness* and the Dalai Lama's *Ethics for the New Millennium* became my new spiritual compass. *Inner Revolution* spoke to my highest value of personal freedom, and how to apply basic principles of Buddhism into my daily life to experience more of that freedom. *Ethics* laid out a moral system based on universal—rather than religious—principles, through which every single person, no matter their religious beliefs, could be happy.

I'd seen the world firsthand, often travelling off the beaten track to countries on the US Department of State's danger list. Most of the information touted by the State turned out to be pure propaganda, in that the US was equally dangerous for women and children (for example, human trafficking, sex slavery, and rape culture). It certainly would've been dangerous for a female to travel solo to war zones and other legitimately unstable hotbeds, especially just weeks prior to 9/11. But none of the places I landed had ever posed a threat to me—except Karachi in Pakistan. Granted, the reason I hadn't felt threatened was because I wasn't the typical American tourist. But, in general, the Department of State manipulated the perceptions of danger and safety in other countries. My self-training to escape from the Amish, and then to survive in the world, gave me the skills to inform myself sufficiently about the places I planned to visit. Once on the ground, I relied on my instincts, not on what the State said.

What I got from those places—by talking with and observing the local, non-Western people—was a very different education on and perspective of the US. I learned how they saw us, how they interpreted political events and history, that history was written by the victors in a light that made the victors look good—or, whoever wrote history wrote it to make themselves look good, period, never mind the actual facts if the facts were uncomfortable or inconvenient—that the "facts" about all the wars fought past and present were different depending on which side you talked to, and that every side believed that they had the correct version. The people I met often expressed similar sentiments in our conversations:

"You Americans, your American imperialism imposing your politics and religion upon us. . . ."

"You Americans orchestrate coups and elections in other countries."

"You Americans invade countries because of your greed for oil and other natural resources, not because you care about creating a better life for the everyday people."

I empathized with those views because of my personal struggle for freedom from Amish authoritarian oppression and because of the untold genocide and holocaust by white Europeans who invaded what is known today as the Americas. White Europeans—and subsequently Americans— deliberately mass murdered and slaughtered the Natives—stole the lands, natural resources, and freedoms from the native peoples and exerted their authoritarian control over them, in the name of religious righteousness. I was, and am, against *all* religions and customs that practice hypocrisy and oppress personal freedom. Humans as a whole, no matter the skin color—not just white—tended to be barbaric. Prof. Thurman was right about that.

One day I walked into Thurman's office with a burning question: "Why does the Dalai Lama eat meat?"

Every week I'd shown up during office hours with a list of questions about the course material that didn't make sense to me or felt incongruent. Buddhism's hierarchy of karmic gravity put killing sentient beings at the top. For the Dalai Lama to eat meat, then, which required the killing of a being, seemed hypocritical to me—not walking the talk or practicing the preaching. Thanks to my personal experiences, I was particularly allergic to hypocrisy and attuned to the cracks, or hints of cracks, in a system.

I expected Thurman to jump to the Dalai Lama's defense, put me down, blow me off, or give me some sort of excuse or justification. I still didn't know if he was the real deal—how authentic he was—but his answer solved that for me: "I don't know. Ask the Dalai Lama."

Hearing someone of his status say "I don't know" impacted me deeply. I was just a lowly undergrad student with no academic or royal pedigree. He could've easily dismissed me. Instead, he didn't pretend to have the answer and speak for the Dalai Lama. The fact that Thurman actually said "I don't know" shocked me. Equally shocking was the suggestion that I could go directly to the Dalai Lama and ask him myself. That response was so unlike my Amish and corporate experience—where you were supposed to stay repressed,

go through the chain of command, or be denied
access to whomever was at the top because you
were deemed too unworthy to speak directly to the
leadership.

During that semester, my long journey seeking
the truth came to a disconcerting end. In the pri-
or three years, I'd taken a break from college and
travelled around the world looking for what made
sense to me. Even before I escaped at age fifteen,
my dream was to visit every country in the world,
including outer space. I wanted knowledge. Answers. I wanted to know the Truth. Would I go to
hell when I died? Was the Judeo-Christian God
actually real? Where exactly was heaven? Why was
I born? Where was I before I was born? What was
my purpose in life? If God was a loving, all-knowing, and all-powerful God, why did he allow wars?
If God was a good God, why did he let me get
raped? Repeatedly. Where was God when those
things happened? How were those things loving
and good? Why didn't my parents love me? Would
I ever have the life of my dreams? The life I fought
so hard for, the life I gave up *everything* for? My
community, family, culture, the only people and
things I'd ever known. Would I ever be happy? And
not poor and barely surviving? Would I ever find
anyone who loved me? Unconditionally?

I wanted answers to all the hard existential
questions in life. There had to be an ultimate truth.
Who was right? Of all the religions in the world,
which one was the *right* religion? Almost all of
them claimed to be the one and only. I flew to as
many countries as I could to experience the cul-

tures for myself, asking questions directly of the people, instead of merely relying on what Americans' versions were.

What I discovered in Buddhism that was so disconcerting was that the Buddha said that there were many paths up the mountain. And that no one else could walk my path for me or do my work for me. Buddhism distinguished between absolute and relative truths, and the only absolute truth was that there was no absolute truth. The implications of that profoundly reshaped how I thought about my past and how I viewed the future. What that meant was that there was no definitive answer to life, the universe, and everything. There was no black and white. The world didn't exist in that way—in absolute rights and wrongs. Rather, it existed in shades of gray. Truth was fluid and contextual.

I reflected on the tendency for students to either love or hate Prof. Thurman, and the irony of that. Buddhism was gray—about the middle way—but Thurman's likability was black and white. I also recognized the irony that I had never liked being told what to do and what to believe as a child—I wanted to figure things out for myself—but then when I finally stumbled across a belief system that told me to find the answers for myself, I was disappointed. The uncertainty of that—that unknown—unsettled me.

Through Buddhism, I learned to become comfortable with the ever-present and all-pervasive uncertainty of life. Buddhism said that the only constant in life was change. Nothing was permanent. I had to become okay with that idea of impermanence and of things constantly changing. What did that mean in terms of real-life applications? Such as loss. The loss of family, parents, community. So desperately wanting a real father and mother who loved me unconditionally, but never having that. Wanting people I could trust implicitly, who'd neither betray me nor abandon me. Buddhism didn't promise any of those things. The only thing Buddhism said was a certainty was that life was uncertain.

That questioned my deepest heart's desires, including why to invest in a romantic relationship if it would inevitably end. Why bother if the relationship could never be permanent? I wanted my fairy-tale knight, my Prince Charming, and I wasn't promised that. Buddhism didn't even pretend to promise that.

"If the buddhas and bodhisattvas who are so infinitely compassionate were able to rescue you, don't you think they would have already?" Prof. Thurman asked in class one day. "The buddhas are omniscient—all-knowing—but they're not omnipotent—all-powerful. You have to save yourself."

In a matter of several seconds, that insight ripped out the threads of everything I'd fantasized about and thought I needed to do with my life. I thought it was my mission to save the world, to make it a better place, to create peace and harmony, to rescue people from pain and suffering. If even the buddhas couldn't save anyone, then certainly I couldn't. And . . . no one was going to save me either.

That was a blow.

Just exactly *how* do I go about saving myself?

What Buddhism did promise was that there was a way out of suffering. This was the opposite of the message I received as a child. The Amish way to *stop* suffering (that is, get to heaven) was *by* suffering. The more you suffered for your faith, the better your chances were at getting through the pearly gates. In Buddhism, suffering wasn't a virtue. Only when you became free of suffering did you get into "heaven" (that is, become enlightened and experience eternal peace).

I loved the promise that it was possible for me to become happy and freed from my traumas. What I didn't like were all the rules and regulations that Buddhism set forth in order to attain that freedom, rules that turned out to be just as unpractical and nonsensical for me as the Amish rules and regulations. Today, although there are many things I love about Buddhism—and although I have immense respect and appreciation for the Dalai Lama—I don't believe in its karmic hierarchy. I don't subscribe to the notion that physically killing someone or something is the worst possible sin or crime. Rape is far worse. Rape is a murder of the soul.

I also don't subscribe to the notion that those who have committed heinous crimes against me in this lifetime will pay the consequences for their actions in a future lifetime, if not in this one. What good does that do me or the rest of the world? Where is my justice? What about all the innocent children or other victims that these sexual predators will destroy because they're allowed to roam free on this planet? What about the safety of society in general? Waiting for some future lifetime for justice makes no sense. Those sexual predators won't remember what they did and neither will I— *if* there even is a future lifetime.

And exactly who in that future lifetime is the one deciding what kind of consequences, if any, the criminals are paying for their actions from a past lifetime? If it's really up to me to save myself, as Buddhism says, then I can't rely on some nebulous force to restore the scales of karmic balance on my behalf at some undetermined point in the future.

To me, waiting on karma is no different from the Amish saying "Turn the other cheek. Don't make them pay for their actions. God will punish them in hell when they die." If the predators even go to "hell," that still doesn't do me any good in this lifetime. I haven't received justice and restitution for my lifelong terror and trauma.

Rape is a weapon of war. It's a practice that's sanctioned and kept alive by political, religious, and social institutions. It isn't some hazy force of nature or karma that just happens and can't be stopped. Sexual assault in all its forms is an *intentional* strategic weapon embedded in all structures of society in the effort by those in power to continue maintaining that power and control. This practice of rape is terrorism, at its very best. It needs to be stopped in *this* lifetime. I—and all sexual assault victims—need justice *now*.

I graduated from Columbia with three years of classical Tibetan language under my belt, and a

personal introduction to His Holiness the 14th Dalai Lama. In 2005, I produced a four-hundred-per-
son, by-invitation-only, high-profile event that featured the Dalai Lama as part of Columbia's World
Leaders Forum, which coincided with the General
Assembly of the United Nations. As the executive
assistant to Prof. Thurman—who was responsible
for bringing the Dalai Lama to campus—I was put
in charge of organizing the conference. [It just so
happens that out of over one hundred heads of
state and world leaders in the span of fifteen years,
the picture on Columbia's World Leaders "About"
web page is the one that was taken of that event.]

Several years after I graduated, the Dalai Lama
made a statement at the Vancouver Peace Summit
that went viral on social media: "The world will be
saved by the Western woman." I wondered what
the hell he meant. I couldn't wrap my head around
the possibility that women would actually make a
stand and clean up this world. Nothing I'd seen in
my Amish childhood pointed to the likelihood that
women would wake up in my lifetime. Nothing
in my post-escape life backed that up either. Until
the MeToo movement. The fact that the movement
didn't die out and that it kept going, relentlessly,
on a near-daily basis in big media for months on
end, was what led me around to the Dalai Lama's
foresight. Then I finally saw what he saw eight
years before: we women *will* rise before I die.

Music for the Soul

———

*Here are several selections that helped me get through the
events or period of this chapter, or reflect musically what I
felt during this time. I understood very little of most
lyrics—even today my ears don't process most words—but
the melodies and instruments fed my soul. Had it not been
for music, I wouldn't have survived until I finally got to
therapy at age twenty-nine.*

- Compilation album by Hypnotic Records.
  "Take Me Away (feat. Jessica Jean)."
  Dubstep - Chillout, 2012.

- Bob Dylan. "Blowin' in the Wind." *The
  Freewheelin' Bob Dylan*, 1963.

- Inner Splendor Meditation Music and
  Yoga Project. "Healing Tibetan Singing
  Bowl Meditation." *The Healing Power of
  Tibetan Singing Bowls*, 2009.

CHAPTER 15

My Freedom Is Not for Sale (A Billion Dollars Didn't Buy Me)

Earlier that year, I'd met someone who wanted to marry me.

"You don't want me," I told him after several months. "I'm fucked up." I didn't say, I don't want to marry you because I don't love you. I was afraid to just say no. I assumed that bluntly telling him that I was messed up would scare him off.

Aidan was convinced that he wanted me, and I was extremely attracted by the prospect of at last leaving poverty behind and experiencing financial security and stability. With him, I'd never need to worry about how to afford healthy food—or just eat, period—how to pay the bills, how to keep a roof over my head, and how to come up with a backup plan if I lost my job or had an emergency. Aidan lived a glamorous lifestyle in Dubai with a villa on the Palm Islands and enjoyed a fortune worth over half a billion. All my basic necessities would finally be met, plus I'd experience luxury as a way of life.

But I hadn't been able to make myself love him.

One of the things that bothered me about him was that he didn't support my dream to earn an Ivy League degree. He wanted me to quit Columbia and move halfway around the globe with him right away. I had only one year left.

"You don't need a degree. You can do anything you want with me," he said, sipping coffee from a white European-designed mug. Sharply dressed à la European fashion—fitted charcoal gray wool blazer, tailored trousers, pastel linen shirt, Italian leather pointed shoes, belt, bespoke luxury watch—he looked the part of my dream man.

We sat in the breeze by a table outside one of Dubai's high-end restaurants, in a glitzy part of downtown. An early weekend morning, the sun hadn't yet risen all the way above the sand dunes and the city hadn't yet fully woken up. I loved the smell and taste of Turkish coffee in the mornings and the unhurried sounds of the merchants setting up their stalls in the open markets nearby.

Aidan lived in a world in which money, not so much degrees, talked. At least, degrees didn't matter to him when it came to a future spouse.

"Okay, I wanna make a film about my life. Would you support me in that?" I shifted back in my chair to get a good read on his body.

One of his eyebrows lifted and a tiny frown crossed his face. "Why do you want to do that?"

"It's something I've been meaning to do for years. But I want my degree, too. I went through unbelievable challenges to pay the tuition every year, and I'm not gonna quit now that I'm this close."

"You don't need to work if you marry me." The way he said it made me feel that that was the end of the discussion. He'd decided what was best for me.

All sorts of thoughts raced through my head. I'm *not* a trophy wife. And why wouldn't you want your spouse to have a degree? Wouldn't that make you proud? "I *want* to work. Start my own business."

"You love travelling. Let's travel around the world together. Just be with me."

While I'd be seen everywhere by everyone as a gold-digger wife, not as someone who is intelligent, smart, and respected? And then what would happen to me the day you decided you want a divorce? I'd have no business of my own, no brand-name recognition in the US, and no degree. All my years of struggles to get somewhere in life gone down the drain.

But I didn't express any of my feelings to him. I never did with male authority figures who wanted something from me that I didn't want to give them. I felt backed into a corner and unsafe. What if he got angry with me, left me at the table, took off in the car alone, and abandoned me in the middle of a foreign city with my passport and belongings still at his house?

The appeal of travelling and not having to worry about bills enticed me. Maybe I could make it work with him. I offered a compromise: "I'll marry you and not start my own business if you let me finish out my last year."

His jaw tightened and he took another sip. "Okay, but only one more year. No more school after that."

That's not a good look. I don't like this feeling.

A few weeks later, I sat on the bed in a room at the Ritz Carlton in New York City. Aidan, pulling a shirt out of the closet, had brought up the subject of marriage again. I couldn't keep faking my feelings but I was still scared of saying no to him.

I'd always wondered if I'd relinquish my personal freedom for financial security if the offer were big enough. My hands shook and I kept looking down, eyes locked on the floor. So that I'd have the courage to stand my ground with Aidan, I repeated to myself, *No one* buys my freedom. *No one* buys my freedom. "I wouldn't make a good wife."

"What. . . . What do you mean?" Aidan asked. He seemed genuinely concerned—not the response I was expecting—stopped what he was doing, and came over to sit down next to me.

"There's a lot of things wrong with me. I've had a really tough childhood."

He laughed a little, his voice bemused. "You're not messed up," he said, with a touch of condescension.

Fuck, this isn't going the way I thought. I'm gonna have to tell him. "I was raped. Many times. You don't want me. I'm really fucked up." I stared through him and then back down, my hands locked over my stomach above my vagina, my legs clenched up, my heart beating fast. *He'll leave me now.*

But Aidan reacted completely appropriately. The way every person should: he was supportive. "What?" His expression froze for a second, his mouth open, his body stiff. Then, "Who?" He reached for my hand. "Who did this to you?"

"Don't touch me!" I screeched and jerked my hand away. My body lurched to the other side of the bed, an auto-response to put distance between myself and the predator who was flashing back through my PTSD state of mind. Aidan represented the violators and I couldn't handle his touch. "My uncles."

"Your mom's or dad's brothers?"

Why does it matter? "My dad's. I've never told anyone."

Aidan stormed up from the bed, angry, and blurted out, "Your dad knows."

"Huh?" It was my turn to be shocked.

"They're brothers. Brothers know these things about each other."

"I've never told anyone. You're the first person. One uncle threatened to kill me if I ever said anything. Don't tell anyone, please." *What does he mean, my dad knows?*

Several years later, my brother Al told my parents—Henry and Ida Bontrager—what the uncles Harvey Bell and Enos Bontrager (both my father's brothers) had done.

When I asked what their response was, Al said, Mom didn't say anything. Just sat there at the table. Dad got up and left the room, not saying anything either. It was so strange. He just left the room."

"What the fuck, are you kidding me? He didn't say anything at all?"

"No. I think he's a rapist, too. I don't think he's

raped any of the sisters, though."

That's when it dawned on me: my father's energy, demeanor, and attitude were the exact same as my rapist uncles. I have a rapist father. The father who I'd thought did no wrong when I was a child. The one I'd tried to get to love me for thirteen long years post-escape. That father. The father who'd treated me as the favorite child and then did everything possible to destroy me. Such as telling me that I was evil and going to hell unless I converted to his right-wing, fundamentalist, evangelical, born-again Christian religion. It was okay for him to have resigned from the Amish Church after my escape, but I was still going to hell because I disobeyed him. That father. The father who went around proselytizing in Guatemala and Haiti and who knew where else. The father who ran an orphanage in Guatemala called "God's Little Children." That father. What was he *really* doing down there?

For years, I'd wondered if he ran drugs, because he and Harvey had a weird, dark connection. During my time in Montana, Harv would talk to me a lot about the massive cocaine operation he had run in the eighties and tell me that the Feds still had their eyes on him. I had no doubt that Harv would kill me—or send someone after me to do the job—if he suspected that I'd report him for the rapes. Maybe my father ran the operation with him. And human trafficking and child sex slavery, too. Missionary trips and orphanages were perfect covers for all sorts of sick, heinous, criminal activities. An orphanage provided an easy supply of vulnerable children to rape and victimize.

If my father is a rapist, too, it certainly explains why neither he nor my mother have ever bothered to express any acknowledgment for what happened to me. Not a word. Ever. In all the eight years to date from Al's disclosure on my behalf, not one word from them. Not even a single expression of regret or sign of empathy when Al told them.

Who is Henry Bontrager really? What is he hiding? And what is Ida covering up for him? These questions run through my mind constantly.

"I hate to say this because he's your father, but. . . ." My maternal uncle Daniel stayed up late one winter night to visit with me. The flickering light from the kerosene lamp cast shadows of his unkempt beard and hair onto the wall. I'd made a trip to see that side of the family—all still in the Amish Church—for the first time in around twenty years. His ornery hair, unruly beard, and long, crooked nose made him look like one of the wizards from *Harry Potter*.

"I'm interested only in the truth."

"There's nothing good to be said about your father. He's a self-righteous asshole. Sorry."

"Your father has no heart," my uncle Samuel said. He didn't soften the blow with "I hate to say this, but." I'd called him to learn more about my father's character before he married my mother. "He's always been like that."

My father has no heart? I felt the hit—stunned—on my end of the line as I stood in my kitchen searching for answers about how it's possible for a father and mother to not love their child. To not care that their child had gone hungry, to not care that their child had been homeless, to not even care enough to acknowledge that their child had endured multiple rapes.

"And Ida, your mother? My parents . . . you know, your grandparents, didn't want her to marry Henry. But she begged and begged and begged until they said yes."

Some of the pieces of the puzzle finally came together for me. During all the years, instead of leaving him, she made all of us children suffer at his hands—and hers. We're the ones who are paying for her mistake and her refusal to accept the responsibility for her actions. What kind of mother puts her children through such hell? And what kind of father?

Shortly after our conversation in the hotel, I broke things off with Aidan. He didn't support my career aspirations, and I wasn't interested in being his accessory of a wife. But his declaration—"Your dad knows. They're brothers"—never left me. He'd said it with such emphasis. "Brothers know these things about each other."

Had I been some sort of prize in Henry, Harvey, and Enos' rape business?

Intended to be passed around among the brothers?

Groomed from birth for that purpose?

NOTE: The names of some of these characters and other identifying details have been changed to protect the privacy of individuals.

Music for the Soul

_____

Here are several selections that helped me get through the events or period of this chapter, or reflect musically what I felt during this time. I understood very little of most lyrics—even today my ears don't process most words—but the melodies and instruments fed my soul. Had it not been for music, I wouldn't have survived until I finally got to therapy at age twenty-nine.

- Phish. "Free." *Billy Breathes*, 1996.

- Hisham Abbas. "Habiby Dah." *Habiby Dah*, 1999.

- Fairouz. "Sallimleh Alayh." *Legend - The Best of Fairuz*, 2006.

CHAPTER 16

The Queen of Rings in the Asian South Seas

In the jungles of Indonesia, a poor Balinese boy and a poor Columbia University student made a pact. He'd brought with him a ring, a small, simple, and beautiful silver band set with a pearl fished out of the South Sea. He slipped it on her finger and they clasped their left hands together, held each other's gaze and said, "In the next lifetime, husband and wife."

Desak was married and a responsible husband. I was single and afraid of commitment. Even a promise to a future lifetime scared me so much that I silently inserted, *If it's meant to be.*

I had arrived in Bali several weeks earlier for a summer vacation before my final year of school. Ubud was known as the artistic and cultural heart of the island and it was filled with white American and European expats, vacationers, and wannabe spiritualists. Ubud, unlike most of Indonesia, was not Muslim but a hybrid of imported Hinduism blended with the traditional, local animism. Every day I woke up to the crystal clear sun streaming in my face as it rose over the mountains. Every day I walked out of my villa to the fragrance of burning incense on my doorstep. Every day at dawn a small cake of white rice appeared, decorated with fresh pink and yellow flowers and the incense stick in the center. A hotel employee had tiptoed by with it as an offering to the gods and ancestors and spirits.

Every morning was the same: bright lush green rolling hills and valleys dotted with thatched roof huts and smoke from the temples and shrines rising to meet the heavens. A hushed peaceful-ness enveloped my walk to the front of the hotel complex before I exited onto the street toward the village center.

"Good morning, Ms. Bontrager," the sculp-ture-like girl with exquisite eyes, ruby red lips, and dangling jewelry said, backing away quickly if I emerged from my room too early and caught her sweeping the veranda. "Sorry to disturb you."

Sometimes I met a dark-skinned male, clothed in a colorful Balinese uniform, rounding the bend from the other way. "Good morning, Miss," he said, smiling and nodding shyly, stopping quickly to move off to the side of the narrow stone pathway, and bowing until I passed.

"Good morning, Madam." An old gardener planted in a flower bed with a spade in his wrinkly hands spotted me and stopped his work as I went by, as if pausing his activities to recognize my pres-ence with a moment of attentiveness was one of his daily duties.

I always felt as if I was treated and recognized as some sort of royalty. Some wealthy white queen or diplomat who was deserving—or demanding—of the highest protocol at all times.

I spent six weeks in that villa that summer. And never once did this royal regard for me diminish. I'm poor, just like you, I'd think. Haven't you picked up by now that I have no money and I struggle for my daily necessities no differently from you? That I've just been randomly lucky to swing a trip here? That I work remotely for an American boss out of an internet cafe every day? I'm dependent upon that paycheck for survival, just like you. I'd never be able to afford a villa and six weeks in a beautiful place with amenities like this in the US.

That summer marked a radical shift in my perceptions about money and wealth. In how I saw myself and how I began to see the relative value, and accompanying attached perceptual status, of money. In the eyes of the relatively far poorer Balinese, I was indeed a rich white American woman living a life of luxury and ease. In their eyes, I was privileged, a member of the elite class of the world, a status that some of them dreamed of—and could only dream of. In their eyes, because I was kind to them, I deserved royal treatment even more. Perhaps I was one of their reincarnated ancestors and merely seeing me from a distance, serving me each morning, and being in my presence as I walked by, smiled back, and acknowledged their presence in return, was a blessing in their day. The nice, pretty American woman who didn't treat them like meaningless servants inferior to her. Who didn't treat them as if she were a tourist from the United States.

"You're American? US? You don't act like one." The questions came at breakfast or lunch—when I was dining alone—from whomever had stopped by my table to take my order. Usually the servers were young, with a good command of English.

"Thank you." I smiled because of their surprise and for the compliment. "I'd like a bowl of mangoes and poached eggs this morning."

"You don't look American either. Your face is not American. . . ." They accepted the menu from my outstretched hand, curiosity and puzzlement etched through their expressions as they retreated to the kitchen. Who was this unusual person?

In roughly thirty countries around the globe, I've gotten this same response. No one places me for a US tourist or traveller:

"You're Romanian."

"No."

"Ah, Czech."

"No."

"Polish. . . ? Russian?"

In that order, without fail. Never "US."

That afternoon, after the storm had washed the terraced rice paddies and thick rain forests, Desak came to my villa. He was a gifted tattoo artist and spoke American English unusually well because of his clients. I'd been one of them, who had temporarily turned into more than a client after he tattooed the Japanese-Chinese character "death" onto my body.

Desak took me on adventures into the countryside and off the beaten track. We did touristy things, too, like visiting the Monkey Forest, an open sanctuary of hundreds of wild monkeys climbing trees, scampering across trails, and begging for food from human visitors. But far more important to me was learning about Desak's world from his perspective. I learned that his name indicated a specific order of birth and societal rank in Balinese tradition. He was from the aristocratic, warrior, or ruling class.

Desak believed fully the indigenous views of his culture. That a living force breathed through everything: human, animal, rock, plant, the elements, physical, nonphysical, visible, and invisible. That there were ghosts and spirits and beings and some that appeared human but weren't human. That certain humans were psychic and had the power to shapeshift and perform acts that defied known scientific laws of physics. And that it was possible for us to find each other after death in this lifetime.

Desak pulled me toward the bed. "You're so beautiful." He ran his fingers through my hair and kissed me on my lips. He slid the straps off my shoulders and pulled the top of my dress down.

I looked at the ring on my finger and wondered if I'd made a mistake. *What if this pact really held into the next lifetime?* My flight back to the US was leaving the next day, and the bubble I'd lived in with Desak for three weeks started to crumble. *I'm not sure I wanna be tied to him. . . .*

The sun had set behind the mountains and twilight was stealing softly across the valley and over the hills, tucking in the temples and shrines and villas and huts. With it came the tinny, xylophonic sounds of the gamelan from Ubud Palace, drifting to us through the open window. Dancers and singers, dressed in ethereal costumes, performed each night at the Palace. For the last time before my departure, we made love. Like the fire dancers swaying under trance-like rhythms, we moved to an exotic world of our own.

"I have to go now," Desak said.

I watched him walk out my door to go home to his wife and children. I felt guilty that I'd slunk in an amendment to my contract with him. He was a good person and, had he been single, I would've married him.

For a year afterward, I wore his ring. He'd given me a pearl, not a diamond. Because pearls were known as the "queen of gems."

NOTE: The name of this character and other identifying details have been changed to protect his privacy.

Music for the Soul

Here are several selections that helped me get through the events or period of this chapter, or reflect musically what I felt during this time. I understood very little of most lyrics—even today my ears don't process most words—but the melodies and instruments fed my soul. Had it not been for music, I wouldn't have survived until I finally got to therapy at age twenty-nine.

- Gotan Project. "Epoca." *La Revanch del Tango*, 2001.

- Sia. "Elastic Heart." *1000 Forms of Fear*, 2015.

- P. J. Harvey. "Angelene." *Is This Desire?*, 1998.

CHAPTER 17

Following My Own Way (Part III of a Trilogy)

I grew up on fairy tales and nursery rhymes, just like many American children, but those stories came through books and not through TV, movies, internet, radio, or music. In a culture that actively censors and shuns outside influences as much as possible, and prohibits intellectual inquiry, books became my passport to the universe. I couldn't wait until I was old enough to go to Amish school so I could learn how to read and not have to depend on my mother for stories and knowledge.

One of my favorite stories was about King Arthur and the sword in the stone. The only part of the plot I knew was that once upon a time in a land far away, there was a boy named Arthur who pulled a magical sword out of a rock. That meant that he was the rightful king of England. No one else had been able to remove it.

During my last year at Columbia, I took Professor Karl Kroeber's *Children's Literature* course to fulfill my literature requirement. One of the first books we were assigned to read was *The Once and Future King*. Through that, I got the background to the Arthur story that I'd been fascinated with as a child.

"What did Merlyn mean by 'education is experience and the essence of experience is self-reliance'?" Prof. Kroeber's fluffy snow-white hair, glasses, and bearded face looked like Santa Claus. His was a popular class, restricted to around twenty upper-level students who each had had to submit a special application in the hopes of getting on the roster. Being a Columbia student didn't guarantee that one would learn from Prof. Kroeber. One of my fellow Gsers—School of General Studies, the undergrad school for nontraditional students—had raved about him one night over drinks on a rooftop bar, and I felt very lucky that he'd accepted my submission—even more so because he was battling cancer and it was possibly his final class.

Throughout the entire semester, Prof. Kroeber talked to us about his views on education and the potential of children. He challenged us with an intellectual intensity and unconventionality rarely seen in a classroom, even at Columbia. He seemed to believe that we students sitting in our posh, Ivy League environment possessed no independent thinking skills. He wasn't a fan of institutionalized education, which he thought encouraged parroting our professors' opinions or the CliffsNotes instead of coming up with critical answers ourselves.

"I don't agree with that at all" was one of his favorite lines in class. It was frustrating to get snapped with that response every time he asked for my thoughts on the material. He was impossible to please. Eventually I became so disheartened that I no longer spoke up. I'd sit toward the back instead of the front, crouch down in my seat, and do my best to disappear from his view so he wouldn't call on me for an original analysis.

Before Arthur had become aware of his true royal origins, the wizard Merlyn took him under his wing and groomed him to become king. Merlyn taught the boy about the magic of the natural world. Part of Arthur's education included getting turned into birds and animals and experiencing the world from those perspectives. Prof. Kroeber frequently referenced the passage in which Merlyn turned Arthur into a fish:

> "Oh, Merlyn," [Arthur] cried, "please come, too."

> "For this once," said [Merlyn], "I will come. But in the future, you will have to go by yourself. Education is experience, and the essence of experience is self-reliance."

I don't remember if Kroeber ever revealed what he thought about that concept of education—if he were still alive, I'd ask him. What I do remember is that he never stopped asking us what we thought Merlyn meant. Looking back, I think it's obvious that Kroeber was beating us with this passage in an effort to shake us out of our educated hypnosis. Real education is about acquiring experiences in order to figure out one's own path (one's own truth based on personal experiences) rather than blindly following external sources or authority figures who claim to have the answers. It's about trusting yourself and no longer looking to others for approval. It's about refusing to give away your power to other sources (books, texts, articles, news) or figures (priests, pastors, preachers, politicians, parents), alive or dead (Jesus, Moses, Mohammed, the Buddha, the government), and to look within yourself for the answers. To know that you know what is best for you. Kroeber wanted us to make our own rules, instead of unquestioningly following the rules that society had predetermined for us. That's why he provoked us so much.

During the week that we covered *Winnie-the-Pooh*, Prof. Kroeber harped on the spelling in the book. "Honey" was often spelled "HUNNY" and Christopher Robin would write strange-looking notes: "GON OUT, BIZY, BACKSOON," for example. "These aren't necessarily misspellings. The rules of spelling are completely arbitrary. Who made these rules? They only work because we, as a society, follow and uphold such dictates. They're not set in stone."

The most profound thing I learned from Kroeber wasn't about anything that made me a better academic—or employee, or boss—but it made me a better person in both life and love. The topic got started from a discussion of a passage of *Winnie-the-Pooh* in which Piglet asks Pooh, "How do you spell love?" and Pooh answers, "You don't spell it. You feel it." I distinctly remember Kroeber, in professorial garb, standing at the head of the class asking us, "How do you know when you really love someone?"

I raised my hand. "You love them despite their

faults."

"No, you love them *because of* their faults."

Blown away by the profundity of that difference, I never forgot his perspective; it remained embedded in my consciousness. I was a disaster at love. I had no positive models for romantic relationships, no idea what it took to create and maintain a healthy partnership. I yearned for my fairy-tale knight, but I was terrified of betrayal and broken trust, and hence I was commitment-phobic and unable to cultivate a relationship that allowed me to develop deep emotions. In order to protect myself, I coped by blocking my feelings—even though I couldn't help but feel. Constantly. Deeply. Painfully. Silently.

During my years at Columbia, I learned that the Ivy League system is no different from the Amish system: you're expected to toe the party line. On a broad level, being a "good" student means working the system, regurgitating what your professors say, and not challenging them (so you get good grades; so your GPA doesn't take a hit; so you get grants, scholarships, and a degree; so you get into grad school; so you get your dream job). You're trained in how to think—specifically how to think in the way that your professors want you to think—and if you deviate from or challenge those ways of thinking, you're punished with bad grades, which have long-term ramifications: losing financial aid, not getting accepted into the grad school of your choice, not getting the job, or even career, of your choice, and so forth. Higher education, just like the Amish Church, practices a specific form of brainwashing. Both Ivy League students and Amish children are specially trained—brainwashed—to become and remain "good" little members, stay within the system, and never venture outside. If you do dare to deviate and peek behind the curtain, the shock of what you see is so traumatizing that you're forced to return. Unless you're the rare, tiny percentage that somehow is born with the fortitude and luck to make it despite the odds.

I don't diminish the value of higher education. Everyone should become as exposed as they can to as many different opinions, beliefs, and facts as possible. Knowledge is power. Learn the rules so you know how to break them successfully. However, higher education, just like the Amish Church, was created to control and manipulate knowledge for the purpose of manufacturing good little boys and girls who grow up to serve an overlord. Colleges and universities—like the Amish Church and Amish school—provide a very strategically curated curriculum that's in the best interest of those ultimately in authority. Those in control in the world use higher education to program the general public, whether the ulterior motive is to design the masses to consume in the name of patriotism, to live from paycheck to paycheck, or to remain enslaved within American oligarchy and corporatocracy. Similarly, those in control inside the Amish program their members to isolate from outside engagement, to believe that suffering is a virtue, and to remain enslaved within Amish totalitarianism and authoritarianism.

Neither system allows topics such as remote viewing—or other psychic skills—and the existence of extraterrestrials to be taught or genuinely acknowledged. These topics are considered heresy, and good little American boys and girls are those who do not question what they've been brainwashed into believing from birth: that they have no psychic powers; that aliens don't exist; that there's no secret space program; that there are no military bases on the dark side of the moon; that there's no galactic commerce including alien and human trafficking and slavery; and that age regression, genetic manipulation, predictive programming, subliminal messaging, and time travel aren't routinely carried out—despite the vast body of evidence in existence on all these matters.

[Thankfully more and more individuals are coming forward to disclose the truths about humanity's existence, history, and capabilities. One of the positives about social media is that it provides a platform for the masses to speak out. The downside is that it's extremely challenging to discern the bits of truth from the made-up stuff. Take a look at shows that discuss secrets and cover-ups at www.gaia.com or search on YouTube for information about the Secret Space Program and humans' origins. Many things that sound like science fiction can be verified, such as the CIA's remote viewing programs. I don't believe one hundred percent anyone's claims about things that can't be verified, but there's definitely more to this planet than what the history books and politicians tell us.]

Sitting in a classroom and copying everything a

professor says, or indiscriminately following your boss or a religious figure isn't educational, meaningful, or fulfilling. There's a difference between authentic learning and indoctrination. I think Prof. Kroeber was trying to get us to become aware of the fact that, at some point, someone decided to create spelling and to make rules about spelling (metaphorically and literally) and that everyone else decided to follow those rules, or were coerced into following those rules. By failing to question and examine the rules independently, we lose our self-reliance. If we lose the skill of self-reliance, then we're living someone else's experiences, not our own. What kind of education is that? Real education comes from experience—and experience relies upon the self. That's what Merlyn meant when he said, "in the future, you will have to go by yourself."

A good professor, boss, leader, religion, or belief system encourages you to genuinely question, to think for yourself, and to learn from personal experience. When you find such a mentor, I hope you have the maturity and smarts to recognize the gold you've stumbled upon. Respect that person. Take every opportunity to learn from them. This is why Kroeber remains one of the few Columbia professors whom I truly admire. I'll forever be grateful for having had the fortune to be in his class.

A big, fat C stared at me. For the umpteenth time. "You're not comprehending the message in the material," Prof. Kroeber had scrawled across the first page of my essay. His handwritten notes were barely legible, but not so illegible that I didn't get *his* message: "This is terrible writing." The image of his monstrous, unyielding C—in plain view for all my better, smarter classmates to see as he handed back our essays—burned. I felt humiliated. *What does he want me to say or write? It's a fucking kids' literature class. This was supposed to have been easy!*

After collecting enough Cs, I showed up at his office hours one week. I knocked on the foreboding, heavy wood door, a feeling of dread flooding my soul. I needed to pass with at least a B or my GPA would drop and I'd lose my partial scholarship. It would take a miracle to recover at this point in the semester.

"Come in." Prof. Kroeber sat behind his desk in a solid wood banker's chair—the kind of chair seen in old libraries or imposing offices—and motioned me to take a seat opposite him. Overloaded bookshelves crowded out the light from the one and only window in his office.

"I can't write. I have ADHD," I said, flinging my worn backpack crammed with textbooks and papers for the day's classes on the floor.

"You're definitely challenged, but you do *not* have a *learning disability*." Prof. Kroeber looked me dead in the eyes. "Learning." "Disability." He pronounced each word separately, with emphasis.

What did he mean? "But I was diagnosed with ADHD. . . ."

My conversation with Kroeber that day turned into one of the best memories I have. He didn't like that I was on Ritalin. I could see his concern, and I agreed with him that doping children was harm-

215

ful. "The educational system suppresses children's imagination and creativity," he said. "It doesn't let them learn in ways that are unique to them." After that day, I felt a kindred spirit in him, even though he continued to give me Cs.

Toward the end of the semester, he gave me one B-minus and stated that I was finally starting to show some improvement. For my overall grade, he called me in to his office to say, "I'm giving you an A for effort. You haven't earned an A in your writing, but you have potential and you've been improving."

Tears oozed out. I tried not to cry, from shocked gratitude and relief, until I left his office. No professor had ever shown such empathy toward my creative-writing challenges.

A few years later, Prof. Kroeber passed away. Cancer had triumphed. I didn't attend his memorial service, because I wanted to keep the memory of him teaching in our classroom: the musty smell of old books lining one side of the walls, wooden desks with metal hinges that looked like they came from an Amish one-room schoolhouse, creaky hardwood floors, and heavy castle-like doors—with a view that overlooked Butler Library and the campus center plaza outside, the afternoon sun's rays dancing off the edges of Kroeber's glasses, lighting his face in shades from the setting sun, and me praying for the semester to end so it'd all be over: *I'll never become a writer; this is too fucking hard.*

Following our own way doesn't mean that we have to do it alone, without the help of others.

Arriving in New York City, in 2003, made that clear to me. For the first time I felt what it was like to not be alone. I wasn't the only unique person in the world anymore. I wasn't the only misfit in society. Here, in this beautiful city, uniqueness and individuality and "different" weren't only accepted, but were embraced and encouraged and celebrated. That's why I revere the City, why it's my home and my deep love. New York is, and always will be, my heart and blood.

Despite the downfalls of an educational system that doesn't encourage individuality and independent thinking, I have Columbia's School of General Studies to thank for embracing my story and giving me a chance; for bringing me here to experience the world through the eyes and soul of NYC; and for exposing me to special professors like Karl Kroeber, Robert Thurman (who taught me about the nature of reality according to Tibetan Buddhism), David Albert (who taught me about the philosophy of science, the realities of time and space, and the science fiction-esque possibilities of quantum physics), and Achille Varzi (who taught me symbolic logic, which is a method of representing logical expressions through the use of symbols and variables, and makes you far smarter in life when you learn it). They expanded my mind and encouraged my potential. They're key individuals who helped me find my own way, while I acquired the experiences in life to create myself.

As I evolve—as I experience more—many of my truths change or become more refined. This comes from the self-reliance that the wizard Merlyn talks about, and reflects the Buddhist view that truth is not absolute but is relative. Even my own path is right only relatively, not absolutely. Even when I have the freedom and gumption to follow my own way, what becomes true for me one day doesn't necessarily remain true for me in the future. For example, I thought Buddhism had all the answers for me—and everyone else!—but after graduating from Columbia, I felt stuck.

There's a saying in Buddhism that a being who's genuinely enlightened won't tell you that they're enlightened and to run away as fast as you can from anyone who claims to be enlightened. Well, if the premise of Buddhism is that enlightenment is possible but there's no way of proving that enlightenment (whatever the hell *that* is) actually exists—unless you yourself inexplicably become enlightened one day and just so happen to know that you are now enlightened—then that premise is just as faulty as any other religion or belief system's. To continue with Buddhism meant that I'd need to operate out of pure faith that what I was told was true, with no verifiable external evidence. So I tossed out Buddhism completely for a year and began to read self-help books such as Eckhart Tolle's *The Power of Now*, Deepak Chopra's *The Way of the Wizard* (the only one of his books that I like), and Debbie Ford's *The Dark Side of the Light Chasers*. When I no longer clung to the belief that Buddhism was the one and only way for me and opened myself up for answers from somewhere else, the brain-boggling concepts that I hadn't been able to comprehend in Prof. Thurman's classes suddenly made sense.

This is what was meant by *x*, *y* and *z*! Presented or colored in other ways, I finally got them. I'd needed to get off my own path in order to get on my own path.

The principles I rely on to guide me in life today are to listen to my heart, to trust myself, and to know that I know what is best for me. And to remember that my truth evolves as I evolve. It takes guts to become comfortable with such uncertainty, and it took me a long time to get there. It's not easy—but it *is* worth it.

Music for the Soul

Here are several selections that helped me get through the events or period of this chapter, or reflect musically what I felt during this time. I understood very little of most lyrics—even today my ears don't process most words—but the melodies and instruments fed my soul. Had it not been for music, I wouldn't have survived until I finally got to therapy at age twenty-nine.

- Moby. "Live for Tomorrow." *Last Night*, 2008.

- Moby. "Last Night." *Last Night*, 2008.

- Tiesto. "Just Be (feat. Kristy Hawkshaw)." *Just Be*, 2004.

CHAPTER 18

My "Heroes" Are Julian and David Bowie

I sat in Julian's austere, neat apartment on Chrystie Street in New York City's Chinatown one rainy Thursday evening. Vinyl records and awards, piled up on the floor against the wall in his hallway, had outlined a jagged path toward the back kitchen. Certified gold and platinum plaques provided the only obvious evidence of the glamorous lifestyle and celebrityhood the occupant of this top-floor apartment, in a no-doorman building, enjoyed.

Is this this real or am I tripping? I'd wondered when I first arrived. I'd tried to walk past nonchalantly as Julian led the way, asking me how my week had been. I tried not to stare at the haphazard stacks of shiny objects, as if all my friends were rock stars and this was normal, everyday. I'd never even seen physical music industry awards before. Only pictures. This scene was the stuff of dreams, not real life. Certainly not real for a no-name wannabe musician girl from Amish country.

I'd been introduced to Julian through a mutual friend at a film screening in Tribeca several weeks before. Typical pop culture–deficient Amish me hadn't realized with whom I was having a fascinating, cerebral conversation that night until several hours later when I asked, "Um, what's your name again?"

The look that shot across Julian's face was priceless. He was at the height of his career and world-famous. But to me he was just another of countless guys interested in my personal story, asking the exact same list of questions I'd been asked a million times before. I recognized his name only because one of my friends had happened to mention his breakout album a few years earlier.

Julian brought over a bottle of wine and poured two glasses at the dining room table. Music I hadn't heard before played in the background. Whimsical. Lilting. With a female voice. "French music," he said when I asked him what it was.

He didn't waste any time getting personal. "What was your first time like?" Julian pulled back a chair, sat down across from me, and studied my face.

I felt his stare penetrating me for what seemed like an eternity. He expected a serious response. The way he sat, the way he held his glass, and the way he fixed his eyes on me made me feel like I was backed into a corner. In that moment, something in me knew that he'd know if I didn't give him an honest answer. He wasn't someone I wanted to lie to. I liked him a lot. Shit, I thought. This isn't a topic I want to discuss right now. Definitely not on a first date. Shit.

I glanced at Julian, gripped the stem of my glass a tad too hard, and focussed on my drink. *Fuck it.*

You asked. Don't ask the question if you can't handle the answer. "I hated it." I dreaded the next question.

For the first time, I answered truthfully about my initial sexual experience. None of my romantic interests—not even the ones I'd been engaged to— had ever asked me, but other people who were curious about my Amish sex education had inquired. I'd thought that it was supposed to feel good so I'd said great. No one asked further.

By late 2006, the rapes from ten years earlier pillaged my psyche. I couldn't repress the realities of my past anymore, and I was tired of what felt like covering for my rapist uncles by saying that my first time was good. I fought daily to stave off the memories and flashbacks enough to just barely make it through my last year at Columbia. My laissez-faire dormmate Oliver owned a huge glass bong and welcomed my regular visits in the evenings before I headed off for bed. Without that, I probably wouldn't have graduated. I wasn't in therapy yet and didn't even know I had PTSD—I'd never heard of post-traumatic stress disorder. Weed was the only thing that made it possible for me to fall asleep at night without the flashbacks overpowering me. On the nights without weed, I had to imagine chopping off penises with high-powered grinders and flying bits spewing everywhere, in a psychological and symbolic battle of fighting back. Killing, crushing, annihilating the monsters who'd murdered my soul. Until I was finally able to sleep, the rapists dead again for one more night.

Julian looked surprised—and impressed—by my answer. "Most girls lie about it and say it felt good.

But you didn't. The first time hurts."

I just nodded, grateful for the information, and feeling lucky that fortune had smiled upon me: he didn't suspect I'd been raped. I hadn't wanted to answer his follow-ups. Julian was smart and the type who would've probed if he thought I was hiding anything.

That night still ranks as one of the best sexual experiences, out of a hundred-plus guys, I've had. I'd been frightened shitless by the possibility of sex with Julian. As much as I wanted to die, because of my daily struggles to just survive the darkness of my past, I didn't want to die from AIDS or contract STDs. Statistically, a celebrity came with a higher risk than the average person.

"Condoms. You *have* to wear a condom," I said when it became obvious to me that he intended to get me naked. "I don't want to get an STD."

I hadn't thought the evening would get to that point with him. I found it hard to believe that he could be sexually attracted to me. I had such low self-esteem and such huge body image issues that I honestly thought he was just charmed because of my brain when he'd invited me over. A famous person interested in me? From New York City, with a million beautiful women? Impossible.

"Don't worry." He held my face in his hands and brushed a strand of hair out of my eyes. "I'll be safe."

For the next several hours, Julian treated me like a queen and asked nothing of me. Not even a blow job. That night was my night. He focused so much on me that I genuinely wanted to pleasure him, too. He took me on the sofa, the furniture, and the floor, my body a piece of art that he sculpted and painted and played into a mind-blowing experience.

He sent me into an out-of-body, altered state of consciousness. Like an acid trip. The hours with him turned surreal. I'd never felt anything like that before. The intense pleasure, the sensations, the colors, the sounds. The otherworldliness.

I had no point of reference for what Julian did for me. That was long before my days of dropping LSD and becoming comfortable with my sexuality. I was so out of touch with my physical body that it was hard for me to absorb what was happening. He knew what buttons to press, what made me tick, what made me feel good. And he did it all without sticking his penis in me. Safe. Just like he'd promised.

"I wonder where we went," he said after it was over, lying next to me on the floor, and resting his head on my shoulder. "Don't you wonder about that?"

"Yeah," I lied. I didn't know then what he meant, but I do now.

"Let me tell you what David Bowie told me about fulfilling your dreams: 'When I started walking like a rock star, that's when I became a rock star,'" Helene said. Her elegant fingers touched the handle of a china teacup and her spiral-square silver earrings caught my eye. Helene embodied an air of aged sophistication and confidence that I desperately wanted.

I was twenty-three and had run across her while doing research for a paper in a music literature course at Columbia. Among many other things, she was a meditation teacher who'd been an activist on the West Coast music scene in her youth and had just re-released an album as a fun side project. I was intrigued by her accomplishments as a musician and multi-entrepreneur. A successful creative and business mind combined, Helene was the first such powerful female I knew. She was someone with whom I felt a kinship, a female role model I could look up to and possibly learn from as a mentor.

Her bio dropped names up the wazoo. Yoko Ono. Hugh Jackman. Michael Franti. But this was New York City, and in New York, everybody knew somebody. And everybody was somebody.

Helene's words left an indelible mark in my consciousness. They were the single best piece of practical business and life guidance I'd received at that point—and they're still one of the most valuable guiding principles I aspire to incorporate: carry yourself as if you already are who you want to be; be like David Bowie. That changed my approach to life and shifted my trajectory in a permanent way.

It wasn't until the night with Julian that I realized that the song that had gotten me through some of my darkest years post-rape was David Bowie's. Julian had wanted to know what my favorite music was.

"Lots of stuff but Pink Floyd, The Velvet Underground, Roxy Music, and Iva Davies & Icehouse are what I listen to for therapy."

His eyes lit up. I could tell he was surprised but pleased by my taste in music. "How does a young Amish girl come to appreciate those artists?"

"I had a music mentor. He liked the sixties."

"He did a good job. I've never heard of Icehouse. What are your favorite songs?"

"'Heroes' and 'All Tomorrow's Parties'."

"'Heroes'? That's a David Bowie song. And 'All Tomorrow's Parties' is The Velvet Underground's."

That's when it clicked. George, my music mentor, had given me an album *The Berlin Tapes* when I was nineteen. "They're covers but remarkably composed and influenced by some big names. You need to listen to these."

I hadn't understood what "cover" meant. I thought they were originals. But all this time I'd been listening to David Bowie's lyrics.

The opening "I, I will be king / And you, you will be queen / Though nothing will drive them away / We can beat them just for one day" and the refrain "We can be heroes just for one day" carried me through every day—for one more day—when my world had crashed post-escape. When I'd jumped out of the frying pan of childhood abuse and into the fire of routine sexual assault. When all my dreams had shattered. When isolation and darkness crushed me. When I had nowhere to turn, no parents who loved me, no family who cared. No one who had my back. If I had died, no one would have come looking for me. My Amish parents wouldn't have cared and would have relished using the story to brainwash my siblings even more into not leaving. "This is what happens if you disobey your parents and leave the Amish" is what they would have said.

I'd lie on the floor in a ratty studio apartment on the outskirts of Houston, Texas, and fall asleep to David Bowie's belief in me that I could be a hero for just one day. I could beat "them" for one more day.

During my brief time with Julian, I acquired a wealth of knowledge on how to navigate romantic relationships, handle fame, and craft a public persona. He possessed an unusually gifted business mind that helped me become a better marketing professional. In the end, we parted ways on a note of betrayal—like all my romantic fuckups—never to speak again.

Sometimes I wonder if he was someone from another lifetime or planet sent to help train me for my path in the public eye. But then I think, *He's such a fucking asshole.*

NOTE: The names of these characters and identifying details have been changed to protect their privacy.

Music for the Soul

Here are several selections that helped me get through the events or period of this chapter, or reflect musically what I felt during this time. I understood very little of most lyrics—even today my ears don't process most words—but the melodies and instruments fed my soul. Had it not been for music, I wouldn't have survived until I finally got to therapy at age twenty-nine.

- David Bowie. "Heroes." *Heroes*, 1977.

- Icehouse. "Heroes." *The Berlin Tapes*, 1995.

- Icehouse. "All Tomorrow's Parties." *The Berlin Tapes*, 1995.

- Roxy Music. "Avalon." *The Best of Roxy Music*, 2001.

- The Velvet Underground & Nico. "All Tomorrow's Parties." *The Velvet Underground & Nico*, 1967.

CHAPTER 19

Suicide Meditations

"**H**e's dead."

The tone of her voice was as cold as the word "dead." His mother had never had any shred of love for me but couldn't she at least have used a gentler, more loving word? Like "passed away"? Or "gone"?

No.

Just "dead."

And no condolences. No "I'm sorry."

I hung up.

It was over. I was free.

The last several months with my fiancé had been a voyage into the outer spaces of seriously fucked-up darkness. I watched him spiral out of control on a path that consumed him. I tried to save him, steer him onto a trajectory that would help him deal with his demons and become the person I knew he had the potential to be.

I loved him with all my heart. He was my soulmate, I thought. In the end, I had to choose between loving myself or going down with his wreckage. I chose myself and watched him sink. Slowly. Steadily. Nothing I tried helped him.

There's a saying "If you love someone, let them go." I let him go. That kind of pain was the most agonizing and heart-wrenching that my heart had ever felt. Unconditional love hurt. I couldn't do anything. I couldn't save him. I couldn't rescue him.

The day I was going to leave him, he killed himself. He abandoned me on the side of the interstate in the middle of nowhere after an argument. I had to walk half a mile to the nearest gas station, and wait for two hours for a friend to pick me up because my purse was in the car. I was stranded with no cash, no credit cards, no ID.

That afternoon I stood under a perfectly beautiful blue sky and watched the world move in surreal slow motion around me. I felt relieved. Profound relief. I was free of him.

. . . But not free of the hells to come:

From his IBM employer, who sicced his boss on me *on the day of the memorial service* to recover their assets.

From his parents, who hated my guts and held his ashes ransom in an attempt to extract all our belongings from me, down to the last plastic spoon, and tried to blackmail me into giving them the passwords to his bank accounts.

From his psycho ex, who'd used the children to get whatever she wanted from him, and who'd succeeded in getting the children taken away from him by filing false sexual assault allegations when he didn't give her what she wanted.

From his thieving, meth addict sister.

From even our Unitarian Universalist minister, who sided with his non-UU, Catholic parents and delivered a message on their behalf in the memorial service address—despite knowing that it was against my wishes and against what would've been my fiancé's wishes.

From my siblings, some of whom made a show of appearing at the memorial service I held but then refused to help me move out of our house. I wasn't allowed to mourn first. I had to move out within two weeks after his death because I wasn't safe alone. His parents, ex, or people on their behalf drove past the house and made threats.

And, of course, from my father, who wrote, "If you just were a Christian, bad things wouldn't happen to you." Considering that he never expressed any regret when my brother told him I'd been raped repeatedly, I can only assume his sentiments regarding that were the same: "If you just were a Christian, my brothers wouldn't have raped you." The meaning in both cases was that I deserved what had happened to me. It was God punishing me for daring to have fled at age fifteen from parental abuse.

Death opened my eyes. When I lost the only person I loved—the only person I cared about in the entire world—I learned that death is the first lesson of life. It's not the last one, reserved for the end. I started living when I died.

I no longer cared about the pettiness and absurdities of everyday life, and even less than before about people's opinions of me. This kind of death set me free in ways I hadn't been free before and gave me a pristine clarity on what was really important to me. I can die at any second, completely out of the blue. Literally. Is this really what I want to be doing with my energy and time today, right now? Do I really give a shit about your attacks and crusades against me?

For a long time, that clarity stayed with me. And then it wore off. Faded. Just like all hits of mind-altering experiences do.

Meditations and Poems on Death

I meditate on death a lot. Even before my fiancé died, I'd practiced a meditation from the Tibetan Book of the Dead called *'pho ba* (also spelled *phowa* or *powa*), which means "transference of consciousness." The method visualizes chakras and channels and the dying process one goes through, according to Tibetan Buddhism. Staying aware of death helps me to stay in touch with myself, judge myself less, and be more loving and kind toward myself.

Some of my favorite poems on death are by the Lebanese writer Kahlil Gibran and the Chilean poet Pablo Neruda. Gibran expressed the philosophical depths of my encounter with death, and Neruda expressed the determination in me to make it through the fires of the aftermath of losing who I'd thought was "the one."

Here are a few of my favorite lines from the poem "On Death" in *The Prophet*, by Gibran:

> But how shall you find [the secret of death] unless you seek it in the heart of life?

. . . .

If you would indeed behold the spirit of
death, open your heart wide unto the
body of life.

For life and death are one, even as the river
and the sea are one.

My friend Antonio's father read Neruda's "La
Muerta" aloud to me when I was grieving in Ecua-
dor. Since then, both Antonio and his father have
passed on, too: Antonio from an out-of-the-blue
tragedy shortly after I last saw him, and his father from cancer. I still find solace in that poem.
It touches my heart and soul and reignites warm,
comforting memories of the two and their families, who opened up their hearts and homes to me
during such a heartbreaking and intense juncture
in my life. Whenever I read this poem, I hear Antonio telling me, "He would've wanted you to be
happy. It's okay to be happy."

It's hard to translate Neruda's depth of color,
emotion, and beauty into English. If you can read
Spanish, it's far more potent than the English
translation:

> Si tú no vives,
> si tú, querida, amor mío,
> si tú
> te has muerto,
> todas las hojas caerán en mi pecho,
> lloverá sobre mi alma noche y día,
> la nieve quemará mi corazón,
> andaré con frío y fuego y muerte y nieve,

mis pies querrán marchar hacía donde tú
    duermes,
pero
seguiré vivo,
porque tú me quisiste sobre todas las cosas
indomable,
y, amor, porque tú sabes que soy no sólo un
    hombre
sino todos los hombres. (excerpt from "La
Muerta," by Pablo Neruda)

If you do not live,
if you, darling, my love,
if you
have died,
all the leaves will fall in my chest,
it will rain over my soul day and night,
the snow will burn my heart,
I will walk with cold and fire and death and
    snow,
my feet will want to go where you sleep,
but
I will still live,
because you [wanted] me above all things
untamable,
and, [my] love, because you know that I am
    not only [a man]
but all men. (excerpt from "The Dead
Woman," translated by Curtis Bauer)

Death Doula

I'm a death doula. When I was twenty-six, I tattooed the Japanese-Chinese character "death" onto my body. It was a way for me to own death instead of fearing it. Carrying death with me every day helped me to become friends with it. The tattoo is a daily reminder that what we think of as death is just a point of shifting from one form of existence to another—or perhaps no existence at all after this lifetime.

 When you're no longer afraid of dying, you have the freedom to live.

How to Stop Wanting to Die

(March 24, 2017)

I got a message via Facebook from someone late last night: "How do you stop wanting to die?"

My answer: "You find a reason to live. And if you can't find a reason to live and you can't kill yourself, then you make up a reason. That was a significant piece on how I made it through my last suicidal crisis."

I'm not against suicide. That's an unreasonable societal taboo. Sometimes you find a reason to live when you give yourself permission to die.

Suicide Is Okay

Sometimes suicide is the best option for a person. Sometimes that's the only option to stop one's suffering. I've contemplated it seriously six times in the past twenty-two years.

Suicide is not okay if it's used as a cowardly method of escape (for example, to avoid prison when you've committed a crime). But I see no virtue in suffering unnecessarily.

Making a thoughtful, rational decision to end my life is not a crime. Society needs to stop using the term "commit suicide" and start accepting the fact that we each, individually, are the sovereign owners of our bodies and lives and have the innate right to end our life in this lifetime whenever we choose to do so. Using the term "commit suicide" is an attack—loaded with judgment and preconceived notions—on my personal sovereignty as a living being and whatever situation I'm going through.

Spiritual suicide is something no one talks about. Isn't that the real tragedy? Why are we so hell-bent as a society on accusing people of committing a crime for killing themselves physically, but we're not concerned at all for all the ones who have already died spiritually? Physical suicide is often the result of a soul that had long been tortured, lived in agony, and felt neglected and uncared for by this world.

Suicide, PTSD, Depression, and Psychedelics

(March 17, 2016)

In the past several months, I've experienced a depression unlike anything ever before. This one was completely and utterly debilitating. So debilitating that I thought I wasn't going to be able to return to writing my memoir. Not because I didn't have anything to say, but because I had nothing positive, hopeful, inspiring, or encouraging to say about humans and this world we live in.

I wanted to kill myself, but unfortunately I'd acquired so much knowledge and so many ideas about what might (or might not) happen if I killed myself that I simply wasn't willing to take the risk of landing in a possibly worse situation than the hell I was experiencing at the time. I tried *everything* to fix myself. I felt like a coward because I didn't have the guts to put myself out of this horrendous suffering, yet I had nothing left to live for: I was being tortured 24/7 by images and memories of my childhood/teenage traumas (rape scenes looping and coursing through my brain night and day) and nothing I tried made those images and memories stop. I was completely powerless to halt the flashbacks and, despite that, I still wasn't willing to kill myself.

There I was, wondering why I was alive and honestly not feeling that I could ever authentically be happy again. How could I create meaning for myself in this world in which rape is virtually celebrated, with at least one presidential candidate having raped at least one of his ex-wives and publicly indicated he'd f*ck his own daughter if she weren't his daughter? How could I rationally and authentically find meaning to continue to live? How could I ever again sincerely send a message of hope to anyone in this world that life is worth being alive for?

So I remained silent—waiting as the days and weeks went by and, during that time, testing out ketamine infusions (legal in the US if administered by a licensed medical professional) and iboga (legal in Mexico) based on one of my friend's recommendations. Those were things I hadn't tried before, and it is in this specific moment as I sit here writing that I'm feeling genuine spontaneous gratitude for my friend coming to my rescue.

Today for the first time in at least three months, thanks to those psychedelic medicines, combined with energy work by a healer friend who had had a clinically-dead experience, I can say that I genuinely feel a sliver of gratitude and lightness. I'm finally seeing consistent progress toward relief. I'm only operating at one percent of my normal functioning capacity—but I'm genuinely grateful for that, and I feel that the needle is going to keep moving forward again.

What has changed? Or what created this change? In this particular experience, no amount of positive thinking, therapy, coaching, and bodywork did a damn thing. My neurons were—most still are—damaged or destroyed by seventeen years' worth of extreme constant trauma. From birth to fifteen, my Amish parents abused me physically, verbally, psychologically, spiritually, and emotionally until I literally left in the middle of the night to escape that. Then, immediately after that, two of my uncles raped me repeatedly over the course of a year. Looking back at all of this now, it's no wonder that my brain cells couldn't process any of the positive messaging I sent them in the past year: I needed help on a physical, neurological level. That's what ketamine infusions and iboga gave me (as well as the psychedelics I did in the past that had given me one and a half years of freedom from PTSD[1]).

This post is the beginning of easing back into writing my memoir daily. I can write again because I genuinely feel tiny slivers of gratitude again, because I genuinely feel tiny slivers of hope again, because I genuinely see tiny slivers of positive, steady progress in my life again. I haven't changed my mind about the horrors and evils of this world and the rampant rape culture that exists in almost all levels and types of societies everywhere. Those things haven't changed at all.

What *has* changed is that psychedelic medicine is saving my life. It stopped the relentless onslaught of torturous memories, took away my chronic, severe physical pain that prevented me from getting a decent night's sleep, restored my appetite, fixed my metabolism so that I'm now consistently daily losing the thirty pounds of weight I'd gained within the past year—and is bringing color back into my life. Music sounds beautiful again, artwork is visually pleasing again, and I can smile and appreciate good food again. What science knows so far is that these medicines encourage the growth of neurons, neurons that didn't develop due to childhood trauma.[2] And that is the miracle I need if I'm to remain on this planet.

I'm sharing this because the best leaders are those who share their challenges and not just their triumphs. It's a myth that successful and wealthy people and companies have no problems or didn't face challenges—and sometimes extreme challenges—to get to where they are today. If you follow me regularly enough, you're seeing a bestselling memoir in the making and getting the often brutal, agonizing, and emotionally taxing up-and-down, real-time picture of what it's taking me to make this book happen.

When you see it hit the media outlets, you'll know that I'm not an overnight success or that I just magically effortlessly wrote it. You'll remember, you'll have read here, that I hadn't known if I could pull it off, and that there'd been a point in the process where I felt that I couldn't authentically continue to write because I saw absolutely nothing good in the world anymore. I hope that seeing this and remembering this will help fuel you in your endeavors.

Most of all, I hope that sharing my story—with all its colors, light, and darkness—will help you love yourself a little more, or help you learn to start to truly love yourself. Because what this world needs and what we all want is love. To just be loved.

Notes

1. Dr. Glen Brooks uses both the terms "post-traumatic stress disorder" and "post-traumatic stress." I'm not sure if his use of those terms are intended to mean the same thing or two different things.

Personally, I agree with General Peter Chiarelli that we do not have a disorder: "...The Army's No. 2 officer and top mental-health advocate, General Peter Chiarelli, used PTS repeatedly before opening up about the change. "I drop the *D*," he said. "That word is a dirty word." Chiarelli said the use of "PTSD" suggests the ailment is "pre-existing," when in reality it is a predictable reaction to combat stress" (qtd. in: Thompson, Mark. "The Disappearing "Disorder": Why PTSD is becoming PTS." *TIME*, 5 Jun. 2011, nation.time.com/2011/06/05/the-disappearing-disorder-why-ptsd-is-becoming-pts. Accessed 25 Mar. 2019.).

Also read the following article: Rittenhouse, Laura. "Will Google Learn That PTSD Got A New Name?" *Forbes*, 3 Jun. 2017, www.forbes.com/sites/laurarittenhouse/2017/06/03/will-google-learn-that-ptsd-got-a-new-name. Accessed 25 Mar. 2019.

Post-traumatic stress is a normal response to rape and other forms of extreme violence and we should not be stigmatized for that, or characterized as having a "disorder." In my writing and speaking, I try to use "PTS" rather than "PTSD" but because Google still hasn't learned that the D should be dropped, I often use that word so people new to the term can research it.

2. I am alive today only because of regular ketamine

infusions. For more details about PTS/PTSD and ketamine, read chapter 25 or watch this episode in which I interview my doctor, Dr. Glen Brooks: "What Ketamine Is + How It Helps with PTSD, Depression, and Pain." *Amish Entrepreneur Show with Torah Bontrager*, season 3, episode 8, www.amishheritage.org/what-ketamine-is-how-it-helps-with-ptsd-depression-pain. I also share more details about how I found ketamine in this article: Bontrager, Torah. "PTSD and the Designer Drug That Saves Me From Suicide." *Our Stories Untold*, 10 Apr. 2018, www.ourstoriesuntold.com/ptsd-design-er-drug-saves-suicide. Accessed 25 Mar. 2019.

Music for the Soul

Here are several selections that helped me get through the events or period of this chapter, or reflect musically what I felt during this time. I understood very little of most lyrics—even today my ears don't process most words—but the melodies and instruments fed my soul. Had it not been for music, I wouldn't have survived until I finally got to therapy at age twenty-nine.

- Phish. "If I Could." (*Hoist*), 1994.

- Pink Floyd. "Comfortably Numb." *The Wall*, 1979.

- Pink Floyd. "The Great Gig in the Sky." *The Dark Side of the Moon*, 1973.

- Willie Nelson. "Roll Me Up." *Heroes*, 2012.

CHAPTER 20

The Baddest Motherfuckin' Guitarist in Existence

A black South Side Chicago boy once told me, "You can't dance to the blues."

Aghast, I wanted to slap him awake. How could he not know essential music history? From his own culture? How was it possible that this naive Amish girl knew more about the origins of R&B and hip-hop than he did? It wasn't that he wasn't smart. He was incredibly intelligent and well-educated, with a solid ten years more of life over me *and* a mother who had protested in the civil rights movement of the sixties.

I wanted to tell him that if you can't dance to the blues, you don't know how to dance. Or you've never heard real blues: Buddy Guy. For my Amish and white friends, Buddy is the Elvis of the blues. But to even make that analogy makes me cringe. Because Elvis ain't got nothin', nothin' at all, on Buddy. Buddy is in a whole universe of his own, the greatest guitar player alive—the greatest guitar player alive or dead. The baddest motherfuckin' guitarist in existence.

When Buddy plays, something changes in you.

He shoots straight into the bloodstream, into your
DNA. You don't need drugs or psychedelics—weed,
acid, ecstasy, DMT—when you take a hit of Buddy
Guy. Put on a pair of earbuds, turn on his 2012
album *Live at Legends,* and get transported into an
altered state of consciousness. Then listen to all his
other stuff, too.

Music got me through the many years of dark
days and dark nights post-escape, especially in
the never-ending aftermath of repeat rapes that
had occurred over the course of my first year outside. Music nurtured what was left of my soul. If
it hadn't been for music that spoke my pain, that
understood the endless torment screaming inside
me, I wouldn't have survived.

I didn't discover Buddy Guy until 2012, but
he'd been in my life through the many rock musicians I listened to in my young adult years. One day
while sitting at my writing desk, with the TV on
the blues channel, a deep primal wail pierced my
brain and paralyzed my pen. Who the fuck is this? I
wondered. I ran to the screen and stood captivated,
frozen, until the electric guitar solo was over.

Why had George, my Santa Barbara, California,
music mentor from my late teens and early twenties, never mentioned Buddy Guy to me? George
had instilled in me a deep reverence for Jimi Hendrix. From him, I got the message that Jimi was
the greatest guitar player in history, that there was
something very special about Hendrix, and that his
work was the standard for me to aspire to if I wanted to become a good guitar player.

I wanted to be a professional musician. That

was my number one childhood dream, and for years I tried unsuccessfully to find my voice. When I finally got into therapy, in 2010, I realized that the reason I hadn't been able to make music when I was younger was because I couldn't let myself feel. If I'd allowed myself to feel, I wouldn't have survived, made it through Columbia, and gotten myself to a place in life that afforded me the luxury of facing my demons—of opening the box into which I had put all the bad memories, to wait for the day when I'd be strong enough to deal with them.

I was eleven years old when I had a dream one night that I played the guitar in a huge stadium filled with thousands of people. Just me sitting on a stool on a round stage with a spotlight on my face and a guitar in my hands. I didn't understand the setting in my dream. I'd never been to a concert or inside a stadium. Except for the harmonica in some communities, playing or creating music wasn't allowed in the Amish; the only thing allowed was singing hymns a cappella in church—or in some communities, Hank Williams and Beatles tunes that crept in from the outside, set to German lyrics—that we didn't understand—about our persecuted and martyred ancestors.

I wanted to learn how to play the guitar and resented being told what to do simply "because the Bible said so." The Amish Church leaders cherry-picked the parts of the Bible that suited them and made up rules based on whatever twisted interpretation they wanted. Religion tells you what to do, I thought. I'm sick of being forced to follow other people's rules. How do I change the world without ordering people around? The thought occurred to me that music was something that everyone understood without words. That's how I can speak without forcing my beliefs onto anyone and make the world a better place, I thought. I'm going to be a musician.

Years later when I was around twenty, one of the first shows I saw was Def Leppard, who happened to play at a venue with a round stadium. Then I understood what I'd seen in my dream.

After I stumbled upon Buddy Guy, I found out that Jimi Hendrix had learned his moves from Buddy and that Buddy had influenced "Voodoo Child," one of my favorites. Supposedly Jimi once said, "Heaven [lies] at Buddy Guy's feet while listening to him play guitar." I agree. Whatever your idea of heaven is, that's where you go when you listen to Buddy. He makes you *alive* in the parts of you that you didn't know existed or thought had died out long ago.

Many of the guitarists I love are "the best"— David Gilmour of Pink Floyd, Trey Anastasio of Phish, Carlos Santana, John Lee Hooker, Joan Jett, Neil Young, Lou Reed—but if I could learn how to play the guitar from just one person, it'd be Buddy. That would be a dream beyond my wildest dreams come true. I hope he stays alive long enough for me to say thank you in person one day. Or at least see him live at his Legends club in Chicago, on Wabash Avenue.

"'You can't dance to the blues'?" Tristan, sitting on a cherry red sofa across from me, shook his head. He leaned forward and propped his elbow on

the sofa's arm. "You can dance to silence."
An electric blue guitar rested at his side.

Saxophone Goddess
(a love poem)

Tonight when it's just me in this house,
*   On a hill with cars passing by*
And the night sounds clear
Crickets chirping and stars twinkling
And the river softly splashing along
I have this fantasy of being a saxophone player
Except the sax can't be played
She has to be loved
Listened to
Cared for
And only then will she let you play **with** *her*
She's the most beautiful instrument in the world
An extension of myself
Who feels what I feel
Hears what I feel
And says what I can't say without her
Primal sounds
Longing, sadness, joy, bliss
An extension of myself
The goddess breath
The call to live
The magic in-between worlds in the between worlds
Secret
Hidden
Unexpressed
Expressed.

The night river

The saxophone
The goddess
Eternal.

I am not a saxophone player.
I only see her and revere her.
From the shadows.
She is who I want to be

Music for the Soul

Here are several selections that helped me get through the events or period of this chapter, or reflect musically what I felt during this time. I understood very little of most lyrics—even today my ears don't process most words—but the melodies and instruments fed my soul. Had it not been for music, I wouldn't have survived until I finally got to therapy at age twenty-nine.

- Buddy Guy. "Feels Like Rain." *Best of the Silvertone Years*, 2005.

- Buddy Guy. "I Smell Trouble." *Best of the Silvertone Years*, 2005.

- Buddy Guy. "Turn Me Wild." *Born to Play Guitar*, 2015.

- Jimi Hendrix. "Voodoo Child." *Electric Ladyland*, 1968.

- John Coltrane. "I'm Old Fashioned." *Blue Train*, 1957.

CHAPTER 21

Dolls Without Faces

Several years ago I happened upon a drive-through cemetery lying in an evergreen forest along the Connecticut River. The grass looked like a freshly vacuumed verdant carpet, perfectly tailored to fit around the base of each soaring tree, not a pine needle out of place. The firs, unmoving and formidable, stood like palace soldiers overlooking and guarding the remnants of the dead.

I no longer believed that depositing human remains in a plot in the ground was a good idea. What was the point in using up precious natural resources for storing bones? Why store bones in the first place? Yet I was still drawn to beautiful, peaceful cemeteries. This one was unusually serene. And pretty. Whoever designed it had made it fit in with the natural landscape, not take away from Earth's beauty.

I spotted what appeared like a driveway around a particularly stately tree—like the half-circle drives in front of mansions with Bentleys and Porsches. The irresistible lure of the surrounding solitude pulled me in. I parked the car and turned off the engine.

Kicking off my shoes first, I exited the car and walked barefoot across the grass to the perfect spot. There. Right there. I settled in and looked around. Not a living human materialized, not a breeze stirred, not a bird or insect emerged to reveal itself. Just me and the trees where the sun shone through the canopies and warmed up the clearing below.

The grass felt good and I noticed the flash of orange polish on my toes popping against the greenery. Lost in thought, I reviewed my life. *Why am I here? What made me stop? Why do some humans bury their dead and others not? What's the point? All the money that gets dumped into funeral expenses. What a waste.*

Then it hit me. Graveyards are the photos of my past, the pictures of ancestors unseen. They're the only tangible link I have to my Amish progenitors. We weren't allowed to have cameras or have our pictures taken. I wanted to see photos of my aunts and uncles and grandparents. Of my past, my history, and my future. But there was no evidence of where I came from except the faceless genealogy books and oral accounts. Graveyards served as the pictures. Graveyards became the proof that my ancestors had actually existed.

As a child, I felt a loss—deprived—because I couldn't know what my grandparents looked like when they were young. Nor what I looked like when I was a baby. I felt undocumented, an unacknowledged citizen of a country foreign to me.

Now I understand why I took so many photos of myself and of mundane events during my travels in the first ten years of post-escape life. I wanted a visual record of myself. I wanted proof that I existed. That, yes indeed, I had visited those places, done those things. That they weren't just made-up stories or facts or details lost within the generations that passed down oral history.

I wanted my heirs and descendants to have a permanent fixed identity, not one that fell between the cracks of time. Here are the pictures of my trip to India, I'd say and walk them through my volumes of photo albums. Here is me on an elephant ride going up to a palace that was featured in the James Bond movie *Octopussy*. Here are the open-air courtyard-style huts with no interior doors, windows, and floors on the side of the mountain up the road to Dharamsala. Here is the poor Hindu woman who couldn't speak English but offered me, an uninvited stranger who knocked on her door, a piece of bread when she didn't have enough food for herself and her children.

Here are the pictures of me on my first international trip, on the train in Germany. Here are the castles and countrysides I passed through and the moment that I felt a sense of déjà vu: I'd been there before, long ago. I hadn't yet learned about rebirth, reincarnation, time travel, and parallel lives, so I didn't understand the feeling.

Here is what I did in the Persian Gulf, in the Caribbean, in Asia. Yes, this actually happened. This is the hotel I stayed at. This is the Arab who told me about Rumi and recited his poetry from memory to me. This is the first sugar cane and guinea pig I ate. This is the ninety-year-old shaman woman who couldn't speak English who gave me a nasty-tasting concoction and said, "Drink this. It will open your eyes." These were real stories that I'd tell my nieces and nephews and other descendants when I was old. The photographs were proof of life, *my* life.

A vehicle pulled up behind my car. An old man and a woman with short gray hair got out. She carried a bouquet of fresh flowers and he held her arm as they trekked across the grass. They stopped in front of a headstone in the center of the grounds. The woman dabbed her eyes with a tissue and the man hugged her.

I spotted it after church services were over. Laura was playing with it. The white miniature-sized, plastic English doll with delicate features looked so pretty. I admired its tiny, beautiful brows with open eyes, its dainty nose and lips, and its cute defined hands and feet, the tiny fingers and curly toes. She was exotic, a non-Amish doll dressed in proportionately scaled-down Amish clothes—the first time I saw an English one in our clothes.

I played with a set of white cloth twin Amish dolls. My mother had crafted them from scratch when I was too young to remember. They were about twelve inches tall and outfitted in a matching set of dark brown clothes: a dress and black Amish cap for the girl, and a shirt and black pants for the boy.

The dolls had no faces. No eyes, no nose, no mouth, no fingers, no toes. Featureless shapes denoted the head, hands, and feet.

"Mom, look. I want a doll like that." I dragged my mother's attention away from the church women she was visiting with.

My mother pressed her lips together. "No, it's

zu hoch."

Zu hoch meant "too prideful" or "too arrogant." *Hoch* also referred to all non-Amish, non-Anabaptist people: *die hoche leht.* "The prideful, arrogant people." *Er is hoch gah.* "He left the Church and joined the English." It was a sin to be *hoch.*

"But Laura and Mandy have one. Why can't I have one, too?"

My mother's forehead creased and her body stiffened. *"Heich mich!"* That meant "Obey me and stop questioning or I'll spank you."

Laura and Mandy's parents are so nice to them. Someday I'll have an English doll like that. "Can I play with your *dolle?"* I asked Laura.

"Yes." Laura smiled and gave me a turn.

Later that year, after begging often enough for the little English doll, my father ordered my mother to buy one for me. My mother was upset that my father had taken my side. She threw away the doll's English clothes but refused to make Amish clothes for her. So, at eight years old, I taught myself how to measure and cut material from scraps that my mother tossed into the wastebasket when she was sewing. I didn't know how to make separate pieces for the arms and upper and lower parts of the body. So I made a cloak for my precious English doll—a cloak with a hood like Little Red Riding Hood's—and fastened it shut with a safety pin that I found in my mother's sewing drawer. I named her Guinevere, like King Arthur's queen.

On rainy days, I spent many hours in the attic playing with her and telling her the fairy tales that I'd memorized. Whenever I heard a new name that

I liked from the books I read, I changed Guinevere's. All my Amish dolls assumed fluid monikers,
too. I never had enough dolls for the long list of
enchanting names I liked and made up.

A few years later, my parents moved from Wisconsin to Michigan. My Guinevere caused a scan-
dalous uproar. The community in Michigan was
far more modern in terms of material possessions.
They allowed indoor bathrooms, phones in the
barn, gas-fuelled generators, air-powered tools, and
bicycles. But a doll with a face. . . . That was impet-
uous, too English, too *hoch*. "Thou shalt not make
unto thee any graven image" meant having neither
photos of our faces nor faces on our dolls. Even
drawing eyes, a nose, and a mouth on the blank
white blob, as I had once done, turned the toy into
a forbidden idol.

"You can't take your doll to church anymore,"
my mother said. "It's against the rules."

"Get rid of the doll," my father said. He sat at
the table eating homemade popcorn after church
and barely looked away from the article he was
reading.

"Can I keep her and just play with her at home?
I won't tell anyone I have her."

The stony silent glare on my father's face
warned me not to say anything more.

You were the one who said I could have her and
you break the rules all the time, I thought. Why
can't I keep her? My bottom lip stuck out and my
shoulders drooped. I hoped my expression would
change his mind.

My father slammed his magazine shut, shoved

back his chair, and shot his full attention onto me. "Where is that doll? Go get it."

Why does he want her? I wondered as I brought her down the stairs from my room.

"Give it to me." He yanked Guinevere out of my hands and stomped to the kitchen. Then he threw her in a trash bag and burned her behind the barn.

Faceless dolls and inscriptionless tombs, I contemplated on the grass. The English belonged in the world and mourned their dead. We Amish didn't. "We must remain separated from the devil's playground," my mother said and the preachers preached. "We're not part of this world. Our home is in heaven, if we're good enough when we die. If not, we go to hell."

Music for the Soul

———

Here are several selections that helped me get through the events or period of this chapter, or reflect musically what I felt during this time. I understood very little of most lyrics—even today my ears don't process most words—but the melodies and instruments fed my soul. Had it not been for music, I wouldn't have survived until I finally got to therapy at age twenty-nine.

- Madonna. "Rain." *Erotica*, 1992.

- Crosby, Stills & Nash. "Guinevere." *Crosby, Stills & Nash*, 1969.

- Grateful Dead. "Peggy O (Live at Palladium)." *Download Series Vol. 1: 4/30/77 (Palladium, New York)*, 2005.

CHAPTER 22

Time Travel and Memory Wiping: My Real UFO Experiences

"Um, aren't we having a briefing tonight?" I walked into the main department. It was 11 PM but the conference room, where I had stopped at first, had been eerily empty. Usually other members of my team were there, drinking coffee or catching up on the news before our shift started.

The looks on my colleagues' faces were as confused as mine. "What do you mean? Of course we had a briefing."

Morgan, my supervisor, walked over. "Glad you're here. I was worried when you didn't call in."

What on earth are they talking about? I wondered. I'd arrived exactly on time. In fact, I'd verified what time it was when I parked, right before turning off the ignition: *11 o'clock on the dot.* "Are you playing a joke, trying to pull some prank? Funny."

By this time, several of my teammates had pooled around me, but everyone else stayed hunched over their computers. No one showed any signs of getting up to make their way to the briefing room. "Here, get these flights handled," Lisa shoved a report in my face on her way from the printer and back to her desk. "I need you on the phone the instant the Milan office opens."

I guess there's some sort of emergency tonight. "Guys, what's going on? And are we doing the briefing later?"

"Are *you* joking? You're late," Morgan looked half-concerned, half-confused, and sounded as if he wasn't sure whether to yell at me or take me to the emergency room.

"It's twelve o'clock." Shannon, Jen, and Lee all pointed at the clock hanging on the wall behind me.

I turned around. 12:06 AM. ***What the.*** . . . It can't be twelve o'clock. I just walked in from my car. My clock said eleven."

Rick, at the computer station closest to me, swiveled his chair around. "What, you got caught in a time warp?" He chuckled. Everyone else burst out laughing.

Holy fucking shit. That's what happened. Did I lose time? What the fuck?!

For the next twelve years, I sought an answer. What had happened to me during that missing hour of time? Until that night, I hadn't believed extraterrestrials existed. One of my friends believed she'd been abducted by aliens and would tell me stories about her experience. I'd thought she was just a crazy Californian hippie. I believed her now. But unlike her story of horror, I didn't feel that anything nefarious had happened to me. My "abduction" felt benign. What had they wanted with me? And where did I go?

At the time, I didn't believe in anything that couldn't be proven to me. I did, however, know just enough about quantum physics that I started wondering how a lost hour could be explained by time travel, memory wiping, and other theories. "A good hypnotist could help you recover some of those memories," a NASA insider told me.

I was too poor to afford hypnotherapy sessions from a credible practitioner. So I shelved what had happened until the day when I'd be rich enough to pay for hypnosis.

I stood on the second floor and gazed out over the solar system. This, the Rose Center for Earth and Space, was my favorite wing of the American Museum of Natural History. I felt a tap on my right shoulder. Not a gentle tap. More like a finger jab. Polite but a little too hard.

Slightly annoyed, I looked over. But no one was there. *Weird.* I looked left, wondering why the person hadn't just stayed on my right after poking me. Again, no one. *What the fuck? Is he behind me now?*

I did a three-hundred-and-sixty-degree turn and still, no one. At that point, I began freaking out a little. *I know I felt that. There's no way this person could've disappeared.* I looked up and down the hallway in both directions but it was completely empty. The fact that the entire corridor was absent of people—not a single person but me—was unusual. This was New York City and one of the largest museums in the world. How could this section be empty, and in both directions?

Not knowing what to make of what just happened, I resumed my contemplation on the stars. With no warning, tears started flowing. *I just want to go home*, the thought looped through my head. *And home isn't here, not on Planet Earth*. I buried my head in the corner of my arm and tried to muffle my sobs.

I felt a presence next to me. No one was there, but it was "him." The one who'd tapped my shoulder.

That presence stayed with me, and less than a year later, he gave me some answers into the mystery of the missing time. My mind almost exploded. It took me days, then weeks, then months to process.

I still have more questions than answers.

And I still don't know where home is.

Music for the Soul

———

Here are several selections that helped me get through the events or period of this chapter, or reflect musically what I felt during this time. I understood very little of most lyrics—even today my ears don't process most words—but the melodies and instruments fed my soul. Had it not been for music, I wouldn't have survived until I finally got to therapy at age twenty-nine.

- Moby. "We Are All Made of Stars." *18*, 2002.

- Snow Patrol. "The Planets Bend Between Us." *A Hundred Million Suns*, 2008.

- Johann Strauss II. "The Blue Danube."

- David Bowie. "Space Oddity." *Space Oddity*, 1969.

CHAPTER 23

Writing as Therapy: Scientifically Proven Physical and Mental Benefits

"The mere act of disclosure is a powerful therapeutic agent," James W. Pennebaker wrote in an *American Psychological Society* article, "Writing About Emotional Experiences as a Therapeutic Process." "Even though a large number of participants report crying or being deeply upset by the experience, the overwhelming majority report that the writing experience was valuable and meaningful in their lives."

In the eighties, Pennebaker, a Professor of Psychology and a leading authority on the growing field of expressive emotions therapy (EET), discovered the power of expressive writing in helping people process traumatic experiences. His—and subsequently other researchers'—studies revealed that writing about deeply personal issues boosted the immune system in students, employees, and patients, resulting in less trips to the doctor and less sick days from work. Participants reported that "writing about upsetting experiences, although painful in the days of writing, produced long-term improvements in moods and indicators of well-being compared with writing about [mundane] topics."

I didn't hear about Pennebaker until after I completed the first edition of my memoir. It was fascinating for me to see that his writing technique was similar to the independent approach I developed to write my traumatic story, and that his findings reflected my personal experiences as a result of this type of writing. I've included Pennebaker's technique here, so you can compare it with my *12-Minute Writing* process:

> For the next 3 days, I would like for you to write about your very deepest thoughts and feelings about an extremely important emotional issue that has affected you and your life. In your writing, I'd like you to really let go and explore your very deepest emotions and thoughts. You might tie your topic to your relationships with others, including parents, lovers, friends, or relatives; to your past, your present, or your future; or to who you have been, who you would like to be, or who you are now. You may write about the same general issues or experiences on all days of writing or on different topics each day. All of your writing will be completely confidential. Don't worry about spelling, sentence structure, or grammar. The only rule is that once you begin writing, continue to do so until your time is up. (Pennebaker. "Writing About Emotional Experiences as a Therapeutic Process." American Psychological Society, vol. 8, no. 3, 1997, pp. 162–166.)

Torah Bontrager's *12-Minute Writing* Process

My *12-Minute Writing* process teaches you three easy steps that instantly cut through the over-whelm to let you write with confidence, calm, and peace. This process works whether you're an emerging writer, advanced writer, or writing for therapeutic purposes only.

Step 1:
Set a timer countdown for 10 minutes.
(Once it goes off, set a final timer for 2 minutes to wrap up.)

Step 2:
Pick a prompt. (You can download a free list of 365 unique prompts from my website, www.TorahBontrager.com/book, prompts you won't find anywhere else online.)

Step 3:
Handwrite nonstop for 12 minutes.

You *must* handwrite! This process won't work if you use a digital device.

The only rule is to write by hand (not with an electronic device) and to keep the pen moving for the entire twelve minutes. If you don't know what to write, then write "I don't know what to write." Don't write any other phrase or sentence; this part is critical to the success of the process.

I've successfully tested this method on others and if you'd like to learn why it works or hear what people are saying about it, you can get my free ebook online. Just search for *The 12-Minute Writing Process: How to Begin Sharing Your Personal Story—Even with Little or No Previous Writing Experience.*

Music for the Soul

Here are several selections that helped me get through the events or period of this chapter, or reflect musically what I felt during this time. I understood very little of most lyrics—even today my ears don't process most words—but the melodies and instruments fed my soul. Had it not been for music, I wouldn't have survived until I finally got to therapy at age twenty-nine.

- Phutureprimitive. "Kinetik." *Kinetik*, 2011.

- Jefferson Airplane. "White Rabbit." *Surrealistic Pillow*, 1967.

- Nellie McKay. "Inner Peace." *Get Away from Me*, 2004.

CHAPTER 24

What Forgiveness Is and What It Isn't

For most of my life, I struggled with the idea of forgiveness, searching for a concept that resonated with me.

Today, my understanding of forgiveness is the following:

1. Forgiving does not mean forgetting.

2. Forgiving does not mean not holding the perpetrator accountable for their actions.

3. Most importantly, forgiving is personal. That is, I can forgive only myself. I can't forgive anyone else. Why? Because I'm not responsible for anyone else's actions. Forgiveness is only relevant within the domain within which I can control.

So, no, I do not forgive my parents and uncles for violating me. I never will. I do, however, forgive myself for having blamed myself for what they did to me.

How to Write a Letter of Forgiveness to Yourself

One of the most powerful healing effects I've experienced through writing is by disclosing on social media that I'd been sexually assaulted. This was long before MeToo, and the thought of publicly sharing what had happened to me was terrifying. Thanks to the outpouring of support from a compassionate online community, I became more comfortable with disclosing more of my personal fears, shames, and struggles. One such disclosure is a letter of forgiveness I wrote to myself on my thirty-sixth birthday.

Forgiveness for sexual assault and other trauma survivors can be very triggering. I recommend that survivors write anonymously, in a safe and supportive group setting, or just for themselves first, before taking the leap to disclose in public.

Whatever your belief about forgiveness is, I encourage you to do a seven-day challenge in which you write for twelve minutes daily on the topic of forgiveness. Your prompt is "What is forgiveness?" or "I forgive myself."

Use my *12-Minute Writing* method (explained in the previous chapter) and at the end of the seven days, I think you'll be pleasantly surprised by how your beliefs and outlook on life have changed. At that point, write a letter of forgiveness to yourself, incorporating what came through from your stream of consciousness results.

If you feel comfortable enough to do so, I'd love to get an email from you about your experience with this. Send it to forgiveness@TorahBontrager.

com and I'll respond.

A Letter of Forgiveness to Myself on My 36th Birthday

Below is an excerpt of the letter of forgiveness I wrote when I turned thirty-six. I wrote what I'm proud of myself for first. That led to the forgiveness—and bawling my eyes out at the end.

*D*ear *Me,*

I forgive myself for feeling that I'm not good enough. That I'm not doing enough. That I "should" be further along in the vision I have for my life on this planet.

I forgive myself for expecting so much of myself that I forget that my physical body just isn't equipped to keep up with the quantum speed of my spiritual and mental bodies.

I forgive myself for feeling that I'm inadequate.

I forgive myself for second-guessing my brilliance, my intuition, my knowingness on what is right for me.

I forgive myself for comparing myself with the hundreds of people I admire and think are so much further ahead than I am.

I forgive myself for forgetting about what really matters: love—loving myself, celebrating myself, trusting myself, nurturing myself, and growing an energy gar-

den of love.

I forgive myself for forgetting that I'm the queen of my universe and that all the beautiful people I admire are invited guests in my queendom, not people to be intimidated by or to feel inferior to or to destructively compare myself to.

I forgive myself for being unreasonable with myself, for demanding perfection when it's impossible to be "perfect" in this human physical realm.

I forgive myself for not caring for my inner child and being afraid to express who I truly am. I'm so proud of the little Amish girl me. That the little girl inside of me dared to dream, to dream big, and to keep dreaming. That she believed in herself no matter the odds. That she did it. And will keep doing it.

Thank you, all the humans-who-are-more-than-human in my life, for having touched me in so many ways. For having supported me and loved me no matter what. For being there for me through all my shit and anger and despair. Unconditionally. Because you really do love me. Thank you.

Torah

Music for the Soul

———

Here are several selections that helped me get through the events or period of this chapter, or reflect musically what I felt during this time. I understood very little of most lyrics—even today my ears don't process most words—but the melodies and instruments fed my soul. Had it not been for music, I wouldn't have survived until I finally got to therapy at age twenty-nine.

- Bon Iver. "21 Moon Water." *22, A Million,* 2016.

- Tiesto. "A Tear In the Open." *Just Be,* 2004.

- Gareth Emery. "Beautiful Rage (feat. LJ Ayrten)". *Drive,* 2014.

CHAPTER 25

PTSD and Ketamine, the Designer Drug that Saves Me from Suicide

PTS(D) Strikes Again

Summer 2015.

Out of nowhere, I found myself clutching my body and rocking back and forth on my bed.

You're okay. This is a flashback. You're not in actual danger right now.

Five years earlier, I had finally found a therapist who was actually skilled in handling sexual assault cases. I was twenty-nine years old, dealing with my childhood traumas for the first time. That is, after a failed first attempt with a Columbia University clinical psychologist who re-traumatized me when I went for help during my last year of school. Those sessions with her opened up a Pandora's box of nightly gruesome flashbacks that nearly prevented me from surviving and making it to graduation.

In 2010, after nine months of intense five-days-a-week therapy or therapy-related activities, I'd acquired the self-awareness and tools to manage my triggers and PTS (post-traumatic stress)[1] for the first time since age six or younger. I felt I hit a ceiling in terms of recovery: I was about as close to healed as a recurring child rape survivor could ever hope to be.

Hunched over on my bed, my knees pulled up to protect my vagina, I expected the flood of flashbacks to stop after the aware adult observer me acknowledged the triggered child panic-stricken me.

But, unlike past results, the PTS escalated. Even right now while writing this, the exact sequence of events is a blur. The next thing I knew, I was in a fetal position and screaming at the top of my lungs—in overpowering, sheer terror. It shocked the adult me.

What is happening?

What exactly triggered me?

Was it this? That?

I don't know why or how exactly I got there, but I became aware that I was now on the bare floor, still in the fetal position, pulling my knees up so tightly against my body that my arms hurt. Internally I kept clenching my vagina in a futile attempt to add another layer of protection. But still I didn't feel safe from the penis weapon approaching me, looming closer and closer.

The terror intensified. Following another blurred sequence, I felt myself rolling around all over the floor, trying to get away from that penis. I couldn't let my hands go from maintaining my protective posture, and that made it impossible to roll away fast enough to keep from getting attacked.

This is the daily fear, the terror, I lived under when he was raping me? This is how I felt that first year all alone in his house?

I lived with this for fifteen years!

I don't remember having attempted to ever physically evade or retreat from the first uncle, Harvey Bell (last known location: Alder or Sheridan, Montana, and/or Alaska), who raped me repeatedly. The day after the first night, he bought my silence with a death threat. If I told anyone, he'd kill me. I didn't dare resist subsequent attacks from him; the only way to save my life was to endure the rapes until I could figure out a way to escape.

I think the event on the floor was an indication of how trapped I felt during the first half year of my escape—from my Amish parents, Henry and Ida Bontrager, in Ovid, Michigan. For as long as I can remember, I endured some form of abuse or another: physical, verbal, emotional, psychological, spiritual/religious, and sexual. At age eleven, I made the conscious decision to leave, which led to four years of planning a way out. During my last year, I'd collect-call Harvey after my parents and siblings were asleep. Harv, my father's oldest brother, had also escaped the Amish when he was a teen. I trusted him completely; he was the only person I knew by whom I felt understood. I'd crawl out of the bathroom window at night and run out to the phone in the barn. Never once had it occurred to me that he would rape me, or that I wouldn't be safe with him.

Instead of being free, I was trapped again: a fifteen-year-old, alone in his house. I'd jumped out of a frying pan of parental abuse and into a fire of routine sexual assault. I couldn't protect myself from Harv and I had nowhere else to go. I was his hostage.

The surreal part of the PTS strike was that I was fully aware as the observer that I wasn't in danger in that present moment, yet I was simultaneously rendered powerless to stop the danger from the past playing out as if it were real in the present. That past was just as real to my body as the con-currently safe present was to my adult mind.

Why can't I make this stop?

Then, the part where the adult me lost it: *What's going to happen if I can't extract myself from this scene?*

I think the possibility of never being able to recover control in order to get out of that mo-ment overrode the terror of the flashback itself. Somehow I jerked myself out of it. The screaming stopped. My hands gradually loosened their grip. I got up, off the floor and back onto the bed. *What just happened?*

That particular event led to 24/7 memories looping through my head. The flashbacks started out relatively mildly, gradually becoming more in-tense and then taking over my conscious awareness until I was suffering full-blown memories day in and day out. I even began to see a therapist again, but like most therapists, she wasn't trained to deal with sexual assault (despite her claims that she was experienced in this).

In short, that counselor began gaslighting me. Thankfully, I retained enough of my developed, ed-ucated adult self throughout the sessions with her to recognize what she was doing. I called her out

on her abuse via an email and her response to me
was, in effect, "You're the problem, not me."

I wanted to sue her but the re-traumatized,
fragile child part of me wasn't able to go through
that process at the time. My adult self had to
protect her child and shelter her from even more
trauma, which the litigation process would have
incurred.

Although I've mentioned these incidents briefly
in some of my writings, this is the first time that
I'm publicly disclosing the names of the therapists
who abused me. Unqualified and untrained mental
health professionals who misrepresent their experience with sexual assault cases need to be called out
publicly, just like sexual predator criminals are.

The Therapists Who Harmed Me

Dr. Addette Williams, who forced me to recount
in 2006 in X-rated graphic detail all the rapes
that I could remember, worked as a clinical psychologist in Counseling and Psychological Services
at Columbia University. As a student, I was limited
to only six or so free counseling sessions. I couldn't
afford paying for further therapy, and Dr. Williams,
after continuing to insist that I needed to recover,
revisit, and retell all the assaults by both rapist uncles in detail, didn't even let me know that I could
get free services from the Crime Victims Treatment
Center (CVTC) adjacent to St. Luke's Hospital.
CVTC was literally across the street from Columbia's main campus, within walking distance from
my dorm at the time.

I was refused further treatment by the University but given no free alternatives, of which New York City, I learned many years later, has an abundance. Over the next several years, my untreated mental, psychological, and emotional state led to an increasing downward spiral that resulted in suicide attempts, homelessness, desperation, unemployment, and extreme poverty.

CVTC is who I found in 2010, and where I, for the first time in my life, learned that I had PTS, what "triggers" are, and how to face my traumas.

"Why didn't the Columbia therapist tell me about you in 2006?" I asked one of the staff. "I guess you don't reach out to the University to let them know about you. . . ."

"They do, and did, know about us. We were actually formed because of a rape that took place on Columbia's campus in 1977. We've been trying for years to develop a relationship with Counseling and Psychological Services, to get them to tell the students about us. But they refuse to."

"Are you kidding me?!"

"No."

[Even today, as of 2018, Columbia University still refuses to take sexual assault seriously. The University has dumped $2.2 million into a research project that positions campus sexual assault as a matter of health, instead of crime (www.newyorker.com/magazine/2018/02/12/is-there-a-smarter-way-to-think-about-sexual-assault-on-campus).

I'm eternally grateful to Columbia's undergraduate school for nontraditional students, the School of General Studies, which embraced me and my story and gave me the chance to become, to my knowledge, the first first-generation Amish[2] person in history to graduate from an Ivy League school. But this blatant disregard for women's—and any person's—safety is unacceptable and Columbia needs to stop protecting and making excuses for sexual criminals.]

The therapist who gaslit me in 2015, and actually told me—after building up my trust with her—that I chose the rapes to happen is Rebecca Jeffers, M.Ed., LPC of Evolve Hypnosis & Wellness Center in Fort Worth, Texas.

"In a past life, you chose these rapes," she said, "so why are you upset about it?"

Other than CVTC, two of the best resources I know of for finding free and more likely qualified help for sexual assault survivors are Survivors Network of those Abused by Priests (SNAP) and Rape, Abuse & Incest National Network (RAINN). I list several credible New York City resources in the "Resources" section, but if you live outside the city, reach out to SNAP or RAINN.

SNAP is the largest and oldest peer support group of sexual assault survivors in the US and is comprised of chapters throughout the country. One of its chapters is called "SNAP Amish," which offers monthly free, online support meetings for survivors and their advocates; as part of its services, the Amish Heritage Foundation facilitates the meetings.

RAINN offers a free 24/7 number that anyone can call at any time just to talk and to be believed by someone who's trained and empathetic. I'm also a member of the RAINN Speakers Bureau.

If you need help and don't know who to turn to:

AHF - Call or text 212.MEG.HALL (634-4255) to be connected with Torah or a trained staff member who will give you confidential support, information about the laws, and referrals for safe, in-person help. AHF also offers a monthly free, online, confidential support group meeting and a private Facebook support group at www.AmishHeritage.org.

SNAP - Call 877.SNAP.HEALS (762-7432) to be connected with a trained staff member who will give you confidential support, information about the laws, and referrals for safe, in-person help. You can also reach SNAP's Survivor Support Coordinator, Melanie Sakoda, at 925-708-6175 or find lots of information for survivors and advocates at www.SnapNetwork.org.

RAINN - Call 800.656.HOPE (4673) to be connected with a trained staff member who will give you confidential support, information about the laws, and referrals for safe, in-person help. RAINN also offers a 24/7 confidential chat service at www.rainn.org.

I always try to mention a resource whenever I talk about my experiences, because so many of us suffer in silence, like I used to, with no information or knowledge. When I share my story, I want to also offer practical tools and tips for potential healing. Like any other organization, there are no guarantees that you'll find a skilled therapist through RAINN or SNAP, but I feel the chances are far higher and hopefully you won't have to go through what I did.

The Medicine that Saved Me

January 2016.

The detective assigned to investigate my case against my uncle Enos Bontrager (last known location: Fond du lac, Wisconsin; prior location: Friesland, Wisconsin; place of business: Pride Originals furniture company, Cambria, Wisconsin) dragged his feet. Detective Sgt. Michael Haverley, Jr., of the Columbia County Sheriff's Office in Wisconsin, wasn't interested in helping me, and his lack of support exponentially exacerbated my flashbacks, PTS, and re-traumatization. His treatment toward me and his refusal to conduct due process turned me suicidal.

I posted on Facebook that I was about to kill myself, or something to the effect that I saw no further reason for living. I'd done everything I could to stop the flashbacks and to get justice. I was at the end of the road, especially now that even law enforcement actively refused to help me, despite the fact that the statute of limitations for the State of Wisconsin was still in effect for my case.

[To date, Detective Sgt. Haverley, Jr. still hasn't investigated Enos Bontrager, which is part of the required due process when sexual assault is reported and the statute of limitations is still in effect. The District Attorney's Office hasn't taken my case seriously either. They are aware of my reports, as well, but no one from any agency has bothered in over two years to conduct an investigation.

The Trempealeau County, Wisconsin, detective (a female whose name I've forgotten) likewise has never gotten back to me to conduct an investigation after I reported that Enos had molested me when I was around age five or six.]

After reading my suicidal posts, one of my friends, Liam, urged me to try ketamine.

"That's for depression," I said. "I'm suicidal, not naturally depressed. I'm only depressed as a result of the conditions that are causing my suicidal state."

"You said you tried everything but you haven't tried ketamine. Will you just give it a try?"

I didn't believe it would help me but Liam was so insistent that I thought, What the hell. I have nothing to lose. I'm going to kill myself anyway so why not cross ketamine off my long list of alternative therapies, modalities, psychedelic plant medicines, and pharmaceuticals before exiting this life.

What I learned about this "designer drug," thanks to finding Dr. Glen Brooks' website (www.nyketamine.com), is that it isn't necessarily for depression, contrary to my misinformed belief based on popular myths floating around. In fact, ketamine tends to most help those of us with a background of childhood traumas.

"Based on decades of ketamine research," Dr.

Brooks said, "post-traumatic stress[1] isn't a chemical imbalance and is really much more of a structural problem." He explained how ketamine can fix the neurons in our mood centers—which never developed due to early childhood abuses—so that we PTS sufferers can have a normal mood.

When I showed up in his office in Lower Manhattan on a bleak winter afternoon for my first infusion, I didn't think I'd ever see the light of spring again.

But Dr. Brooks was optimistic: "Statistically, you're a perfect candidate for it. You fit the profile for success."

After just one infusion, the 24/7 flashbacks stopped their incessant loop. I noticed only brief moments that first day, but the moments were real. The flashbacks took a tiny break.

Two years later, my health stabilized. But I need to remain on a maintenance routine of ketamine infusions for the rest of my life in order to keep that health.

I'm still not well enough that I can work a normal eight-hour day. I still haven't found an attorney who's willing to handle my cases against my predators, abusers, and enablers of those abusers. And I still have to constantly monitor my exposure to and shield myself from attacks by my birth parents Henry and Ida. (They resigned from the Amish Church many years ago and claim to be born-again Christians, but neither of them believes that Harvey Bell and Enos Bontrager raped me. None of my siblings, all younger than me, believe me either. They all actively defend the uncles.)

What has changed radically for me, despite the nearly insurmountable ongoing challenges, is that I see that the MeToo movement is here to stay. For the first time, I don't feel all alone anymore. Most encouraging is that I'm finding incredible, amazing Mennonite women who are standing up and not backing down. This kinship type of support had been one of the major missing links to the success in my work. Innumerable women outside our Anabaptist heritage support me, but change ultimately comes from within: the Mennonites are the closest group to us Amish who have resources, and I need that inside support to bring light and justice to survivors.

I see this spring, 2018, as a women's spring, and I'll continue the fight to enforce change inside our Anabaptist culture. I've decided to give up trying to kill myself because this fight is worth staying alive for. Even if I'm the only woman who remains committed to MeToo, I won't back down. But I hope that you'll join me in this, so the battle doesn't get so lonely.

Please consider sharing your story on my podcast—or anywhere. What's important is that you speak up, when you feel safe enough to do so. Your voice matters. Speaking out is the only way that we'll see peace and justice manifest in our communities and make the world safer for us and our children. This is our time.

What Exactly Ketamine Is + How It Helps with PTSD, Depression, and Pain

I had the great honor of interviewing my ketamine doctor, Dr. Glen Brooks, for my *Amish Entrepreneur Show* podcast. I've included the summary and transcript of that conversation here. You can see the episode itself (S3Ep8) on iTunes and YouTube:

www.TorahBontrager.com/iTunes
+
www.TorahBontrager.com/YouTube

Dr. Glen Brooks of New York Ketamine Infusions—with locations in New York City; Pittsburgh, Pennsylvania; Madrid, Spain; and www.NYketamine.com—is the only doctor whom I can recommend to go to if you're interested in checking out ketamine for post-traumatic stress (PTS/PTSD)[1] or pain. I don't get the infusions for pain; I get them for PTS from repeat rape and extreme childhood traumas.

One of the reasons that I wanted to do an episode with him was to let people know that ketamine is an option if they're suffering from post-traumatic stress. And, just as importantly, to let them know that ketamine is extremely safe and not addictive at all, when administered properly by a trained clinician such as Dr. Brooks.

In the episode we cover some of the common objections that the general public have about ketamine. We also cover Dr. Brooks' protocol, which is very different from any clinic out there that I've looked into. Or at least it was as of two years ago.

When you're doing your own research, please refer to the episode or transcript to ask the kinds of questions that you should be asking when you're considering which clinician or doctor to select to give it a try.

If you feel that ketamine is an option for you, or something that you'd like to explore to help alleviate PTS, do whatever it takes to get treated by Dr. Brooks. He's incredible, beyond amazing, and so empathetic. He's literally helped save thousands of lives, including my own. Two years ago, I was on the verge of suicide. I would've gone through with killing myself if I hadn't found Dr. Brooks.

Please help me spread this information. Share it with your friends. Do whatever you can to circulate the episode or transcript in order to educate the general public. This medicine might be the key to saving your friend, colleague, or child's life. Thank you.

Summary

Dr. Glen Brooks explains, based on decades of ketamine research, why post-traumatic stress

(PTS/PTSD)[1] isn't a chemical imbalance and is really much more of a structural problem. He explains how ketamine can fix the neurons in our mood centers so that we PTS sufferers can have a normal mood again.

Ketamine is a very good drug and it's a very safe drug. Dr. Brooks' success rate is eighty-five percent to ninety percent for someone under age thirty. Between ages thirty and fifty, the success rate is eighty percent. For over fifty, the success rate is worth giving ketamine a try if nothing else has worked for you.

Unfortunately there's a lot of material about ketamine that frightens patients and frightens the parents of young adults who should be getting treated. There's the argument that ketamine is a recreational and addictive drug and that we don't know the long-term consequences of using ketamine. That's incorrect. We do know. It's a proven science.

No addiction comes from any of the clinics that administer ketamine properly. There's absolutely no dependence on this drug at all.

If you're at the end of your rope, call Dr. Brooks to see if you're a candidate for ketamine treatment. He literally saved my life and has treated more patients than the next five or six, or maybe seven or eight clinics, put together. This medicine might be the answer for you, too.

Transcript of Dr. Brooks' Episode (S3Ep8)

Torah Bontrager: Hi Everyone, I'm here today

with my ketamine doctor, Dr. Glen Brooks, and he's going to explain what ketamine is and how it helps people with PTSD,[1] chronic pain, and depression.

Thanks for being here. I really appreciate your. . . .

Dr. Glen Brooks: Thank you.

TB: Maybe you could help us understand what exactly ketamine is and what it does for people with PTSD in particular.

GB: Ketamine's a pretty interesting drug that's been with us since the sixties. It gets a lot of funky press. If you read most of the media articles, you'll think it's nothing but a club drug or a horse tranquilizer. But in fact, for the past fifty years, it's been a very important human general anesthetic agent.

It was first used in Vietnam in the sixties. In the 1970s, it was in pretty much every civilian hospital throughout the country, and it spread throughout the world.

I'm an anesthesiologist and I've been [administering] ketamine since 1974. It really has wide applications. It's used in operating rooms, emergency rooms, intensive care units, burn units, pain centers, radiation therapy, pediatric anesthesia, general anesthesia. . . . It's the only drug that Doctors Without Borders has.

TB: Oh, really, they use it?

GB: It's the only general anesthetic agent they have.

TB: Wow.

GB: And it's on the World Health Organization's list of top ten essential drugs. So it's far more than just a club drug or an animal tranquilizer.

But the discovery that ketamine was very useful in treating post-traumatic stress actually began in the early nineties during the first Gulf War.

That original paper was published by the doctors at Walter Reed and serious research began at Yale in 1995. Here, the National Institutes of Mental Health and pretty much every major medical center over the past twenty-five years or so has been involved in some kind of ketamine research. Right here in New York City, we saw some very large programs at Mount Sinai and Columbia University [Torah's alma mater].

What I treat for the most part is post-traumatic stress disorder. But it's not veterans returning from war; it's survivors of childhood traumas. When you say childhood traumas, people generally go right to physical and sexual abuse, which is true for many of my patients. But psychological traumas can be just as devastating.

Traumas at home. Parents who are either alcoholic or some other substance abusers, divorce, abandonment, insecurities that come because of those, fighting parents, problems at school, body dysmorphias that some patients experience during their adolescent teen years. Bullying can be quite devastating as well.

There are many causes of childhood stress. To understand the implications of childhood stress, we have to understand somewhat mood center development.

We have three important mood centers: (1) our prefrontal cortex, (2) amygdala, and (3) hippocampus.

Most of their development takes place between the ages of two and eighteen. That development is very much dependent on the substance called BDNF, the brain-derived neurotrophic factor. That's the substance that's responsible for the development, maturation, and maintenance that then writes the synapses that allow the neurons in our mood centers to communicate with each other. We need that kind of intact connectivity to have normal mood.

Now childhood stress, for whatever reason, raises brain cortisol levels. During those developmental years, when you raise brain cortisol levels, you end up suppressing the production of the brain-derived neurotrophic factor. So our mood centers never really develop.

TB: Right. So is that actually a brain injury as opposed to a mental illness? Or what's the difference?

GB: It's not really a brain injury. It really has more to do with maturation, mood center maturation rather than brain injury. But if your mood centers don't mature during those adolescent teen years, you are very prone then to lifelong problems that involve the symptoms of post-traumatic stress. Many of my patients begin to crash right after high school, the first year in college, or whatever they're going into.

Now the symptoms of post-traumatic stress disorder vary from patient to patient. Among the patients that I see, depression and anxiety are the two most common, closely followed by obsessive compulsive disorders. Not necessarily ritualistic behaviors, but constant ruminating negative self-deprecating thoughts that often spiral toward suicide ideation. In other patients, it's eating disorders and for some, it's raging anger.

So there's a whole buffet of different symptoms that go along with post-traumatic stress disorder.

Now for the past fifty years, psychiatrists have been treating the symptoms of post-traumatic stress as if each represented some sort of a chemical imbalance. So that's why they prescribe drugs that increase serotonin or dopamine or norepinephrine or lithium or acetylcholine or GABA.

Well, what the ketamine research has been saying for the past few decades is that it's really not a chemical imbalance. That's why most patients really don't respond to these medications. It's really much more of a structural problem.

If you did a biopsy of the neurons in the prefrontal cortex, and looked at them under the microscope, it would be "Oh, my God, how could this lovely young woman possibly have a normal mood when there's such a dearth of the synaptic connectivity that she would need to have for a normal mood."

So what ketamine does different from other medications is that ketamine turns back on brain-derived neurotrophic factor and starts regrowth. Starts to grow those synapses that have been missing. And that's really the science behind ketamine.

TB: Wow, that's awesome! What are the most common objections to administering ketamine for PTS?

GB: Well, again we get back to some of the media articles that are quite commonly read. There's a lot of material that just isn't true. And unfortunately there's a lot of material in these articles that frightens patients and frightens the parents of young adults who should be coming in for treatment. Again, the arguments are always that it's unproven science, that it's really an animal tranquilizer.

People don't understand the important role that ketamine has played for the last five decades in every hospital throughout the world. People talk about problems with addiction. We don't see addiction in this clinic. We don't see addiction in any of the clinics that administer ketamine properly. There's absolutely no dependence on this drug at all.

And then there's always the argument that it's quite popular [as a recreational drug] and that we don't know the long-term consequences of using ketamine. Well, we do. This drug has been around for fifty years and it's been used in much larger doses than we use to treat post-traumatic stress.

Patients in pain clinics get doses forty to fifty times higher than any dose we use here [for PTS patients] and they do it for years in some cases, with absolutely no signs of any organ toxicity.

So the claims really aren't based on reality.

TB: How many patients have you treated?

GB: We've treated over fifteen hundred patients in over the past five years.

TB: Yeah, that's definitely long enough to know whether it's actually a bad drug or not.

GB: It's a very good drug and it's a very safe drug. Ketamine has an amazing safety profile. And even after fifty years of use in hospitals, ketamine's still considered to be one of the safest general anesthetic agents we have. And reserved for some of the [unintelligible] patients that come in to operate. So ketamine safety really isn't a concern.

TB: How would you determine who would be a good fit for ketamine if they're suffering from post-traumatic stress?

GB: There are three things I consider when I first talk to a patient over the phone. The first is a story. I need to hear that there's a childhood piece. That on some level this patient had a pretty traumatic childhood. That's probably the most important, because that tells me that there's a good chance that mood center development was interrupted. Or stymied to some degree. That gives ketamine something to fix.

The second is age. Patients under thirty do much better than patients over seventy. So age is another important consideration. We do see improvements in patients over seventy, but it's much less predictable.

If I get somebody in under thirty, we're looking, in our experience, at eighty-five percent to ninety percent success rate. And between ages thirty and fifty, it's still solidly eighty percent.

TB: Oh, wow, that's a big percentage, all things considered.

GB: Between ages fifty and seventy, it drops off. But it could be two out of three patients. So it's certainly worth considering.

The third factor seems to be sex. There have only been a couple of research papers, but it looks like estrogen does give women a bit of an edge over guys. Here in our patient population, it's pretty much 50-50. I think the women do slightly better.

TB: What factor does estrogen play?

GB: I have no idea.

TB: How is your protocol different from other clinics? When I first looked into it, some clinics wanted me to pay for six sessions up front. Without even knowing whether it would help me. How are you different?

GB: Our clinic's a little bit different because it's really based on experience. We've probably treated more patients than the next five or six, or maybe seven or eight clinics, put together.

TB: Wow.

GB: Through experience, we have a pretty good idea who's going to respond and who's not. So the first thing is patient selection. I'm pretty honest with patients. If I think I can help them, I'll tell them. If I think I can't, I'll tell them I can't. But no patient population is one hundred percent in terms of efficacy.

So what we generally do is that we start with two infusions. For patients over fifty, I might push them to a third infusion before we decide it's not working. If I don't see results in younger patients after the first two infusions, and older patients after three infusions, we stop.

We schedule those generally every other day. If patients do respond, then we complete a full series, which empirically seems to be six infusions. And we can do them as close as six infusions in six days, which is what we do for international patients and patients who come from far away and [have to] stay in expensive hotels here in New York City.

Or we can spread that over about two weeks. But I don't like to go any longer than that because each infusion builds on the one before in terms of encouraging synaptic growth. Large gaps between infusions can interfere with that.

    TB: Awesome. Thank you so much!

Dr. Glen Brooks' Bio

Glen Z. Brooks, MD, has dedicated himself to the treatment of depression and neuropathic pain syndromes with Ketamine Infusion Therapy. A Board Certified Anesthesiologist, he completed his residency and pain fellowship training at Harvard's Peter Bent Brigham Hospital, Boston Hospital for Women, and Boston Children's Hospital. He has been a faculty member at Yale University School of Medicine, Chairman of Anesthesia at Cabrini Medical Center in Manhattan, and is a member of The American Society of Anesthesiologists, The New York State Society of Anesthesiologists, and The American Academy of Pain Medicine.

If you or a loved one is suffering from PTS/ PTSD, disabling chronic pain, or depression that hasn't been well-controlled by other treatment, Dr. Brooks might be able to help:

NY Ketamine Infusions
www.NYketamine.com

NYC: 917-261-7370
Pittsburgh, Pennsylvania: 412-414-9916
Madrid, Spain: (+34) 915-328-924

Notes

1. Dr. Glen Brooks uses both the terms "post-traumatic stress disorder" and "post-traumatic stress." I'm not sure if his use of those terms are intended to mean the same thing or two different things.

Personally, I agree with General Peter Chiarelli that we do not have a disorder: "...The Army's No. 2 officer and top mental-health advocate, General Peter Chiarelli, used PTS repeatedly before opening up about the change. "I drop the *D*," he said. "That word is a dirty word." Chiarelli said the use of "PTSD" suggests the ailment is "pre-existing," when in reality it is a predictable reaction to combat stress" (qtd. in: Thompson, Mark. "The Disappearing "Disorder": Why PTSD is becoming PTS." *TIME*, 5 Jun. 2011, nation.time.com/2011/06/05/the-disappearing-disorder-why-ptsd-is-becoming-pts. Accessed 25 Mar. 2019.).

Also read the following article: Rittenhouse, Laura. "Will Google Learn That PTSD Got A New Name?" *Forbes*, 3 Jun. 2017, www.forbes.com/sites/lauraritten-house/2017/06/03/will-google-learn-that-ptsd-got-a-new-name. Accessed 25 Mar. 2019.

Post-traumatic stress is a normal response to rape and other forms of extreme violence and we should not be stigmatized for that, or characterized as having a "disorder." In my writing and speaking, I try to use "PTS" rather than "PTSD" but because Google still hasn't learned that the D should be dropped, I often use that word so people new to the term can research it.

2. I use the term "first-generation Amish" to refer

to those of us who were born and raised traditional Amish and personally escaped, left, or resigned from the Church. This distinction is different from a child whose parent/guardian escaped, left, or resigned. Such a child could be a first-generation college student or an Amish first-generation college student, but not a "first-generation Amish" college student.

"Amish first-generation" refers to anyone of Amish heritage, whether or not they practice the religion. "First-generation Amish" refers only to someone who was born and raised in the Church and subsequently escaped, left, or resigned from the Church.

In terms of the religion, there are traditional Amish, New Order Amish, Beachy Amish, and so forth. "Traditional Amish" is what the general public understands as simply "Amish"—or most often thinks of when they hear or see things about the Amish. I use the terms "traditional Amish" or "Amish" to define those who prohibit electricity, cameras, and cars.

Some outsiders—particularly self-proclaimed experts—call us "Old Order Amish." The Old Order label is not used by us in our language; neither did we invent that label. We refer to ourselves in our language as just Amish (unless we are part of a subset of traditional Amish, in which case the label "Old Order" is still not used).

There are many groups who spun off from the Amish who include an adjective with the word "Amish" as part of their group's identity, and to separate themselves from traditional Amish. Such spin-off groups include Beachy Amish and New Order Amish, who are more materialistically modern than traditional Amish.

To make things even more confusing, there are groups within the category of traditional Amish who also identify themselves as "[adjective]" Amish. For example, the Swartzentruber Amish are even less materialistically modern than the rest of the traditional Amish. There's a third subset, Swiss Amish, who are not more or less modern than the range of traditional Amish, and who speak a different dialect—so different that I couldn't understand it as a kid.

Traditional Amish range from extremely strict in terms of material conveniences (for example, no indoor bathrooms and no running hot water) to "modern" (for example, indoor bathrooms and phones in the barns). The prohibition to use electricity, drive cars, and have cameras distinguishes traditional Amish from more materialistically modern spin-off groups who identify themselves as "[adjective]" Amish.

Music for the Soul

———

Here are several selections that helped me get through the events or period of this chapter, or reflect musically what I felt during this time. I understood very little of most lyrics—even today my ears don't process most words—but the melodies and instruments fed my soul. Had it not been for music, I wouldn't have survived until I finally got to therapy at age twenty-nine.

- Thievery Corporation. "Epoca." *The Richest Man In Babylon*, 2002.

- Stellardrone. "Eternity." *Light Years*, 2013.

- Cantoma. "Gambarra." *Out of Town*, 2010.

- The Five Stairsteps. "O-o-h Child." *Stairsteps*, 1970.

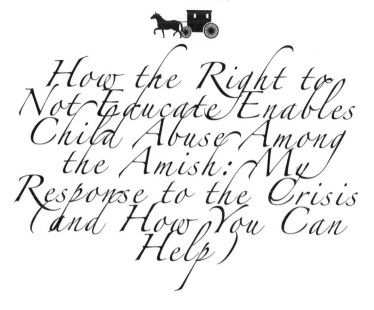

CHAPTER 26

How the Right to Not Educate Enables Child Abuse Among the Amish: My Response to the Crisis (and How You Can Help)

Why I Wanted to Escape

I was eleven years old when I consciously realized that practicing the Amish religion was not for me. For four years I tried to figure out a way to escape from my abusive parents and the only world I knew, and how to provide for myself before I turned eighteen. I craved learning and I wanted to go to high school. None of my dreams—going to school beyond the Amish eighth grade, driving a car, travelling around the world, living by the ocean—were compatible with the Church's rules. I had never even seen an ocean. But I had been to the Mississippi River quite often.

From age three to ten, I lived in a small Wisconsin community only an hour from the state's western border. Sometimes my father would go to Winona, which sat on the Minnesota bank of the Mississippi, or a bit further south to La Crosse, which sat on the Wisconsin bank, for construction jobs or to pick up supplies. The Mississippi looked gigantic, frightening and fascinating me at the same time. The opposite bank seemed miles away. "See how wide the river is. The ocean is even bigger, so big that you can't see the other side," my mother said. I couldn't imagine what it would be like to not be able to see all the way across.

When I was eight months old, my parents dumped me at my paternal grandparents' house and took off on a month-long vacation, their belated honeymoon. They travelled to all the states west of the Mississippi except Nebraska and Hawaii, an unusual trip for an Amish couple, especially back then. Their route took them through the redwood forests and along the coast of California. At most stops, they picked up View-Master reels that documented what they saw. The Amish religion forbids cameras and those reels of photos were as close to a recording as they could get. On rainy days, years later, I'd sit for hours in the attic and rummage through the stacks of disks. I'd pop a thin cardboard reel into the stereoscope and let the photos transport me to colorful and exotic worlds. That was my experience of virtual reality. I couldn't wait until I was old enough to see the world in person.

My mother brought back a conch shell, which she kept in the top drawer of the bureau in the bedroom. She often spoke about how vast and awe-inspiring the Pacific Ocean was, and during special occasions, she'd let me hold the shell to my ear. "That's how the waves sound," she said. Someday, I thought, I'll live by the ocean.

I'm sometimes asked what the defining moment was, the moment I realized at age eleven that I needed to escape. That knowing crystalized when I asked my father to explain how airplanes, extremely heavy objects, could fly in the air. "Don't ask dumb questions." One corner of my father's lip curled up. He glared at me and I knew never to ask that question again. I also knew that he didn't know the answer. If he had, he would have told me. In that moment I realized that something was very wrong with a religion that made it a sin for a child to learn how planes flew.

One of my earliest nicknames was Question Box because I asked so many questions. I was considered cute or funny until I reached adolescence. Then my endless questions were deemed acts of rebellion. To question the rules of the Church or to express a desire to learn about subjects prohibited by the religion was to be disobedient and insubmissive. "Knowledge leads to pride," my father said, pointing at a phrase in 1 Corinthians 8:1. He looked down on his non-Amish clients for not knowing how to build a house or do other manual labor. "They're so stupid. They don't even know how to hang a shelf on the wall." And my mother said, "Read the Bible, Torah. 2 Timothy 2:15 says to study to shew thyself approved unto God." I hated her tone of voice, her martyr attitude. Reading the Bible didn't make my curiosity and hunger for learning about the outside world go away.

At some point during the next four years, I began to read the local daily newspaper, my only source of information about the outside—about current events—to prepare myself for my escape. We had moved to Michigan by this time and my father subscribed to the *Ludington Daily News*. One day the paper ran a front-page story about a boy who divorced his parents.[1] The technical term for that was "limited emancipation." The article explained that a sixteen-year-old could be given the rights of an eighteen-year-old if they were abused by their parents. The list of different forms of abuse included educational deprivation. Aha, I thought, that's how I can leave and go to high school before I turn eighteen. They'll have to emancipate me when I tell them about *Wisconsin v. Yoder*. Throughout my childhood, I endured the gamut of abuse—physical, verbal, emotional, psychological, spiritual/religious, and sexual—from my parents and other members in the community, but I felt that expressing the desire to go to school would be the path of least resistance toward obtaining my freedom.

Not every Amish child is aware of the 1972 Supreme Court case *Wisconsin v. Yoder*, but I grew up hearing stories about it because the protests against public schools started in Iowa, in the community where I was born. One or both of my parents and a number of aunts and uncles on both sides of the family were pupils when the 1965 "Amish revolution" made national headlines. Eventually that led to *Yoder*, which allowed the Amish to send their children to Amish-only schools, for eight years only, with an Amish-approved curriculum, taught by Amish teachers who had no education beyond the eighth grade. It's ironic that both my prohibition to learn and my freedom to learn came about because of *Yoder*. As soon as I turned sixteen, the judge ruled in my favor, citing *Yoder* as evidence that I was educationally deprived. I don't understand how it's legal, according to *Yoder*, for me to have been granted emancipation because *Yoder* says that, simply by virtue of having been born inside the Amish Church, my only future is to remain inside the Church.

Yoder was and still is hailed as a landmark victory for religious freedom, but it was wrongly decided. It violates an Amish child's constitutional right to education, and furthermore, it enables and fosters child abuse, not only among the Amish but also among all other religious groups that use *Yoder* as a precedent for exemptions in the name of religious freedom. *Yoder* was instead, according to attorney and professor Marci Hamilton at the University of Pennsylvania, a landmark victory for extreme religious freedom and it remains an anomaly in the history of the Supreme Court.[2] Per Hamilton, no exceptions before or after have been made by the Court for a religious case such as *Yoder*.[3] The Court decided that the rights of a religion, specifically the Amish religion, outweigh the constitutional rights of living, breathing children, specifically Amish children. A special exemption was made only for the Amish, but consequently that exemption affects *all* children in the United States and Native/

indigenous lands.

To help you understand more about why I'm so passionate about overturning *Yoder*, I'd like to take you back to my origins.

The Amish Revolution that Led to *Wisconsin v. Yoder*

I was born and raised traditional Amish[4] in, at the time, a mostly farming community in the northeast corner of Iowa: Buchanan County. From birth to age three, I lived on my maternal grandparents' farm in the *Doddy haus*, the small house attached to the big farmhouse. Over the course of the ten years leading up to *Yoder*, the Amish in my community protested the public school system's attempt to transition Amish children out of rural one-room schools and into the consolidated local Independent School District.[5] The ongoing battles between the Amish and the Iowa Department of Education[6] came to a head when in 1965 what is now an iconic photo made national headline news. The photo depicted Amish children fleeing to the cornfields to avoid being forced onto a school bus. One of the children in that photo is my uncle.[7]

Public school officials in Oelwein had sent the bus to the Amish-only school, Hickory Grove, expecting to pick up all the children and deliver them to the public school. Having been notified about this plan by the officials the day before, some Amish parents stood waiting at Hickory Grove that morning. When the bus arrived and the officials tried to load the children up, one of the parents screamed, "*Schpring! Schpring zu de velschken feldt!*" ("Run! Run to the cornfields!") A photographer, Thomas DeFeo, who had accompanied the delegation that day snapped the photo that later went viral.

Outrage erupted from all parts of the US by those sympathetic to the Amish. The Oelwein district school superintendent, Arthur Sensor, received hundreds of angry letters. One letter writer accused Sensor of being the Gestapo, the secret police of Nazi Germany. That national outcry worked in the Amish's favor. Local and state officials deemed the controversy a public relations nightmare and subsequently let the Amish Church do whatever they wanted in terms of educating their children.

According to Clayworth and White, in 1947 "all rural one-room schools [in that area of Iowa] were closed with the exception of two that were purchased by the Amish community and run privately with no support from taxes."[5] I don't know that that's true. My mother and her school-age siblings at the time attended a one-room school taught by a state-certified "English"[8] teacher, Mrs. Nolan. Before and after 1965, the Amish in Buchanan County disagreed about whether their children should be taught by English or Amish teachers. My maternal grandparents sent their children to a one-room school taught by a state-certified teacher. My paternal grandparents sent their children to the one-room school taught by an Amish teacher who wasn't state-certified and hadn't attended school beyond the eighth grade. The 1960s conflicts arose due to the lack of state-certified Amish teachers in those one-room schools, not because the Amish children weren't educated past the eighth grade.

The religious right wants the general public to believe that there were no private religious schools before *Yoder*, that overturning *Yoder* will result in one's religious freedom being taken away, and so on. That argument is simply not true. Religions such as Catholic, Protestant, and Quaker had their own schools before *Yoder*. In fact, schools in the US were first started by religious organizations, not by the government. Except Cornell and the University of Pennsylvania, the Ivy League universities—among the oldest educational institutions in the US—were started by churches or individuals affiliated with a church for the purpose of religious instruction.[9] My alma mater, Columbia University, still uses its original motto, which is from a Bible verse: *In lumine Tuo videbimus lumen* ("In Thy light shall we see light") (King James Version, Psalms 36:9).[10] Harvard first used mottos *In Christi Gloriam* ("For the glory of Christ") and *Christo et Ecclesiae* ("For Christ in the Church") before changing to *Veritas* ("Truth").[11]

But let's go back to Iowa. As of 1913, no Iowan child could be compelled to attend school if the child was over the age of fourteen and "regularly employed, or had educational qualifications equal to that of students who had completed the eighth grade."[12] I believe this was applicable through the 1960s as well, which is why the dispute in Iowa wasn't about Amish kids needing an education beyond the eighth grade; what was needed were "educational qualifications equal to that of students who had completed the eighth grade" and Iowa didn't feel, and rightly so, that that qualification was met in schools taught by non-state-certified Amish teachers.

During the unrest of the sixties, some Amish families moved away from Buchanan County to New Glarus, Wisconsin, in response to the school superintendent Ray Habeck's statement: "I don't foresee any points of controversy [between the public school board and the Amish]" (qtd. in Linder).[13] All the Amish in that Wisconsin community, including Jonas Yoder, the lead plaintiff in the *Yoder* case, sent their children to the public school, until it became clear that the state would enforce the compulsory education law. Yoder had no problem with his children being exposed to non-Amish values, until it interfered with his access to free labor: he wanted his children to work for him full-time after the eighth grade.

The State of Wisconsin wasn't as compromising as Iowa when it came to making exemptions from compulsory education after age fourteen. In 1968 the Wisconsin Amish opened their own school in an effort to slide under the radar: none of their children would attend school beyond the eighth grade. However, then local school superintendent Kenneth Glewen checked up on the status of the Amish school's compliance with compulsory attendance and discovered that there were a number of children who should have been attending ninth and tenth grades.

According to Linder, Glewen was motivated to enforce Wisconsin's law because the more students who attended public school, the more state funding his district received.[13] While Glewen's actions seem to have been purely selfish, with no regard for Amish children's educational welfare, that lack of regard was no different from Jonas Yoder's and the other Amish men who refused to send their children to school past the eighth grade. These Amish men were interested only in free child labor. Neither the Iowa nor the Wisconsin conflicts were driven by a genuine concern over the child's spiritual welfare; the disputes were all about Amish men retaining the ability to force their children to work for free and thereby avoid having to pay employees. Making it about religion was a convenient cover.

What outsiders don't understand, and which of course was never revealed in the court hearings, is that Amish children—with perhaps rare exceptions based on a particular family's inclinations—are not allowed to keep any of the money they earn until, depending on the family, the male child is eighteen to twenty-one years old and the female child is twenty to twenty-one years old. Every paycheck a child receives before then goes to the father. And none of it is deposited in a trust for the child. That is slave labor and child abuse.

In most cases, a female child is married before she reaches the age where she would be allowed to keep what she earned, and hence, the majority of Amish women have no idea how to manage money and be financially self-sufficient. Consider also that married Amish women are not allowed to have a paying job; the exception is if the job is a home-based business, in which case the husband—except in rare instances—controls the money even if he himself doesn't earn it from that business. The other exception is if the woman is a widow and hasn't yet remarried.

This financial illiteracy and dependence on the male is designed to maintain control over girls and women and prevent them from upward mobility. This also means that they have no way out of abusive situations. Fathers, husbands, bishops, clergy members, and adult sons all enjoy a higher status than women and girls. How is a female to provide for herself if she doesn't have access to transportation, a roof over her head, and a job that pays enough for her to make the rent? How is she to even begin if she doesn't have a Social Security number? Such challenges are difficult enough for a single woman or girl. Imagine how next to impossible it is for a married woman with a dozen children. How is a woman in that situation supposed to exit an abusive marriage, when the Church forbids divorce, refuses to provide shelter and funding to battered wives and children, and punishes anyone who reports the abuse to law enforcement or outside agencies?

Educational deprivation also makes it next to impossible for any Amish child to smoothly and successfully transition to a life and community outside of the Amish Church. *Yoder* actually explicitly acknowledges this and, furthermore, sanctions it: "During [the adolescent] period, the children must acquire Amish attitudes favoring manual work ... and the specific skills needed to perform the adult role of an Amish farmer or housewife. They must learn to enjoy physical labor. ... And, at this time in life, the Amish child must also grow in [the Amish] faith and his relationship to the Amish community...."[14]

Thanks to *Yoder*, we Amish have been stunted in our development, both as children and as adults. We're a nation of eighth graders, an ethnic minority that speaks English as a second language (and not fluently) with an Amish education at best. A good percentage of Amish do not perform above a C or D grade in middle school or even make it through the eighth grade. A number of my schoolmates did poorly in all or some of their classes. One of my classmates, Marlin Troyer, failed or barely passed most of his subjects every year; Joe Slabaugh, no longer practicing Amish, only made it through the third grade. In general, we learn only the three Rs (reading, writing, arithmetic) from 1950s–1970s textbooks and are taught by Amish community members who went through the same schooling. We are not allowed to be taught science, mental health, technology, world history, music, current affairs, law, civics, and sex education. We don't even have words in our Amish language for "vagina" and "penis." [If you run across anyone Amish who does, I want to know what those words are.] We are not informed adults, because we've been denied the right to learn, to be educated, and to develop and mature with the twenty-first century.

Yoder was justified on the premise that the *only* future for every single Amish child is an Amish agrarian one inside the Amish Church. At a minimum, our curriculum should have evolved enough to at least keep up with other occupational options approved over time by the Church in response to developments in and competition by mainstream society in the past fifty years. We are no longer an agrarian people. We cannot compete with Big Ag, Silicon Valley, and globalization. The Amish child of today does not have the same occupational path as the Amish child of 1972. Yet our children (who grow up to be adults who repeat this educationally deprived cycle) are still stuck with an outdated rudimentary education, with still no knowledge—or no sufficient knowledge—of climate change, artificial intelligence, mercury poisoning, rising sea levels, human gene editing, GMOs, human trafficking, pedophilia, STDs, AIDS, transhumanism, dangerous drugs, and so forth. We're expected to be able to put food on our table in the same way that we did in 1972. *Yoder* fantasized that we would remain frozen in time. The outside world would change, but we wouldn't.

This myth that we Amish remain frozen in time is perpetuated by self-proclaimed experts on us Amish who are not Amish and did not bother to learn our language.[15] Furthermore, with minor exceptions, their publications are based on interaction with Amish men only, men with an eighth-grade Amish education at best. Women's voices aren't represented. Children's voices aren't represented. And in case this hasn't hit home yet, Donald Kraybill's entire body of thirty-plus years of Amish "literature" is based on what male-only eighth graders—who speak English as a second language and don't know what "H_2O" means—said and ignorantly nodded in agreement to in response to whatever narrative Kraybill wanted. The question is, what are the stakes for these "experts" in maintaining an utterly ridiculous narrative about us, one that is comical at best and beyond devastating and heart-breaking in reality? The story that Kraybill, his proteges, and their competitors crank out *enables* the abuse of Amish children. It manufactures an image that denies that Amish children suffer. It makes sure that Amish rapists and child molesters' interests are protected: claiming that there is no crime among the Amish lets criminals continue to freely prey upon victims.

What *Yoder* has resulted in fifty years later is a platform for all religious actors, not just the Amish, to get away with committing crimes against children in the name of religious freedom. These crimes include sexual assault, which runs rampant throughout the Amish Church and diaspora. The criminals thrive because our children don't understand what their rights and responsibilities are as US citizens, or that they even have rights. Neither do the adults understand their rights, except for the one percent of the patriarchy who control the Church and comprehend that their power lies in keeping us illiterate, dependent, and in fear of going to hell if we report them or break other rules. The Amish clergy and the Donald Kraybills work together to keep sexual assault and other abuses of power covered up.

A Vision for Amish Evolution: The Amish Heritage Foundation

When I was around thirteen, I read *Uncle Tom's Cabin* by Harriet Beecher Stowe and learned about the Underground Railroad. Harriet Tubman became my first female role model. For the entire length of our three hundred-plus years of history, no female has held a leadership position in the Amish. Tubman was the first strong, fierce woman I found for guidance in challenging an institution of slavery; the childhood I experienced was that severe. What she did for slaves inspired me to believe in myself and do whatever it took to set myself free, too. I deeply, intensely identified with the slaves' longing for freedom. Tubman solidified my confidence that I could take ownership of myself. I did not have to continue obeying abusive masters. I was not someone else's property. I told myself that if I made it after my escape, I'd help the ones left behind, like Tubman did. Over twenty years later, The Amish Heritage Foundation (AHF) was born.[16] According to what I found, AHF is the first 501(c)(3) organization in history that advocates for Amish people without a religious price tag, promotes compassionate secular values and nonsectarian harmony, and empowers those who leave the Church. No other nonsectarian organization does what we strive to do on behalf of Amish women and children, both inside and outside the Church.

One of the ways my work through AHF addresses the crisis of abuse among the Amish is by overturning, or attempting to overturn, *Yoder* and by providing cultural awareness training to sexual assault survivor advocates, law enforcement, mandated reporters, and other agencies working with Amish victims and cases. Thanks to the Amish religion, and to *Yoder* for enforcing that religion, most Amish children grow up without any knowledge about their body. I didn't even know what my period was the first time I bled. My mother beat me for not telling her that I menstruated—physically beat me—when she found my panties hidden in the bottom of the hamper.[17]

For the Amish, everything about sex is taboo, a topic that simply is not up for discussion. Not once did it occur to me that my uncles Harvey Bell and Enos Bontrager, who helped me escape when I was fifteen years old, weren't safe to be around.[18] I trusted them implicitly. Within a month of my escape, Harv began to repeatedly rape me. He threatened me with death if I ever told anyone and, ultimately, that bought my silence for over thirteen years. When I figured out how to leave Harv with my life intact at sixteen, his brother Enos raped me repeatedly, too. I thought I'd be safe with Enos, who lived in Wisconsin, because he was married and had three small kids. But he was no different from his older divorced brother, who had held me hostage in a dilapidated house on the outskirts of a tiny, isolated Montana town.

What happened to me as a child and adolescent is not an anomaly. These are not unusual crimes. Sexual assault thrives among the Amish, both inside and outside the Church, but it's not talked about. Adults pretend that it doesn't happen: they refuse to educate their children about their bodies and boundaries, and during the rare instances that a rape does get in front of the bishop and Church members, the female victim is required to ask the male perpetrator for forgiveness for having tempted him.[19] That's how the heinous crime of sexual assault is handled by the Amish.

The biggest challenge I run into when trying to raise funds for AHF is the belief that we Amish are perfect. "Why do you need money? What issues? There's nothing wrong with the Amish." That false "peaceful, gentle, crime-free folk" image is advertised, encouraged, and kept alive by Kraybill et al., and it does untold damage.[20] *Yoder* itself states that the Amish never broke the law and Kraybill et al. have run with that for the past fifty years. That we Amish don't break laws was not true in 1972 and it is not true in 2019. Sexual assault—and other violence—has been endemic for generations, but even if no assault cases were publicized in 1972, the reason the Amish were in court was because they broke the law. That willingness by outsiders to put on blinders, to let their eyes glaze over, when it comes to anything Amish, is atrocious. The state's responsibility is to protect the vulnerable, not let predators and others in power sacrifice children in the name of religion.

In an attempt to start correcting the narrative about us, the first thing AHF had to do was to create a credible body of Amish work. We launched with a historic, inaugural academic conference, *Disrupting History: Reclaiming Our Amish Story*, which took place in Lancaster, Pennsylvania, at Franklin & Marshall College.[20] The conference marked

the beginning of raising awareness about what
our issues are, so that foundations, corporations,
and individuals could understand why we needed funding and the general public could become
educated about the real facts of our history, identity, and culture. We recorded all ten speakers'
talks, as well as the panel of women entrepreneurs,
and made the results accessible online as primary
source material via a podcast. In the future when
we have funding, we will develop that content into
other forms of media such as a curriculum for high
schools and universities. Collectively, our speakers
represented five out of the eight Ivy League schools
(as alumni or professors) and two keynotes were
delivered. One keynote, "What About Children's
Rights? Overturning *Wisconsin v. Yoder*," was by
Pulitzer-nominated author Marci Hamilton, who is
an attorney, a professor at the University of Pennsylvania, and the founder and CEO of CHILD USA.
The other keynote, "A Revised Understanding of
God, Belonging, and Freedom," was by Menno-
nite-raised Galen Guengerich, MDiv, PhD, who
is an author, a member of the Council on Foreign
Relations, and the senior minister at All Souls Unitarian Universalist Church in New York City. We
heard from not only Amish but also those raised in
other insular religious communities: ultra-Orthodox Jewish, Muslim, Mennonite, and Navajo (Native American).

One of the things that surprised me the most
from the conference was the revelation that there
was no LGBTQ+ support group on Facebook for
Amish people and their loved ones who wanted

a safe, nonjudgmental space but didn't want to necessarily out themselves. That led to the creation of the AHF Support Group, which, in keeping with our nonsectarian mission, does not allow any Bible quoting. In the following months, thanks in large part to the efforts of then-Board member Mary Byler (who is Amish, lesbian, a sexual assault survivor, and a military veteran), we realized that we needed to explicitly include a welcoming message for LGBTQ+ visitors on our website. That was driven home by a conversation online in response to a homophobic proselytizing Amish organization's actions. One of the comments by Melanie Jones, "this thread is literally the most support I've ever gotten as a gay person from Amish people in 20 years," brought tears to my eyes.[21] I had no idea how isolated and marginalized LGBTQ+ Amish-raised and children of Amish-raised parents felt, but in hindsight it's obvious. AHF really is the only holistic support system for people who don't want to remain inside the Amish Church and don't want to join another church.

Another thing that surprised me was how deeply impacted the members of other insular religions were by meeting each other. "I didn't know how much my ultra-Orthodox Jewish upbringing had in common with the Amish." "I don't feel so alone anymore." "I didn't know that there are any Amish who feel like me and are working on our issues." That cross-insular awareness led to a focus on developing strategic partnerships with ex-fundamentalist organizations. Coming up this year is a one-day conference, *When Rights and Religions Collide*, to address the tension between the rights of a person and the extreme protection of religious freedom, which often infringes on those rights.[22] The event is a collaboration between Malkie Schwartz, founder of Footsteps and now an attorney; Sarah Haider, co-founder of Ex-Muslims of North America; and AHF. Malkie and Sarah met at *Disrupting History* and were so inspired that they wanted to replicate the academic and insular religions format. "I'd like to see more conferences like this that bring together people from various religious backgrounds," Sarah said during the Q&A portion of her talk when a member of the audience asked her what she thought the solution was to creating awareness, acceptance, and support for fundamentalist-raised individuals. Malkie in turn had inspired my model, in part, for AHF; what Footsteps does for ultra-Orthodox Jewish dissidents is what AHF aspires to do for the Amish. I believe very strongly that women and girls hold the key to bringing about local, national, and global transformations and I find it heartening that so many of the organizations tackling religious fundamentalist systems are helmed by women. Another extremely important strategic partner—our first, actually—is Survivors Network of those Abused by Priests (SNAP), which focusses on Catholic clergy sex abuse but has expanded to include chapters from other religions. One of those chapters is a monthly free, online SNAP Amish survivor support meeting that I facilitate as part of AHF's services.[23] SNAP is the largest and oldest peer support group of sexual assault survivors in the US, and I'm beyond grateful for their guidance and support with AHF's survivor advocacy. SNAP was also founded by a woman, Barbara Blaine, who later became an attorney as well.

The women reaching out to me in the past year reflect a distinctive character: strong, courageous, and relentless, with a history of being alone in their work or of having little support from their colleagues. These women are committed to protecting children and vulnerable adults and refuse to back down even in the face of bullying, backlash, and death threats from men in authority. Many of the women have armed themselves with the law as attorneys and/or concealed carry permits. That we're carrying guns may come as a shock, especially when the impression is that the Amish/Anabaptists and clergy members are non-violent. The work we're doing involves encountering dangerous criminals and situations, which warrant security protocols. On a Midwest tour of a number of Amish communities this winter, one of my investigations included being in the same room as two serial rapists, both members of the Amish Church. One of those rapists is actually regarded by the rest of the Amish community as a terrorist; the level of fear is so extreme that both women and men speak of him in frightened, hushed tones. Even the bishop is so afraid that he won't issue any reprimands or punishments when the rapist breaks a rule of the Church.

Despite the terror, several women are privately advocating for this rapist's arrest. I sat in a meeting with half a dozen women, practicing members of the Amish Church, and couldn't believe my ears.

"Ex-communication and sending them to Amish counseling isn't enough. It doesn't work." "This sexual abuse of children starts with bestiality." "We need to report them." "They need to go to jail." I didn't think I'd ever hear Amish women speak out like this until *maybe* on my deathbed, if my life's work was successful. These are women in their sixties, who were abused as children. After all these years, they are seeing the effects of their wounds. Post-traumatic stress (PTSD)[24] doesn't ever fully go away.

At the close of AHF's first year, I can now answer the question "Why do the Amish need funding?" with current cases. AHF needs funding so that abused women and children inside the Church know that they are not alone, so they have the courage to speak out, and so they know where to go for shelter and protection when their safety is threatened by the bishops and rapists.

AHF needs funding so that Dorothy Lehman[25] can get a divorce from her husband. Her husband refuses to sign the papers and the state refuses to intervene as long as she is living with him. Dorothy can't move out because she has no money and no skills to land a job that pays enough to make the rent. She is forced to remain in an abusive situation until she graduates from college, which is years away because she can only afford part-time classes.

AHF needs funding so that LGBTQ+ Amish children and adults have a community and resources. Homosexuality is considered a sin not only in the Amish Church but also by the equally, if not more, fundamentalist churches that recruit Amish escapees or dissidents and charge a religious price tag for their "support."

AHF needs funding so that Daniel Stutzman can go to school to become an engineer instead of working in the West Virginia coal mines. He had to give up on his dream because his lack of math and science skills make it impossible for him to take engineering courses. A prep program that closes the gap between the Amish eighth grade and community college would give him a chance to fulfill his passion.

AHF needs funding so that Aden and Sarah, a young millennial couple, can work for change from within their community. They don't want to leave the Church but they want women's views to be voiced and to be allowed to be part of the Church's decision-making process.

AHF needs funding so that Katie Helmuth can learn money management and Paul Hershberger— and my practicing Amish cousins and friends—can make a living in a tech-driven, globalized world.

AHF needs funding so that young women like Sarah in Kentucky who was raped by her father all her life have a safe house when they get a death threat from the clergy for reporting these kinds of crimes.

AHF needs funding so that we can develop and deliver a sex education curriculum so children like Laura Yoder and me don't grow up getting punished for not knowing what their period is.

AHF needs funding so that we can grow partnerships, share resources, and build community with other ex-fundamentalist groups, so that individually and collectively, we can evolve into a more enlightened, compassionate planet.

The highlights of our second year include developing and launching a prep program that helps graduates of the program get into community college and onward, including Ivy League schools. Designed to fill in the gap from the Amish eighth grade, the program will be open to anyone of any educationally deprived background. Currently we're planning to run the pilot in Lancaster, Pennsylvania, and I'm extremely fortunate to have a former Columbia University Dean of Students as a mentor and advisor in this endeavor.

Another highlight is our upcoming 30-State Summer Media Tour.[26] The purpose of the tour, covering all states with Amish communities, is to find an Amish plaintiff who can help us overturn *Wisconsin v. Yoder* and to inform the general public about why a child's right to a quality education should be enforced. We plan to actually cover 41 states, and 139 cities or towns over the course of four months.

And our key entrepreneurial project in our second year is to develop and deliver a program that helps Amish women and men transition to sustainable farming practices and produce food that can compete in today's marketplace. This program includes financial literacy training.

None of these projects will be successful, though, without funding. Currently the most dire need is for funding to hire staff. Many donors and grant-makers don't want their money to go to staff; they want the funds to go directly to services or programs for recipients, the people we're helping. However, it's impossible to grow AHF and to do anything substantial and long-term for recipients without a paid team of people. Ninety percent of what has been accomplished over the past year has been due to the generosity of volunteers and my life savings, but that's not a sustainable way to run an organization. I feel it's really important for potential donors and sponsors to be aware that AHF is not operating under the prevailing broken model of nonprofits and that we deserve funding for staff, in addition to programs. At AHF, our emphasis is for recipients to graduate out of the need for our services. Our success rate is measured by how many recipients no longer need us, not by how many do. We're providing the tools for people to get to the stage where they can provide for themselves financially and emotionally, while becoming more enlightened contributors to the global community.

In closing, I envision a world in which Amish children are safe, free to learn, and free to choose. We Amish/Anabaptists need to stop enabling evil by virtue of looking the other way, which allows rape culture and child abuse to continue to ravage our homes and churches. We need a new understanding of the golden rule. Our Amish teaching of "do unto others as you would have them do unto you" includes the belief that we're obligated to help our enemies even if it costs us our own lives. This interpretation comes from the Dirk Willems story in the *Martyrs' Mirror*.[27]

Every Amish child knows about Dirk Willems,

the most popular Anabaptist martyr who exemplified all that the Church claims to stand for. The story is accompanied by an illustration of Dirk standing and a man, one of his guards, drowning in a river. Instead of continuing his escape, Dirk had turned around and helped the guard out of the river. "And then they let him go free, right?" I said when my mother first read me the story, "because he saved the guard's life." "No, he was burned alive," my mother said. "No matter what, you must always follow the golden rule and turn the other cheek. Even if it means that you die for our faith, like Dirk did."

The idea is that we'll be rewarded with heaven if we keep turning the other cheek, no matter the personal expense. The fact that our doing so enables rapists and other abusers within our community to keep destroying our children doesn't even enter our Amish consciousness. Where is the compassion toward our children? What about "Take no part in the unfruitful works of darkness, but instead expose them" (English Standard Version, Ephesians 5:11)? The safety of our children must override our religion's demand to harm our children, whether by refusing to allow us to report and prosecute rapists, refusing to allow our children to learn about sex and science, or refusing to recognize that women are equal to men.

Our responsibility is to provide safety, shelter, and freedom. Freedom to choose is, after all, the entire reason our Anabaptist forefathers broke away from the Catholic Church.[28] It is up to us Amish women to step up to the plate and lead this transformation. We are not powerless. We are not alone. We are not worthless. We are good enough and our children deserve our protection. They, and we, have rights: the right to be safe, the right to learn, the right to choose. And the right to be loved, no matter whether we remain inside or outside the Church.

Notes & Works Cited

1. I don't know the article details for this story. I believe the story appeared in the *Ludington Daily News* in 1995 or 1996.

2. Hamilton, Marci. *God vs. the Gavel: The Perils of Extreme Religious Liberty*. Cambridge University Press, Revised 2nd ed., 2014.

3. Hamilton, Marci. "What About Children's Rights? Overturning *Wisconsin v. Yoder*." *Disrupting History: Reclaiming Our Amish Story* Conference, The Amish Heritage Foundation, Sep. 28-29, 2018, Franklin & Marshall College, Lancaster, PA. Keynote Address. And: "What About Children's Rights? Overturning *Wisconsin v. Yoder*." *Real Amish*, season 1, episodes 3 and 4, from AHF, www.amishheritage.org/podcast.

4. In terms of the religion, there are traditional Amish, New Order Amish, Beachy Amish, and so forth. "Traditional Amish" is what the general public understands as simply "Amish"—or most often thinks of when they hear or see things about the Amish. I use the terms "traditional Amish" or "Amish" to define those who prohibit electricity, cameras, and cars.

Some outsiders—particularly self-proclaimed experts—call us "Old Order Amish." The Old Order label is not used by us in our language; neither did we invent that label. We refer to ourselves in our language as just Amish (unless we are part of a subset of traditional Amish, in which case the label "Old Order" is still not used).

There are many groups who spun off from the Amish

who include an adjective with the word "Amish" as part of their group's identity, and to separate themselves from traditional Amish. Such spin-off groups include Beachy Amish and New Order Amish, who are more materialistically modern than traditional Amish. To make things even more confusing, there are groups within the category of traditional Amish who also identify themselves as "[adjective]" Amish. For example, the Swartzentruber Amish are even less materialistically modern than the rest of the traditional Amish. There's a third subset, Swiss Amish, who are not more or less modern than the range of traditional Amish, and who speak a different dialect—so different that I couldn't understand it as a kid.

Traditional Amish range from extremely strict in terms of material conveniences (for example, no indoor bathrooms and no running hot water) to "modern" (for example, indoor bathrooms and phones in the barns). The prohibition to use electricity, drive cars, and have cameras distinguishes traditional Amish from more materialistically modern spin-off groups who identify themselves as "[adjective]" Amish.

5. This paragraph and the following two are based on my memories from childhood stories and the following article: Clayworth, Jason and Rodney White. "1965 Amish school photo started rural revolution." *USA Today*. Published May 12, 2015 in *Des Moines Register*, www.usatoday.com/story/news/nation/2015/05/12/amish-lost-schools-iowa/27204767. Accessed 25 Mar. 2019.

6. The Iowa Department of Education was known as the Department of Instruction in 1965.

7. According to my uncle, he's in that photo but I haven't spoken to anyone else who's confirmed that.

8. Anyone who's not Amish is referred to as "English" by us Amish.

9. Although the University of Pennsylvania wasn't formed for the primary purpose of teaching theology, its first Provost was a minister, Reverend William Smith: Friedman, Steven Morgan. "A Brief History of the University of Pennsylvania." *Penn University Archives & Records Center*, University of Pennsylvania, archives. upenn.edu/exhibits/penn-history/brief-history. Accessed 25 Mar. 2019.

10. "Columbia University at a Glance." *Office of Public Affairs*, Columbia University, www.columbia.edu/cu/ pr/special/cuglance.html. Accessed 25 Mar. 2019.

11. Ireland, Corydon. "Seal of approval." *The Harvard Gazette*, Harvard University, 14 May 2015, news. harvard.edu/gazette/story/2015/05/seal-of-approval. Accessed 25 Mar. 2019.

12. Engelhardt, Carroll. "Compulsory Education in Iowa, 1872-1919." *The Annals of Iowa*, vol. 49, no. 1, 1987, pp. 58-76, ir.uiowa.edu/cgi/viewcontent.cgi?referer=https://www.google.com/&httpsredir=1&article=9217&context=annals-of-iowa. Accessed 25 Mar. 2019.

13. Linder, Douglas. "Yoder v Wisconsin: The Amish Challenge Compulsory Education Laws." *Famous Trials*, University of Missouri-Kansas City School of Law, law2.umkc.edu/faculty/projects/ftrials/conlaw/Yoder-Story.html. Accessed 25 Mar. 2019.

14. Wisconsin v. Yoder. 406 U.S. 205. Supreme Court of the United States. 1972. *Supreme Court Collection,* Legal Information Institute, Cornell Law School, www.law.cornell.edu/supremecourt/text/406/205. Accessed 25 Mar. 2019.

15. With the exception of John Hostetler, I know of no one raised traditional Amish who is or was an academic. It's quite possible more academics exist but I haven't found them or been informed about them. Hostetler, by the way, is a poor excuse of an academic: he doesn't accurately represent us traditional Amish and refused to fight for Amish children's rights to a quality education; instead, he provided expert testimony in favor of the parents in *Wisconsin v. Yoder.* Of all people, he should have advocated for the children because he himself left the Church in pursuit of higher learning.

16. For more information about The Amish Heritage Foundation (AHF), see www.amishheritage.org.

17. I was embarrassed when I saw the dark stain and thought something was wrong with me. My mother never told me that one day actual blood would spontaneously emit from my vagina. This refusal to educate children about sexuality persists within the first-generation nonpracticing Amish population. More than one child of a first-generation nonpracticing Amish parent has confided in me that they, too, had had no idea what their period was.

18. For more details about my escape, read the following article: Simms, Mary. "Survivor Speaks Out Against Amish Rape Culture Ahead Of Sentencing." *HuffPost,* 6 Nov. 2016, www.huffpost.com/entry/

survivor-speaks-out-against-amish-rape-culture-ahead_b_581e7b02e4b0334571e09cfd. Accessed 25 Mar. 2019.

19. It takes tremendous courage for any survivor of sexual assault or domestic violence to share their story with someone. It takes even more courage for an Amish woman or girl to share her story, because we're taught that sexual assault is our fault (we tempted the male rapists) and/or sexual assault is God punishing us (for having broken a rule, for not having been obedient, for having left the Amish Church, etc.). In the Amish Church, when a baptized female is raped, she's required to ask the rapist's forgiveness in front of the entire church membership (*if* the abuse even comes to the attention of the clergy). The female has to ask for forgiveness for having tempted the rapist. This is rooted in the belief that Eve tempted Adam in the Garden of Eden and therefore all the sins and ills of the world is the woman's fault; this is also why, sub/unconsciously, Amish men are almost never held accountable for their crimes. Men cannot be expected to control their actions nor are they personally responsible for their actions, especially when it involves a female.

20. *Disrupting History* took place on September 28-29, 2018 and all the talks are accessible at www.amish-heritage.org/podcast. Amish-raised Elam Zook's talk details the problems with Donald Kraybill and similar self-proclaimed experts on us Amish. In his talk, Columbia and Harvard alumnus Prof. Michael Billig articulates the problems with Kraybill et al from a sociological scholarship perspective. For more information about that and future conferences, see www.amishheritage.org/events.

21. Melanie Jones is a child of Amish-raised parents, who don't accept her. Homophobia and racism don't stop when Amish-raised individuals leave the Church. Due to the lack of education and exposure to more accepting belief systems, the cycle of violence continues among descendants outside the Church.

22. For more information, see www.rightsandreligions.com.

23. For more information, see snapnetwork.org/snap_amish or www.amishheritage.org/events.

24. I am alive today only because of regular ketamine infusions. For more details about PTS/PTSD and ketamine, read chapter 25 or watch this episode in which I interview my doctor, Dr. Glen Brooks: "What Ketamine Is + How It Helps with PTSD, Depression, and Pain." *Amish Entrepreneur Show with Torah Bontrager*, season 3, episode 8, www.amishheritage.org/what-ketamine-is-how-it-helps-with-ptsd-depression-pain. I also share more details about how I found ketamine in this article: Bontrager, Torah. "PTSD and the Designer Drug That Saves Me From Suicide." *Our Stories Untold*, 10 Apr. 2018, www.ourstoriesuntold.com/ptsd-designer-drug-saves-suicide. Accessed 25 Mar. 2019.

25. The name of this person, as well as the names of the people in the following paragraphs, are made up and the details of their situation are based on the situations of a collection of individuals, not just one specific individual. I've done this in order to protect their privacy. That said, the situations I describe are so common that it's possible that you might think you know whom I'm referring to. Some individuals have expressed concerns that they will be found out, but

I can't stress enough that the person you think I'm referring to is not that person. There are hundreds of women throughout the Amish experiencing same or similar problems, and they all think that they're the only ones. The situations I describe are widespread, or at least not uncommon, but we're so isolated from each other—or suffering in silence—that we think these situations are unique.

26. For more information, see www.amishheritage. org/summer.

27. I don't know the details of the *Martyrs' Mirror* version I saw as a child. For more information, read the Global Anabaptist Mennonite Encyclopedia Online's entry "Martyrs' Mirror" at gameo.org/index.php?title=Martyrs'_Mirror. According to that article, the author of the original Dutch version is Thieleman J. van Braght and the full title (translated in English) is *The Bloody Theatre or Martyrs' Mirror of the Defenseless Christians Who Baptized Only upon Confession of Faith and Who Suffered and Died for the Testimony of Jesus Their Saviour . . . to the Year A.D. 1660.*

28. For details, read the following article based on an interview that Elam Zook and I gave: Stella, Rachel. "Dark side to Amish religious freedom?" *Mennonite World Review*, 13 Aug. 2018, mennoworld. org/2018/08/13/news/dark-side-to-amish-religious-freedom. Accessed 25 Mar. 2019.

Music for the Soul

Here are several selections that helped me get through the events or period of this chapter, or reflect musically what I felt during this time. I understood very little of most lyrics—even today my ears don't process most words—but the melodies and instruments fed my soul. Had it not been for music, I wouldn't have survived until I finally got to therapy at age twenty-nine.

- Moby. "We Are All Made of Stars." *18*, 2002.

- Snow Patrol. "The Planets Bend Between Us." *A Hundred Million Suns*, 2008.

- Johann Strauss II. "The Blue Danube."

- David Bowie. "Space Oddity." *Space Oddity*, 1969.

Epilogue

The Amish don't believe that they betrayed me.

They believe that *I* betrayed *them.* . . .

By leaving the Church to escape from the abuse. By speaking out about my experiences. And by exposing the issues embedded in our culture.

For better or worse, they're my people, and I can't betray future generations by remaining silent.

Afterword

To Speak

I am not the voice of the voiceless.
I am the voice of those who have forgotten how to
speak.
I am the voice of those who don't know that they **can**
speak.
I am the voice of those who feel but fear to speak.
I am the voice of those who are dying because they're
not speaking.

I am the voice of the voiceless
until you speak.
You still have your voice.

I wrote this because I don't want anyone to
think of me as a savior. I want people who are
inspired by me, or my writing, to turn inward and
bring out their own voice—to find the courage to
empower themselves and speak their truth also.

I want to see people steal back the freedom that
those in positions of power have stolen from them.
Freedom starts by us standing up and speaking out,

exposing the heinous truths that we were forced to hide. When we speak and name names, we remove the veil of secrecy and power that our captors rely on to keep us enslaved.

Music for the Soul

Here are several selections that helped me get through the events or period of this chapter, or reflect musically what I felt during this time. I understood very little of most lyrics—even today my ears don't process most words—but the melodies and instruments fed my soul. Had it not been for music, I wouldn't have survived until I finally got to therapy at age twenty-nine.

- Pink Floyd. "Lost for Words." *The Division Bell*, 1994.

- Gareth Emery. "Concrete Angel (Original Mix)." *Concrete Angel (Remixes) [Featuring Christina Novelli]*, 2012.

- Tiesto. "Ur." *Just Be*, 2004.

Acknowledgments

Thank You:

Joni B. Cole—the writer's writer extraordinaire—for bringing out the scared and traumatized writer in me, for your tireless encouragement and guidance, for teaching me methods that cut through the overwhelm, and for not letting me quit. This book would not exist without you. Thank you for being the best consultant, coach, mentor, teacher, author, and editor in the universe. All my sentences and paragraphs and sections that are crafted well owe their thanks to you and, of course, all the less-than-stellar content is due to my inability to meet writing deadlines and having had to forego your wise insight and editorial eye.

Michelle Witman-Blumenfeld, for giving me the tools to manage my ADHD during my last year at Columbia, for teaching me how to break down my writing effectively, for giving your wisdom and advice and support unconditionally all the way back in the very beginning of this book over eight years ago, and for believing in me throughout all this time.

Henry Corra (and all my Corra Films family:

Jeremy, Annmarie), for being the first positive male role model in my life and for being the catalyst that got me into therapy, which then finally resulted in the fruition of this book. Thank you for sticking by me through all my ups and downs and for not judging me.

Kieron Sweeney, for giving me the knowledge and wisdom on how to manage money and set myself free financially, for freely giving your time and energy in my struggles and endeavors along my personal growth trajectory, and for still seeing the good in me despite all my failures.

Michael Ellsberg, for editing my basic story over eight years ago that got this book started, for telling me I can write (when I didn't believe I could), for being an inspiration and advocate during all these years, and for rescuing me from my last (and final) suicide attempt.

Yanik Silver, for giving me the courage to own that I'm destined for greatness, for helping me let my inner child play, for having created the Mavericks (my chosen family), and for inspiring me to handwrite all the raw material that seeded this book—much of which was written in the Camp Maverick journal you gave me.

My Maverick family, for having my back. I love you.

Brian Young, for making the podcast possible through your editing, and for all the myriad invaluable contributions you make to help me in my work.

My assistants and interns, for your commitment, dedication, integrity, and wisdom. I'm so fortunate to have you on my team. Thank you.

Joe Treger, for having been the very first patron and benefactor of this book. Thank you for your trust and friendship through all these years and for helping me learn about your culture, which is so similar to mine.

Agi Legutko, for having been one of the very first patrons of this book and for your support and encouragement throughout the years. Thank you.

To everyone whom I've forgotten, for contributing financially so many years ago when I first started writing my story. Please contact me so I can finally deliver on the promise to send you a signed copy and acknowledge your name here.

Debbie Ford, for freeing me from the shame of my shadows.

Paul Hackett, for being a brother to me.

Nisha Moodley, for giving your heart and love that carried me through an earlier suicide attempt.

Michael Brubeck, for helping me get through a long, challenging suicide phase.

Dr. Glen Brooks at NY Ketamine Infusions, for the ketamine that's fixing my brain damage (that is, stunted neuronal development) from childhood traumas.

Cameron Herald, for enlightening me about the emotional rollercoaster ride of entrepreneurs and teaching me the tools to ride that ride with more ease and calm.

James Altucher, for giving me the inspiration to own my betrayals and for the courage to speak my uncomfortable truths publicly.

Selena Soo, for being one of the rare figures in

marketing and branding who consistently operates with integrity—for having been a person of integrity for over fifteen years from when I first heard of you.

Mary Simms, the most badass PR woman and military vet: for your fierce and fearless support in not only getting my story into the media but by also helping me write some of the most triggering dark material I've had to face during a time when so many of the survivors in our entire country were feeling especially re-traumatized by a proponent of rape culture.

Susan Mobley, for continuing to ask me to teach memoir writing and being my first beta tester. And for being my Sister Escapee from another closed religious society.

All the 7-Day Challenge participants who beta tested my *12-Minute Writing* process and proved that the formula I developed to write this book is actually teachable and workable for others, even if they think they don't know how to write.

Mary Wallace, for your reminders to do what makes Torah safe.

Chef Jehangir Mehta, for giving me my very first professional cooking lesson.

Lynzz, for constantly encouraging me and letting me know that my story is helping Amish people inside and outside the Church.

My Amish people, for the positive aspects of our culture.

My Amish maternal aunts and uncles and cousins, for loving me unconditionally from birth to age three, and for being willing during the past several years to tell me the truth about my history and thereby aiding in my healing journey.

Laura Anderson, for buying the very first print copy of the first edition of this book. I'm so thrilled and honored that the first sold copy turned out to go to a fellow Amish.

Elam Zook, for the work you're doing as an educational consultant at Franklin & Marshall College to fight for our people and take back control of our narrative. For twenty years, I thought I was the only one who saw the potential for Amish evolution and the need for us Amish to reclaim and reshape our identity.

Sovilla Coblentz and Lucinda Coblentz, for being some of the bravest, kindest, most courageous, resilient and loving women I know. Thank you for your unwavering support that has gotten me through some of the darkest periods of my life; for standing by me in my fight against Amish rape culture; for facing your demons and grief, too; for being on the podcast to share your stories; and for being bright, shining examples of what Amish women can evolve into.

James Schwartz, for being what I call "the godfather of Amish poetry," for writing and publishing your book *The Literary Party: Growing Up Gay and Amish in America*, for working on behalf of LGBTQ+ Amish, and for being on the podcast and spreading the word to help create a strong community of Amish "expatriates."

For all the strong people (past and future) sharing their stories on my *Amish Entrepreneur Show* podcast, to let the world know that trauma doesn't discriminate, that we're not alone, and that you don't have to be extraordinary to be Extraordinary. Thank you, Season 1 guests: James Schwartz, Fiona Teng, Sovilla Coblentz, Lucinda Coblentz, Elam Zook, Jeselle Hadley-Bacon, Brian Young, Erika Watson, and all the others to come—including all who've appeared on Season 2 and Season 3.

Sarah Kinsley-Brooks and Aaron Kinsley-Brooks, for being part of my heart-soul family.

Vidura Barrios, for being the impetus that finally got me to deal with my money shit.

Celia Maysles, for finding me.

Judith Maysles, for giving me a home so I could go through therapy.

Sebastian Mychel Cruz, for being the energy and light that helped get me through this book, the hardest project I've ever undertaken.

Michael Levin, for loving books as much as I do and for teaching me how to open each chapter.

Dan Poynter, for your book-writing template and self-publishing expertise.

John Eggen, for your book-publishing coaching program.

Janet Tingwald, for your lifeline support and laser coaching sessions that kept me in the game and made me believe that I could get this book completed.

To all the sexual abuse and trauma survivors who are stopping the generational cycle of abuse, thank you and please know that you are not alone. Reach out to me and join our community.

To everyone I've forgotten who's made a positive difference in my life, thank you.

Apple Dumpling and Blueberry Blues, my fierce little dragon protectors: for loving me, eating all my food, and beautifying my life with your colors.

Nikita Borya, for having my back. Thank you for helping me cross the finish line with this book.

Resources

Podcasts

1. *Amish Entrepreneur Show with Torah Bontrager* (podcast about Amish issues and sexual assault in all societies)

"making women safe, one story at a time"

The *Amish Entrepreneur Show* podcast was created to make the world safer for women, one story at a time, by collecting 1,111 stories of sexual assault survivors—from all walks and genders of life.

I believe that that number of voices speaking out is all that is needed to permanently drastically reduce the rate of sexual assault locally, nationally, and globally. Through these stories, the culture of ignoring sexual assault and women fearing for their safety and security is no longer possible. The implicit and explicit condoning of rape and sexual assault will continue to flourish until enough of us speak out and fight back.

Watch the episodes released thus far to be inspired and to know that you're not alone. And that you don't have to be extraordinary to be Extraordinary.

Please consider sharing your MeToo story. We don't go into detail about the horrors that happened to you. Rather, we focus on what tools you use to process and function, and what you're passionate about in your life today.

 Here's how to self-schedule a chat with me to discuss the possibility of sharing your story publicly: www.TorahBontrager.com/appear

Podcast on iTunes:
www.torahbontrager.com/iTunes

Podcast on YouTube:
www.torahbontrager.com/YouTube

Podcast on Website:
www.torahbontrager.com/podcast

2. *Real Amish* (podcast by The Amish Heritage Foundation)

"Real Amish stories from real Amish people."

Watch/listen for the facts about us Amish. TED-style talks, Interviews, and Stories.

Podcast on iTunes:
www.amishheritage.org/iTunes

Podcast on YouTube:
www.amishheritage.org/YouTube

Podcast on Website:
www.amishheritage.org/podcast

Writing

1. Free ebook: *The 12-Minute Writing Process: How to Begin Sharing Your Personal Story—Even with Little or No Previous Writing Experience* by Torah Bontrager
   • Search online for the book

2. Joni B. Cole (consultant, coach, mentor, teacher, author, and editor extraordinaire):
   • Buy her book: *Good Naked: Reflections on How to Write More, Write Better, and Be Happier*

- www.jonibcole.com

3. Michelle Witman-Blumenfeld (educational consultant and ADHD and other invisible disabilities coach extraordinaire): www.sailconsulting.net

4. *Writing the Memoir: From Truth to Art* (the best book on memoir writing, based on my experience) by Judith Barrington

5. Michael Levin (ghostwriter and publishing and writing teacher extraordinaire): www.michaellevinwrites.com

Meditation or Mindfulness and Yoga

1. Mindfulness Training in 10 Minutes a Day with the Headspace App (I like this site because it's a good basic, scientific introduction to meditation for beginners): www.headspace.com (free trial)

2. Inner Splendor Media (for guided meditation and meditation, relaxation and sleep music): www.innersplendor.com

3. Kanta Barrios (yoga instructor offline and via videos): www.kantabarriosyoga.com

Money and Entrepreneurship

1. Kieron Sweeney (entrepreneur's coach, business consultant, and teacher; anything he offers is worth taking; get his free ebook for the exact same money management formula he taught me):
   • Free money management ebook: *Life's Golden Buckets* at www.lifesgoldenbuckets.com
   • www.kieronsweeney.com

2. Yanik Silver (entrepreneur, author, adventurer, and founder of Mavericks1000 for entrepreneurs who want to transform the world):
   • Buy his latest book: *Evolved Enterprise: An Illustrated Guide to Re-Think, Re-Imagine and Re-Invent Your Business to Deliver Meaningful Impact & Even Greater Profit* at www.evolvedenterprise.com
   • www.yaniksilver.com

3. Selena Soo (business & publicity strategist): www.selenasoo.com

4. Mary Simms (founder of The Mary Simms Public Relations Agency; formerly an NBC television news reporter, US Army Veteran, and war correspondent, and past spokeswoman for the US Environmental Protection

Agency; she uses her 15+ years of experience as a media insider to help high-profile clients favorably influence media coverage, embrace their expertise, and land favorable features on top tier media outlets, blogs, and podcasts that lead to increased revenue and exposure): Follow her on Twitter @marysimms or visit www.marysimms. com. Please give her your business. She's a badass.

5. Sebastian Mychel Cruz (marketing genius for millennials): www.expansionmarketing.net

6. Mary Wallace (lifestyle wellness coach): www.marywallacewellness.com

Love and Relationships

1. Maven Communications (Lionel Koh and Lisa Tan-Koh are amazing; anything they offer is worth taking): www.mavencomms.com

Grief Recovery and Death

1. Grief Recovery Method (for physical and emotional losses, to find grief support groups, and for a free ebook for info on the various kinds of grief): www.griefrecoverymethod.com

2. Stephen Garrett (death educator, author, and coach): www.stephengarrett.ca

3. *Farewell to Hollywood* (a documentary film about love, death, art, holding on, and letting go, directed by Henry Corra and Regina Diane Nicholson): www.farewelltohollywood.com

Alternative Medicines and Therapies for PTSD, Suicide, Depression, Trauma, and Addictions

1. New York Ketamine Infusions (in my strong opinion, after thorough research and personally receiving this treatment for several years, this is the ONLY reputable ketamine

clinic in the US—and it just so happens to
be the most affordable, too; they treat for
depression rooted in PTSD, trauma and
chronic pain; tell Dr. Brooks that I sent
you):
- www.nyketamine.com
- NYC location: 917-261-7370
- Pittsburgh location: 412-414-9916
- Madrid, Spain location: (+34) 915-328-924

2. Bluebird Botanicals (CBD Oil for both
humans and animals; they offer a discount
to veterans and disabled and low-income
individuals): www.bluebirdbotanicals.com
or (720) 726-5132

3. Mary Wallace Wellness (Mary is an amazing
friend and has helped me through some of
my health and wellness challenges; get her
book *Lifestyling Wellness: Simple, Healthy Steps
for Taking Care of You*; she comes up with holistic wellness solutions for big energy, high
achievers and can help you manage weight
and stress, regain energy, clarify food confusion, reduce cravings, and more):
www.marywallacewellness.com

Books

1. *The Man Who Sold the World* by Ian Adrian
2. *The Power of No* by James Altucher
3. *Choose Yourself* by James Altucher
4. *Reinvent Yourself* by James Altucher
5. *Writing the Memoir: From Truth to Art* by Judith Barrington
6. *What Should I Do with My Life?: The True Story of People Who Answered the Ultimate Question* by Po Bronson
7. *Stories of Anton Chekhov* by Anton Chekhov
8. *The Way of the Wizard* by Deepak Chopra
9. *Good Naked: Reflections on How to Write More, Write Better, and Be Happier* by Joni B. Cole
10. *The Education of Millionaires: Everything You Won't Learn in College About How to Be Successful* by Michael Ellsberg (and all his other books)
11. *The Dark Side of the Light Chasers* by Debbie Ford
12. *The Prophet* by Kahlil Gibran
13. *Lord of the Flies* by William Golding
14. *God Revised: How Religion Must Evolve in a Scientific Age* by Galen Guengerich
15. *God vs. the Gavel: The Perils of Extreme Religious Liberty* by Marci Hamilton
16. *Stranger in a Strange Land* by Robert A. Heinlein
17. *Double Double: How to Double Your Revenue and Profit in 3 Years or Less* by Cameron Herald
18. *Brave New World* by Aldous Huxley

19. *Sun After Dark: Flights Into the Foreign* by Pico Iyer
20. *No B.S. Marketing to the Affluent: The Ultimate, No Holds Barred, Take No Prisoners Guide to Getting Really Rich* by Dan S. Kennedy
21. *The Love Poems of Rumi* translated by Nader Khalili
22. *The Essential Neruda: Selected Poems* (Bilingual Edition) (English and Spanish Edition) by Pablo Neruda
23. *Animal Farm* by George Orwell
24. *Expressive Writing: Words that Heal* by James W. Pennebaker
25. *Writing Nonfiction: Turning Thoughts into Books* by Dan Poynter
26. *Health Revelations from Heaven: 8 Divine Teachings from a Near Death Experience* by Tommy Rosa
27. *The Literary Party: Growing Up Gay and Amish in America* by James Schwartz
28. *Evolved Enterprise: An Illustrated Guide to Re-Think, Re-Imagine and Re-Invent Your Business to Deliver Meaningful Impact & Even Greater Profits* by Yanik Silver
29. *The Mayan Oracle: A Galactic Language of Light* by Ariel Spilsbury
30. *Life's Golden Buckets* by Kieron Sweeney
31. *The Power of Now* by Eckhart Tolle
32. *Lifestyling Wellness: Simple, Healthy Steps for Taking Care of You* by Mary Wallace

Children's Books (that all adults should read)

1. *The Once and Future King* by T. H. White
2. *Peter Goes to School* by Wanda Rogers House
3. *Winnie-the-Pooh* by A. A. Milne
4. *Pippi Longstocking* by Astrid Lindgren
5. *The Boxcar Children* by Gertrude Warner
6. *Caddie Woodlawn* by Carol Ryrie Brink
7. *A Little Princess* and *The Secret Garden* by Frances Hodgson Burnett
8. *Nancy Drew Mystery Series* by Carolyn Keene
9. *Hardy Boys* by Franklin W. Dixon
10. *The Tale of Peter Rabbit* by Beatrix Potter
11. *Adventures of Huckleberry Finn* **(Third Edition) (Norton Critical Editions)** by Mark Twain
12. *Uncle Tom's Cabin* by Harriet Beecher Stowe
13. *The Wonderful Flight to the Mushroom Planet* by Eleanor Cameron

Films, Documentaries, and TV Shows

1. *Farewell to Hollywood* (a documentary film about love, death, art, holding on, and letting go, directed by Henry Corra and

Regina Diane Nicholson):
www.farewelltohollywood.com

2. TED channel (TED talks are short, powerful talks that cover almost all topics, from
   science to business to global issues):
   www.www.ted.com or search on YouTube

3. *The Matrix* film (the red pill wakes you up to
   the truth about reality, and the blue pill
   keeps you asleep in your current
   mind-controlled reality)

Sexual Assault and Domestic Violence

1. RAINN (Rape, Abuse & Incest National
   Network): www.rainn.org; 800-656-HOPE
   (4673); live chat. Get help 24/7. Free and
   confidential. Call/chat 24/7 if you've been
   violated. Ask them to help you find a sexual
   assault or domestic violence center in your
   location.

2. SNAP (Survivors Network of those Abused
   by Priests): Call 877.SNAP.HEALS (762-
   7432) to be connected with a trained staff
   member who will give you confidential
   support, information about the laws, and
   referrals for safe, in-person help. You can

also reach SNAP's Survivor Support Coordinator, Melanie Sakoda, at 925- 708-6175 or find lots of information for survivors and advocates at www.SnapNetwork.org.

3. AHF (Amish Heritage Foundation): Call or text 212.MEG.HALL (634-4255) to be connected with Torah or a trained staff member who will give you confidential support, information about the laws, and referrals for safe, in-person help. AHF also offers a monthly free, online, confidential support group meeting and a private Facebook support group at www.AmishHeritage.org.

4. CVTC (Crime Victims Treatment Center) provides healing services to survivors of rape, sexual assault, domestic violence, intimate partner violence, and childhood sexual assault: www.cvtcnyc.org. All of their services are confidential and completely free of charge. Call 212-523-4728 for help.

5. Safe Horizon in NYC (the nation's leading victim assistance organization, their mission is to provide support, prevent violence, and promote justice for victims of crime and abuse, their families, and communities): www.safehorizon.org; for domestic violence and child abuse: 800-621–HOPE (4673); for sexual assault: 212-227-3000. Call 24/7 for help.

The Amish Heritage Foundation

This is a brief overview of the vision of The Amish Heritage Foundation. You can find more information by visiting www.AmishHeritage.org.

Objective:
To rebrand the Amish (that is, change how we Amish are perceived by the media and mainstream America), and establish a new generation of Amish leaders who actively engage with the rest of the global community. To do so, we need to reclaim our Amish story and engage our silenced issues.

Problems:
Sexual violence runs rampant within our Amish culture, and there is no female leadership or representation whatsoever. No woman has stepped up to challenge the status quo.

Solutions:
We need to make our women safe—one story at a time—and invest in them to become leaders. By empowering our women and children, we can do something about the wrongdoings in our culture.

Project Outline:
The Dalai Lama says that we have an ethical responsibility to oppose anything that's harmful to the welfare of humanity. "Compassion" means "to

care for the well-being of self and others." In order to equip our Amish—and Anabaptist—people with the skills and wisdom to act compassionately, we need to address the following three overarching issues:

1. *Education:* No library in the world has any section on a credible body of Amish literature. We will deconstruct the 1972 Supreme Court case *Wisconsin v. Yoder,* which directly created an embrace of ignorance and a poverty of literature among our Amish people, and in the process, ran roughshod over our legal rights as Amish children and subsequent adults. We will create a body of work that represents us Amish and, along with that, we will address the problems that speaking English as a second language poses. We will also critically examine the fundamentalist Christianity influence on Amish issues and escapees.

2. *Female-driven Entrepreneurship:* We will teach Amish women and girls entrepreneurship, money management, and financial literacy, which ensures their financially independent future. Economic empowerment facilitates gender equality, poverty eradication, and mitigated abuses of power. Female entrepreneurs can create new jobs for themselves, as well as others, and effectively disrupt our male-dominated economy and male-driven agendas. We will also teach women and girls

the skills to identify opportunities, nego-
tiate agreements, raise capital, collaborate
cross-culturally on a local, national, and
global level, and leverage themselves into
leadership seats at the world table.

3. *Health and Well-being:* The traumatic losses
   that we Amish "immigrants" experience
   when we leave or escape the Church (for
   example, the loss of family, friends, job,
   language, culture, a sense of belonging,
   and so forth) result in debilitating isolation, depression, suicide, and other mental,
   physical, emotional, and spiritual health
   problems. We are routinely manipulated
   and taken advantage of because of our lack
   of resources, neglect, and a stripped sense
   of self-worth. We will connect our population with compassionate, empathetic, and
   nonjudgmental mental health professionals, self-empowerment coaches, mentors,
   sex education programs, self-care practices,
   alternative therapies, complementary medicine, and cutting-edge research. We will also
   educate them on the efficacy of ketamine
   infusions to fix the neurons in our mood
   centers; most of us suffer from PTSD and
   depression because of stunted mood center
   development sustained by early childhood
   traumas. These are services we will offer to
   all low-income members, whether inside or
   outside the Church.

All proceeds from the sale of
this book go to sexual assault
survivor causes.

About the Author

Torah Bontrager, born and raised traditional Amish, speaks English as a second language, and grew up with no electricity, no TV, no radio, no Internet, no cars, and up until the age of ten, no running hot water and no indoor bathroom. She learned how to grow her own veggies from heirloom seeds, raise animals for meat, hunt deer in the fall, and forage for mushrooms, berries, and plants in the wild.

At age 15, Torah literally escaped in the middle of the night, with only what she could carry: the clothes on her back and $170 in her pocket. To her knowledge, she's the first Amish person to graduate from an Ivy League school, Columbia University in New York City, where she earned a BA in Philosophy and focussed on Tibetan Buddhism under the auspices of Prof. Robert Thurman.

Torah is a recurring sexual assault survivor; the host of an iTunes + YouTube podcast, *Amish Entrepreneur Show,* created before MeToo to feature sexual assault survivors' stories; and the founder of the 501(c)(3) Amish Heritage Foundation (AHF), the first secular organization in 300+ years of Amish history that advocates for the Amish (whether inside or outside the Church), promotes compassionate secular values and nonsectarian harmony, and assists those who leave the Church. AHF acts as a diplomatic and cultural attache between the Amish and mainstream society, emphasizes investing in women and girls, who are undervalued assets, and promotes safe workplaces for women, 33% of whom are sexual assault survivors.

Among other initiatives, AHF is attempting to overturn *Wisconsin v. Yoder*, the landmark 1972 Supreme Court case that specifically denies Amish children—and consequently *all* children in the US and Native/indigenous lands—an education beyond the 8th grade. Through projects like this, Torah believes the culture of ignoring sexual assault will no longer be possible.

> *"The survivors of trauma do not have time for karma to come around. We need justice **now**."*
> *- Torah Bontrager*

Self-care is key in Torah's daily routine for remaining sane. She loves gardening, cooking, and hosting dinner parties, and feeds herself and her parakeet babies a non-GMO diet. Despite her many accomplishments in life, she hasn't yet fulfilled her pre-escape childhood dreams of graduating from Harvard and flying into outer space.

Torah's story has been featured on MTV, Forbes.com, best-selling author Tim Ferris' blog, and *HuffPost*, among other outlets.

Check out www.AmishHeritage.org or social media to catch Torah in person somewhere, or to support AHF's pioneering work. Or for an almost FREE print or audio copy of her book, visit www.TorahBontrager.com/GIFT

Founder + Executive Director

TORAH BONTRAGER
speak@AmishHeritage.org
AmishHeritage.org
212.634.4255 (mobile/text/WhatsApp)

#AmishHelp #WIvYoder

Invite Torah to speak on Amish issues. We provide training in cultural awareness, female-driven entrepreneurship, and sexual assault survivor advocacy.

SPEAKING + TRAINING TOPICS:

Overturning *Wisconsin v. Yoder*
We are attempting to overturn *Wisconsin v. Yoder*, the 1972 Supreme Court case that denies Amish children—and consequently *all* children in the US and Native/indigenous lands—an education beyond the eighth grade. Learn why *Yoder* violates a child's Constitutional right to a quality education.

Amish Entrepreneurship
The Amish cannot compete with Big Ag and Silicon Valley. Learn about our programs to help Amish women, and men, transition to sustainable farming practices and produce food that can compete in today's marketplace. Programs include industrial hemp growing and financial literacy training.

Sexual Assault Survivor Advocacy + Cultural Awareness
We wrote an 8-Step Guide to help survivor advocates better support Amish victims. We are LGBTQ+ welcoming and provide cultural awareness training for sexual assault survivor advocates, law enforcement, and attorneys. We also created the SNAP Amish chapter and hold monthly, free online sexual assault survivor support meetings.

Ketamine for PTS(D)
Ketamine for post-traumatic stress is legal in all 50 states, if administered by a licensed doctor. Learn what exactly ketamine is and how it helps with PTSD, depression, and pain. Torah relies on this medicine for relief from repeat rape and extreme childhood traumas.

Feel free to request a topic not on this list. Torah is available in-person and online.

Author of the memoir
An Amish Girl in Manhattan

What Audiences Say:
"We were stunned into silence." - 30th Annual SNAP (Survivors Network of those Abused by Priests) Conference

"We need more conferences like AHF's. . . ." - Sarah Haider, *Executive Director*, Ex-Muslims of North America

"I didn't know my culture had so much in common with the Amish. . . ." - Attendees

Torah's story has been featured:

DONATE
BECOME A PARTNER
BECOME A SPONSOR
www.AmishHeritage.org/donate

Made in the
USA
Middletown, DE